Current Theories of Psychoanalysis

Current Theories of Psychoanalysis

Robert Langs, M.D.

Editor

International Universities Press, Inc.
Madison, Connecticut

INTERNATIONAL UNIVERSITIES PRESS and IUP (& design) ® are registered trademarks of International Universities Press, Inc.

Library of Congress Cataloging-in-Publication Data

Current theories of psychoanalysis / Robert Langs, editor.
    p.   cm.
    Includes bibliographical references and indexes.
    ISBN 0-8236-1094-2
    1. Psychoanalysis.   I. Langs, Robert, 1928-
BF175.C87   1998
150.19′5—DC21   98-13585
                                           CIP

Manufactured in the United States of America

Contents

Contributors

Lewis Aron, Ph.D., ABPP, Diplomat in Psychoanalysis, American Board of Professional Psychology; Clinical Professor and Supervisor, New York University Postdoctoral Program; Adelphi University and Derner Institute Postdoctoral Program; and Associate Editor, *Psychoanalytic Dialogues.*

Jody Messler Davies, Ph.D., Supervisor, New York University Postdoctoral Program; Faculty and Supervisor, National Institute for the Psychotherapies; and Associate Editor, *Psychoanalytic Dialogues.*

Theo. L. Dorpat, M.D., Faculty, Seattle Institute for Psychoanalysis, Northwest Center for Psychoanalysis, and the Center for Object Relations; Training Analyst, Seattle Institute for Psychoanalysis; and Clinical Professor, Department of Psychiatry and Behavioral Sciences, University of Washington.

Robert M. Gordon, Psy.D., Director of Intern Training, Rusk Institute of Rehabilitation Medicine; Assistant Professor of Clinical Rehabilitation Medicine, New York University School of Medicine; and Candidate, Adelphi University, Derner Institute Postdoctoral Program.

Daniel Kriegman, Ph.D., Faculty, Massachusetts Institute for Psychoanalysis; private practice, Newton and Cambridge, Massachusetts; and Founder and Co-editor, *Self and Other: Critical Debates.*

Robert Langs, M.D., Author of 40 books and 125 papers on psychotherapy and related subjects; Visiting Professor of Psychiatry, Mt. Sinai Medical School, New York City; and presently active as a psychoanalyst and psychotherapist.

Richard Loewus, Ph.D., Clinical Consultant and Supervisor of Psychotherapy, Psychological Counseling and Adult Development Center, Graduate School and University Center, The City University of New York; Advanced Candidate, William Alanson White Institute; Editorial Board, *Contemporary Psychoanalysis;* and private practice, New York City.

Michael Lowenstein, M.D., Assistant Professor of Psychiatry, University of California, San Francisco; Member, San Francisco Psychotherapy Research Group; Advanced Candidate, San Francisco Psychoanalytic Institute; and private practice in San Francisco.

Aryeh Maidenbaum, Ph.D., Director, New York Center for Jungian Studies; Adjunct Assistant Professor, New York University; Program Director, Jung On The Hudson Seminar Series; and private individual and group practice in New York City.

Michael L. Miller, Ph.D., Faculty member at the Seattle Institute for Psychoanalysis; Supervising analyst and faculty member, Northwest Center for Psychoanalysis; and Clinical Associate Professor, Departments of Psychiatry and Behavioral Sciences and Psychology, University of Washington.

Stephen A. Mitchell, Ph.D., Editor, *Psychoanalytic Dialogues;* Training and Supervising Analyst, William Alanson White Institute; and Faculty and Supervisor, New York University Postdoctoral Program.

Donna M. Orange, Ph.D., Psy.D., Faculty and Supervising Analyst at the Institute for the Psychoanalytic Study of Subjectivity, New York City.

Eric Singer, Ph.D., Director of Clinical Education, Training and Supervising Analyst, William Alanson White Institute; private practice in New York City and Westchester County, treating adults, adolescents, and couples in psychoanalysis, psychoanalytic psychotherapy, and short-term therapy; and serves as expert witness in cases involving psychological issues.

Malcolm Owen Slavin, Ph.D., Director of Training, Tufts University Counseling Center; President, Faculty and Supervising Analyst, Massachusetts Institute for Psychoanalysis; private practice, Cambridge, Massachusetts.

David Livingstone Smith, Ph.D., Clinical Co-ordinator, Kids Company, London, England; Founder, First Chair, European Society for Communicative Psychotherapy; President, International Society for Communicative Psychoanalysis and Psychotherapy; Editorial Panel, *British Journal of Psychotherapy;* Co-editor, *Electronic Journal of Communicative Psychoanalysis;* Visiting Faculty, Middlesex University, Surrey University, Regents' College and the New School of Psychotherapy and Counselling; and private practice, London, England.

Otto Weininger, Ph.D., Professor of Clinical Psychoanalytic Psychology, University of Toronto; Editor, *Journal of Melanie Klein and Object Relations;* and private practice, Toronto, Canada.

Christina Whyte-Earnshaw, private practice, treating both children and adults, Toronto, Canada; Lecturer; and currently completing Ph.D. in Psychology.

Arnold Winston, M.D., Chairman, Department of Psychiatry, Beth Israel Medical Center, New York City; and Professor and Vice Chairman, Department of Psychiatry, Albert Einstein College of Medicine.

Beverly Winston, Ph.D., Supervising Psychotherapist, Department of Psychiatry, Beth Israel Medical Center, New York City; Assistant Clinical Professor of Psychiatry, Albert Einstein College of Medicine; Adjunct Assistant Professor of

Social Work, New York University; and Faculty, New York
School for Psychoanalytic Psychotherapy and Psychoanalysis.

Foreword

This book, broadly conceived for college and graduate students, general readers, and all levels of practitioners, has been fashioned to open a window into the main trends in present day psychoanalytic thinking. Each chapter has been written by one or more psychoanalytic writers strongly committed to a particular version of psychoanalytic theory and practice. The result is a rather impassioned and captivating presentation of the key concepts and principles of technique of twelve somewhat distinctive, yet in most cases interrelated approaches to the psychoanalytic domain.

For the initiate, the book offers a fascinating opportunity to explore the expanding realm of psychoanalysis and dynamic psychotherapies under the guidance of analysts and therapists who are specialists in various sectors of its territory. For the more experienced mental health professional, the book offers a unique occasion to examine in detail a series of viewpoints that define the current psychoanalytic and psychotherapeutic domains. As reflected in these writings, the varying schools of psychoanalysis have, to a considerable extent, become relatively insular. A graduate of a training program that has emphasized a particular point of view is likely to have little definitive knowledge of the main competing theories. This book will enable such therapists to experience and reflect on the many diverse explorations and thinking that currently characterize the psychoanalytic scene.

While there are notable differences between the approaches presented in this book, there are striking similarities as well. Most obvious is the shift from the now maligned intrapsychic or one-person model of psychoanalysis championed by Freud and his early followers to some type of interactional or interpersonal, two-person model. This new attitude characterizes every chapter in the book. At issue, then, is the problem of how to most incisively and validly characterize such interpersonal transactions as they apply to patient–analyst/therapist

interactions—and parenthetically, to child-mother/parent relationships as well. In this respect, the discussions developed
by the various contributors to this book may be seen as staking
a claim for the accuracy, sensibility, and explanatory power of
their particular positions and therapeutic strategies.

Psychoanalysis is a field that is actively evolving and widening its range of understanding. Its practitioners are striving to
favorably revise its basic propositions and to improve and extend the scope of its clinical applications and the effectiveness
of its techniques. Every writer in this volume is deeply committed to these efforts and the fresh perspectives and insights they
offer place this book at the cutting edge of the field.

All in all, then, these chapters record a singular view of
the present state of psychoanalytic theory and practice, showing both seeming certainties and notable uncertainties. Both
theory and its translation into clinical techniques are to be
found on these pages. We hope that the total effect will be of
great benefit to our readers and promote their personal and
professional growth and understanding.

Robert Langs, M.D.

1.

Interactional Psychoanalytic Theory

Michael L. Miller, Ph.D., Theo. L. Dorpat, M.D.

INTRODUCTION AND OVERVIEW OF INTERACTIONAL THEORY

Interactional psychoanalysis (Dorpat and Miller, 1992) belongs to a group of new psychoanalytic theories (Weiss and Sampson, 1986; Stolorow, Brandchaft, and Atwood, 1987; Lichtenberg, Lachmann, and Fosshage, 1992) that seek to understand a patient and treat his problems by analyzing and working through the interaction between the patient and the analyst. This new perspective unites in theory and clinical practice the development and pathology of the self (self psychological theory) with the normal and pathological influence of a person's relations to others (object relations theory).

The central tenets of interactional psychoanalysis are that the organization and content of a person's mind are the products of his actual, interpersonal history and that the interactions he forms with others, as well as his interpretations of these interactions, reflect this developmental history (Dorpat and Miller, 1992). Recent biological (Shore, 1994) and psychological (Stern, 1985) research supports the idea that the ways in which a person organizes his experience of himself and the world, regulates his emotions, forms his relations with others, and defines his concepts and beliefs, all derive from the internalization of his interactions with others. These internalized interactions form mental representations, called schemas, that non-consciously organize a person's interactions with the world and attribute a meaning to them (Horowitz, 1988). Schemas are activated by the features of an interaction with the social surround, and they function to conserve a person's mental organization and sense of self by organizing and interpreting the current interaction in terms of past experience (Mandler, 1984). People therefore expect others and situations to conform to their schema-based expectations, and they will consciously and unconsciously influence others and situations to match their expectations (Miller, 1996).

Our therapeutic stance is to focus on the interaction between the patient and the analyst because the schemas that organize the minds of the patient and the analyst are manifested in how each of them organizes and interprets the therapeutic interchange and in how they each try to influence the other to validate their schema-based expectations. The analyst comes to know and understand the content and organization of the patient's mind by attending to the patient's emotional reactions to the analyst's verbal and nonverbal communications and to the meaning that the patient attributes to his interactions with the analyst.

In contrast to classical psychoanalytic technique (Greenson, 1967) that aims to detect the unconscious wishes, conflicts, and compromises that distort a patient's thoughts and feelings and correct them, interactional technique treats the patient's reactions to the analyst as nondistorted interpretations that must be understood from within the patient's frame of reference, articulated, and explored. The analyst infers from the therapeutic interchange the conscious and unconscious schemas that the patient uses in organizing and interpreting their interaction. The analyst then makes these schemas consciously available to the patient for his evaluation, testing, and possible alteration.

Any maladaptive behaviors or pathogenic beliefs expressed in the treatment situation reflect the nature and content of the schemas that the patient used to organize and interpret his interaction with the analyst. These pathogenic schemas are not distorted conceptualizations of reality. Rather, they represent a patient's lived experience of trauma, developmental arrest or delay, and inappropriate or inadequate interactions with childhood caretakers and their successors. They cause deficiencies in self organizing and affect regulating capabilities, problems in relating to others, and pathogenic beliefs about the self and others.

Whereas many classical and contemporary psychoanalytic theories (e.g., Greenson, 1967; Stolorow, 1994) hold that the therapeutic power of analysis lies in making conscious, through interpretation, the unconscious fantasies or organizing principles that determined the patient's reactions to the analyst, interactional theory's conviction that schemas are created from lived interactions posits that it is primarily though the creation of new experiences with the analyst that a patient forms new schemas and changes those that he finds to be maladaptive (Weiss and Sampson, 1986; Lichtenberg et al., 1992; Miller and Dorpat, 1996).

THE INTERACTIONAL ORIGINS OF THE MIND

We begin with the premise that human beings are motivated to preserve themselves biologically and psychologically while adapting to an ever changing environment. This motivation is expressed in the human predisposition to detect regularities in lived experience and to use these patterns of experience to organize themselves physiologically and psychologically (Sander, 1988; Shore, 1994). The human infant is born with the innate ability to identify emotional states within herself, to detect particular features of the external environment, and to link these states and features together into temporal, spatial, and causal sequences that create patterns of lived experience (Stern, 1985). These patterns of lived experience organize the brain into networks of neurons and the mind into templates of interrelated features, called schemas, that represent lived events (Shore, 1994).

The ways in which humans organize their experience and regulate themselves physiologically and emotionally are shaped by their interactions with others throughout the life cycle. The influence of others is especially strong in infancy and early childhood when the basic neuropsychological patterns of self-organizing and regulating are laid down.

Sander (1988) for example has shown that an infant's biorhythms are organized into a standard 24-hour sleep–wake cycle through the infant's identification of recurrent states-of-being that are created by her mother attending to her physiological needs and emotional states in an ordered, regular sequence throughout the day. Stern (1985) and Shore (1994) propose that the ways in which a person constitutes and regulates her physiological and emotional states are determined by the nature of the caregiving and playful interactions she has with her caregivers. Lauren's mother, Jan, for example, defines Lauren's happy emotional state by matching it. Lauren's perception of her mother's smiling face stimulates the neural networks in her sympathetic track already activated by Lauren's cheerful state, thereby reinforcing it. If Jan increases her cooing and smiling she amplifies firing frequency of the neurons in Lauren's sympathetic network, thereby increasing the intensity of her emotional state, because Lauren is genetically predisposed to match emotional states with another. Jan can also regulate downward her Lauren's positive arousal by matching her child's aroused state and turning down her own emotional arousal by lowering her voice or slowing her behavior with Lauren. Lauren matches her mother's level of arousal and in so doing conditions her sympathetic track to attenuate the arousal. Lauren too can influence Jan's state of arousal to match hers. Nuzzling noses with her mother she laughs excitedly. Her laughing stimulates Jan to increase the speed at which she touches her nose to Lauren's. When the game exceeds her tolerance, Lauren turns her head away, an action that communicates to her mother to stop the game, and Jan responds by holding her and slowly rocking her to a resting position.

With repetition, Lauren will construct mental representations or schemas of these emotional defining and regulating interactions. She will form a schema of her mother's smiling face paired with her own experience of positive arousal. She will also construct schemas of amplifying and attenuating positive arousal, each with the corresponding changes in her representations of Jan's face, vocal pacing and tone, and other behaviors that characterized the regulatory interaction. These mental representations are used as templates for Lauren's own regulation of positive arousal, even when her mother is not present (Beebe and Lachmann, 1994; Shore, 1994).

ORGANIZING AND CONCEPTUAL SCHEMAS

The type of schemas we have been describing represent a memory for episodes of lived experience. In the heightened state of a nuzzling game, for example, Lauren bites her mother. Jan's physical withdrawal, frown of disapproval, and scolding activated Lauren's parasympathetic nervous system causing a physiological slowing and a corresponding emotional withdrawal and sense of depletion that define the feeling of shame. This experience of shame is mentally captured in a schema representing the sequence of events as it was lived by Lauren from her perspective: sitting in mother's lap Lauren is touching noses with Jan, overly excited she bites her mother's nose, Jan interrupts the game, withdraws her face, frowns, and says no biting. Lauren is physically distanced from Jan, averts her eyes from her mother's face, and experiences a feeling of emotional depletion and shutting down. In addition to depicting the sequence of actions and the context in which the interaction occurs, the schema encodes the reciprocal influence of Lauren on Jan and of Jan on Lauren in the construction of this shame experience.

As these examples illustrate, a person's emotional state and sense of self are defined by the reciprocal influence of the self on others and others on the self that a schema represents. That being the case, a person's experience of others and her knowledge about them are formed by the same schemas that define the self. A schema not only contains information about what the individual experiences and knows, but also about what she perceives that others think and feel in situations defined by that schema. Schemas enable a person to form expectations of how events should unfold and how she and others should feel, think, behave, and interact in the situations defined by a particular schema.

Organizing schemas are those that encode episodes of lived experience. This type of schema orients an individual in time and space; organizes experience; regulates emotions; characterizes the features of the physical and social environments as well as one's interactions with these environments; and depicts the nature of one's emotional relatedness to others and the ways in which subjective experience is communicated and shared between individuals (Mandler, 1984). Each time a schema is used to organize an event, the unique features of that event are added to the schema, modifying it ever slightly. Over time organizing schemas become increasingly general in nature, characterizing the stereotypic set of features of the events that a particular schema has come to organize (Stern, 1985).

As cognitive development progresses, humans are able to abstract from their organizing schemas similar features or experiences and to form them into categories, to construct new schemas out of the data provided by organizing schemas, and to transform organizing schemas in various ways (Piaget, 1970). These second-order schemas are not bound to lived experience as are organizing schemas. Rather, they are the ideas, concepts, beliefs, and theories that an individual constructs to explain her perceptions, thoughts, feelings, and behavior as well as the nature and results of her interactions with others and the environment (Mandler, 1984). For example, Lauren's success in regulating her arousal may create the belief that she can regulate her own experience. In matching her mother's arousal and in getting her mother to match hers, Lauren may create the concepts that she and another can share the same internal experience and that she is interpersonally effective. And, in being withdrawn from for biting, Lauren may form the ideas that aggression creates bad feelings and causes others to abandon her. These second-order schemas embody a person's conceptual knowledge of herself and the world. *Conceptual schemas* evaluate and interpret the events constituted by one's organizing schemas in terms of the beliefs and theories a person holds about herself and the world.

PSYCHOPATHOLOGY OF ORGANIZING AND CONCEPTUAL SCHEMAS

Misattuned, mismatched, and disruptive interactions with one's caregivers create maladaptive organizing schemas that cause disturbances in the organization and regulation of self-experience and in one's attachments to others. For example, when the tickling game between 14-month-old Bill and his mother, Sara, becomes too intense, Bill averts his gaze, but Sara continues to tickle him. When Bill turns his body away from her, she persists in tickling him until he cries. After Bill calms, Sara tries to reengage Bill by tickling him. Bill again turns away from her, but she chases him until he curls into a ball.

Sara is not attuned to Bill's communications, so she increases the stimulation when she should be decreasing it. Indeed, her continuing to increase the stimulation runs counter to Bill's attempts to regulate downward his own arousal as well as her level of stimulation. What Bill will form into an organizing schema is a pattern of interaction in which his positive arousal is disrupted by the person with whom he is interacting. The schema will cause Bill to experience playful interactions as the prelude to uncontrollable agitation and disregulation.

Pathogenic organizing schemas cause disturbances in physiological regulation, as in eating and sleep disorders, and in emotional regulation, as in depression and anxiety disorders. They also affect the maintenance of one's sense of self, as in dissociated or fragmented states, and one's relationships to others, as in the inability to share or coordinate one's subjective experience with another (Lichtenberg et al., 1992).

Now Bill will also construct pathogenic conceptual schemas about himself and his relations with others from the emotionally disruptive interaction he had with his mother. Bill may infer from his inability to regulate his own arousal the pathogenic beliefs that his emotions are too powerful and that he is too weak to control them. Sara's failure to correctly read his communications may cause Bill to form the concepts that his feelings are different from those of others and that they cannot be shared or communicated.

Pathogenic beliefs develop from poorly coordinated, mis-attuned, and traumatic interactions with others. They can also develop from nontraumatic interactions that, due to the imma-turity of the individual's mental processes, had a disturbing or troubling meaning attributed to them. Pathogenic beliefs are painful and constricting ideas about the ways things are or about the ways things should be, and they impede normal func-tioning by giving rise to fear, anxiety, shame, guilt and feelings of inadequacy. Thus, these schemas influence a person's assess-ment of the danger or safety of any interaction (Weiss and Sampson, 1986).

MEANING ANALYSIS

Every interaction with the social surround is organized and a meaning attributed to it by matching the interaction to the past experience and knowledge stored in one's normal and pathogenic schemas. Following Mandler (1984), we call this process of organizing and interpreting interactions with the surround *meaning analysis*. How an individual perceives, orga-nizes, and understands a current event is determined by the particular schemas to which the event is assimilated. The sche-mas that are selected to interpret an event are determined by the features of the current interaction and by the individual's immediate past experience and current preoccupations. The most relevant features of these activated schemas are combined into a *working model* of the current interaction (Horowitz, 1988).

The schemas that comprise a working model are them-selves modified by the interaction that they are employed to organize and interpret. Working models are plastic interpreta-tive states blending past knowledge with current data. Schemas, therefore, continue to evolve and develop throughout one's life cycle as new experience and knowledge needs to be assimilated in adapting to one's changing environment.

Empirical research has shown that humans organize and interpret their interactions with the social surround in fractions of a second (Beebe and Lachmann, 1988) such that the process of meaning analysis is essentially a nonconscious process (Mandler, 1984; Greenwald and Banaji, 1995). Meaning analysis can be a conscious process when data cannot be easily assimilated to the activated schemas because there is too large a discrepancy between what is expected, according to the activated schema, and what occurs, or when there is an interruption in information processing for any reason that requires conscious problem solving.

THE NONCONSCIOUS REPRESENTATION AND COMMUNICATION OF MENTAL CONTENTS

Clinical research and observation have demonstrated that people nonconsciously represent and communicate their experience of an event, the meanings they attribute to it, and the inference they draw from it (Weiss and Sampson, 1986; Beebe and Lachmann, 1988; Horowitz, 1988). This nonconscious depiction and communication can take symbolic and nonsymbolic forms.

The nonsymbolic presentation and communication of one's subjective experience is illustrated in the interactions between Lauren and Jan and Bill and Sara in which they used signals to communicate their current emotional experience to one another and to direct the other to match that experience. Signals are the facial expressions, vocal tones and rhythms, gestures, and postures that are the physiognomic expressions of a person's feeling states (Werner and Kaplan, 1963), and, as such, are inherent aspects of the schemas that represent these states. Organizing schemas, by virtue of their signaling qualities, nonconsciously represent a person's current emotional state and communicate it to others (Dorpat and Miller, 1992, 1994; Beebe and Lachmann, 1994).

Symbols are nonconsciously constructed to represent the content and meaning of the schemas activated to interpret an interaction with the surround (Horowitz, 1988; Dorpat and Miller, 1992, 1994; Lichtenberg et al., 1992). Their form and substance are determined by the nature and content of the activated schemas and by the adaptive demands of the activating situation. Symbols can take the form of mental images, narrative stories, enactments, or any combinations of these. Their content may be taken from the personal experiences embodied by an activated schema, it may derive from shared social signs and symbols that express the schema's meaning, or it may be an imaginary construction that stands for the meaning of the schema. For example, Mr. L felt defeated by his analyst. He symbolically represented the defeat in a story about the time his father beat him in a tennis match. He also communicated his experience of the analyst in a daydream image of a jousting match in which a smaller knight is run through by a greater knight's lance.

THE EXPERIENCE AND CONSERVATION OF THE SENSES OF SELF

A person's experience and knowledge of herself, others, and of her interactions with surround are emergent properties of the activation of her schemas (Horowitz, 1988). By *emergent property* we mean that the experience or knowledge comes into existence with the activation of a schema. One's sense of self and knowledge of the world at any single moment are determined by the schemas selected to organize and interpret the current interaction with the surround. This transitory, situationally determined experience of self and the world is counterbalanced by the genetically programmed aspect of schemas to conserve self-organization and preserve the meaning of life. Schemas ensure the cohesion, stability, and continuity of a person's experience and knowledge of herself and the world by organizing and interpreting each interaction in terms of the past experience and knowledge that her schemas embody

(Stern, 1985; Sander, 1988). Every interaction with the surround is transformed into a representative instance of the schemas that organized and interpreted it. In this way, the variations in self-experience and knowledge introduced by the features of particular interaction are mitigated and the cohesion, stability, and continuity of the self are maintained.

The conservation of self-experience and knowledge is an inherent feature of the operation of schemas. Though schemas readily incorporate variations on the thematic aspects of the experience and knowledge that they encode, they resist taking in data that disconfirm their meaningful organization (Piaget, 1970; Nisbett and Ross, 1980). And, since schemas operate nonconsciously, the conservation of self and the preservation of meaning are nonconscious mental functions. Organizing and interpreting new interactions in terms of past experience creates the unconscious expectation that the interactions will conform to a person's schema-based knowledge. Fulfillment of this unconscious expectation is achieved when an event or person conforms to, actualizes, or confirms an individual's schema-based expectations and inferences (Weiss and Sampson, 1986; Lichtenberg et al., 1992; Miller, 1996). Humans are, therefore, nonconsciously as well as consciously motivated to validate their experience and to prove true their concepts and beliefs.

People expect events to conform to their beliefs and to unfold according to the scripts contained in their schemas. In their interactions with the surround they search for evidence that supports their expectations, and if the evidence is lacking they infer it (Mandler, 1984). If the data contradict their schemas, the evidence is ignored or disbelieved (Nisbett and Ross, 1980). People will also behave in stereotyped, repetitive ways to ensure that events will fulfill their schema-based expectations (Horowitz, 1988). Humans also expect others to behave in accordance with their schemas. If others deviate from what is anticipated they try to influence them to conform to their expectations (Beebe and Lachmann, 1994).

Using her schemas as a guide for how an interaction is to unfold, a human being consciously, but more commonly unconsciously, communicates her experience of the interaction to the person with whom she is interacting and then influences the person to validate it. She accomplishes these acts of communication and persuasion by signaling her subjective experience to her cohort in her tones of voice, postures, gestures, and facial expressions, and by using personal and social symbols to communicate her understanding of the interaction, what she expects of the other, and what she wants the person to think or believe. Additionally, she may create an interaction that provokes in the other person the feelings, thoughts, and behaviors that she desires, or she may directly express to the person her expectations and attributions.

If a person is successful in getting her cohort to meet her expectations and thereby validate her experience and the meanings she attributes to it, her sense of self is both actualized and conserved. What the individual experiences may be described as a vitalization of feelings, a sense of knowing, of being grounded, and of a continuity with who she has been. This sense of self may be a conscious experience, but it is usually an unconscious state similar to Sandler's identity of perception and background of safety (1960). It communicates to the individual that her current experience is authentic or true and that its meaning is consistent with her knowledge and beliefs.

DEFENSE AND RESISTANCE

A person will enact *defenses* when he expects, based on previous experience, that an interaction with the surround will result in trauma or pain. In these situations the individual will marshal an intrapsychic defense, an interactional defense, or both. The aim of the defensive activity is to protect the self from experiences and information that will (1) disconfirm the organizing and conceptual schemas that maintain a person's sense and concept of self; (2) place in jeopardy his ties to the important people in his life; and (3) lead to a recurrence of a traumatic interaction. The threats to a person's schemas, relationships, and adaptation may come from his own thoughts and feelings or they may emanate from others or events. Though these threats may result in the conscious experience of psychic pain, anxiety, guilt, or fear, these threats may also cause unconscious psychic pain and anxiety (Shore, 1994). Like most cognitive processes, these defensive strategies are usually employed unconsciously.

Intrapsychically, a person may protect himself from experiencing certain emotions or having certain thoughts by inhibiting the activation of the schemas that organize these thoughts and feelings in situations in which they would normally be activated. If these feelings and thoughts do become activated, their contribution to the formation of the working model of the interaction can be blocked. In place of these inhibited and sequestered schemas would be substituted schemas constructed to provide experiences, coping strategies, or interpretations that would work with the person's current operating schemas without disconfirming them as well as provide ways of relating to others and adapting to previously traumatic situations (Dorpat and Miller, 1992).

A person may also defend his experience and beliefs from disconfirming data by adjusting the ways in which he perceives and processes information (Lichtenberg et al., 1992). He may, for example, selectively perceive elements in his environment to avoid encountering data that disconfirm his current operating schema or place in jeopardy his relationships and adaptation. Or, he may maintain such rigid categories of experience that disconfirming data will be held in categories separate from the schemas they might conflict with, when ordinarily the data would be assimilated to the conflicting category.

Interactionally, a person may defend himself from disconfirming or disruptive experiences by trying to influence the person with whom he is interacting to behave in ways that preserve the integrity and continuity of the schemas that are currently defining his sense of self (Langs, 1978; Dorpat, 1994). Dorpat (1994) describes three defensive styles of communication that protect an individual's self experience by influencing the other to behave in a particular manner. All three types disrupt emotionally meaningful, symbolically encoded (stories, images, metaphors) communication with the analyst. In the first type an individual protects himself from feelings and thoughts he does not want to experience by denying them in himself and then by manipulating others in such a way that they experience those feelings and thoughts instead. With the second type, the person protects his subjective experience by inhibiting the expression of any emotion such that he prevents the other person from knowing how he feels and what he is thinking and, thereby, from interacting with him in a meaningful way. The last communicative style is one in which the individual protects his authentic and true feelings and thoughts by expressing inauthentic feelings and thoughts that are designed to comply with what the other person desires. When a defense manifests itself in the interaction between the patient and the analyst we refer to it as *resistance* (Dorpat and Miller, 1992).

HOW SCHEMAS CHANGE

Schemas are constantly being modified as new experiences and information are accommodated by the schemas to which the novel data are assimilated. Indeed, humans are genetically motivated to seek novelty and to create novel experiences (Piaget, 1970; Stern, 1985). They enjoy finding or creating variations on what they know and can do. If the variation on a theme is too great, however, change is resisted. Schemas are programmed to maintain their thematic structure. Thematic changes can occur, but these are usually achieved by creating a new schema that competes with the existing one, letting the schema that ensures the optimal adaptation gain precedence (Shore, 1994).

   Since schemas are created out of lived experience, it is the actual experience with the analyst that will induce schemas to change. In organizing and regulating one's subjective experience, the patient's organizing schemas will interface with those of the analyst. If the analyst is optimally responsive to the patient's feelings and psychological needs, the analyst will provide an interaction that will aid the patient in better organizing her experience, regulating her emotions, and coordinating her experience with that of another (Bacal, 1985; Miller, 1996). That is, by interacting with the analyst's appropriately responsive or developmentally advanced schemas the patient is challenged to accommodate to her schemas to fit the responses of the analyst. If the patient's schemas cannot accommodate the analyst's responses, new organizing schemas will be created.

A patient's conceptual schemas can also be altered in treatment as she tests the concepts and beliefs that she holds about herself and the world in her relationship to the analyst (Weiss and Sampson, 1986; Miller and Dorpat, 1996). If the patient's own behavior or that of the analyst deviates from what is expected, based on the concepts and beliefs held by the patient, the patient is forced to reevaluate the schemas, modify them, or create new ones that better account for her experience with the analyst.

PRINCIPLES OF THERAPEUTIC PROCESS AND BASIC TECHNIQUE

The aims of our interactional approach to psychoanalytic treatment are to identify a patient's schemas as they are used to organize and interpret his interactions with the analyst and others; to enable the patient to assess the adaptive adequacy of these schemas; and to empower the patient to change those schemas that he finds to be maladaptive. To this end, the analyst analyzes the patient's experience of his relationships and the beliefs that he uses to understand his interactions with others.

THE THERAPEUTIC INTERACTION

Like any social exchange the psychotherapeutic situation is one to which both the patient and the analyst must adapt. The patient comes to the interaction with certain schemas activated, the content of which may or may not be in his conscious awareness. These schemas embody the emotional states, preoccupations, and specific issues relevant to the patient's current life circumstances as well as the patient's expectations of the analyst's reactions to these concerns and to the patient himself. The features of the treatment setting and the analyst's initial expressions and behaviors activate additional schemas in the patient that encompass emotional states and memories associated with previous interactions with the analyst and others. The patient then blends these activated schemas into a working model that renders the analytic encounter a coherent and meaningful experience. He may or may not be consciously aware of his working model, though its contents are available for conscious self-reflection.

The patient's working model of the therapeutic interaction is constructed out of the normal and pathogenic schemas that organize the patient's experience and define what he believes about himself and the world. By organizing and interpreting his own and the analyst's behavior in terms of this situationally specific model, the analytic interaction becomes a representative instance, or living example, of these schemas. As such we define the psychoanalytic concept of *transference* as the ways in which the patient organizes his experience of the interaction with the analyst and the meanings he attributes to this experience.

In constructing the initial and all subsequent working models of the analytic interaction the patient assesses the analyst's emotional reactions, utterances, and nonverbal behavior to determine whether or not these responses sustain his experience and confirm his concepts and beliefs. If the analyst's responses do not match what the patient expects he will try to influence the analyst to behave as his schemas prescribe.

As detailed earlier, the process of organizing and interpreting the analytic interaction and of influencing the analyst to meet the patient's expectations are chiefly unconscious processes. The patient's meaning analysis of the interaction is non self-reflectively represented and communicated to the analyst through his nonverbal behavior, such as tone of voice, posture, facial expression and attitude; by his narratives about current and past events that have a meaning similar to the meaning the patient is attributing to the here-and-now interchange; and in the types of interactions that he engages the analyst and the responses that these interactions arouse in the analyst.

The analyst too comes to a session with emotional states and preoccupations activated by issues in his personal life, the previous patient or activity, and what he expects from the current patient. These schemas are blended with those evoked by the patient's initial presentation into a working model of the analytic interchange. We conceptualize *countertransference* as the analyst's organization and interpretation of his interaction with the patient. The analyst conserves his sense of self and his concepts about himself and the patient by having the patient validate his experience and interpretation of their interaction. If the patient's behavior and reactions fail to confirm the analyst's expectations or support his beliefs, the analyst unconsciously influences the patient to meet his expectations.

The therapeutic interaction can be characterized as a conscious and especially unconscious dialogue in which the patient and the analyst try to influence one another to conform to their schema-based expectations. The form and content of the analytic interchange are products of the interface of the patient's schemas with those of the analyst.

Though self-knowledge and continuing self-analysis aid the analyst in monitoring and controlling his countertransference, the primarily unconscious operation of these schemas makes it difficult for the analyst to identify the content and implications of these schemas prior to their expression in the analytic hour. Thus, the analyst's personality, his ways of regulating emotion, processing information, forming relationships, and the concepts and beliefs that mediate his reactions and interpretations will all influence the patient. The analyst controls for his influence on the patient by understanding that his conscious and unconscious behavior are the proximal stimuli to which the patient is responding in organizing and interpreting the analytic interchange. The analyst therefore makes his interpretations and interventions in reference to the patient's experience and interpretation of the analyst's behavior.

HOW THE ANALYST LISTENS

A patient tries to maximize her adaptation to the therapeutic interaction by having her schemas validated by the analyst. The

patient engages the analyst in interactions that will aid her in
conserving, affirming, and vitalizing her senses of self and in
confirming the beliefs she holds about herself and the world.
The patient is, therefore, communicating the nature of her
subjective experience in types of interactions she involves the
analyst and the content of her beliefs in the meanings she attributes to these interactions. From the perspective of how the
analyst listens, the analyst's aim is to uncover, with the patient's
help, the form, function, and content of the nonconscious
schemas the patient used to organize and interpret their interaction.

The analyst always tries to understand the therapeutic interaction from within the patient's point-of-view and experience. This does not mean that the analyst neglects her own
experience and perspective, but that she uses these in the service of understanding the meanings and expectations that the
patient attaches to their relationship. The analyst adopts what
Stolorow and his colleagues (1987) have called an attitude of
sustained empathic inquiry into the nature of the patient's subjective experience and the meaning attributed to that experience. This investigative stance seeks to explain the patient's
behavior, emotional reactions to the analyst, and inferences
about herself, the analyst, and the world that the patient draws
from their interaction. To this end the analyst attempts to infer
from the relationships that the patient forms with her and the
patient's reactions to her the organizing, regulating, and affirming functions that she is performing for the patient. The
analyst also tries to infer the concepts and beliefs that determine the meanings a patient attributes to their interaction by
abstracting from the patient's narratives about current and past
events meanings that may apply to the current interaction.

The analyst's inferences are not made solely in terms of
her immediate experience of the patient. They are informed by
her understanding of human emotional, cognitive, and social
development, psychopathology, and the patient's history as
well as the problems she is currently working on. The analyst
uses her informed inferences to formulate approximations of
the patient's nonconscious organizing and conceptual schemas. She makes these schemas consciously available to the patient, by interpreting the current interaction in terms of the

proffered schema, for the patient's assessment of their adaptive adequacy. The analyst also infers the function and content of the patient's schemas for her own use in constructing interventions.

INTERVENTIONS AND INTERPRETATIONS

Interventions are the ways in which the analyst interacts with a patient that enables the patient to alter his schemas. *Interpretations* are statements that characterize the unconscious experience, inferences, and meanings that the patient attributed to his interactions with the analyst. Interpretations make these experiences and meanings consciously available to the patient for assessment and testing as well as for formulating, with the analyst, the nonconscious schemas from which these experiences and meanings derive.

Though interventions and interpretations are an analyst's principal tools for bringing about change in a patient's schemas, they serve a second very important function. They create an environment of safety for the patient so that he can test his schemas and experiment with changing them. A patient will be open to changing his experience and beliefs only if he knows that the analyst understands and accepts him. The patient feels a sense of safety when his schemas are confirmed and validated (Sandler, 1960; Miller, 1996). A patient's organization and interpretation of the interaction are validated when the analyst responds as the patient expects or when the analyst interprets the patient's expectations and inferences, especially when his responses may deviate from what the patient expects.

INTERVENTIONS

As a participant in creating the therapeutic interaction, how the analyst intervenes will influence how the patient organizes and interprets his experience of their interchange. The analyst formulates his interventions to be *optimally responsive* to the

patient's needs (Bacal, 1985). By optimally responsive we mean
that the analyst responds in a manner that is appropriate to
the patient's emotional experience and tailored to the psychological functions that the patient requires. The analyst does
not contrive an interaction in order to cause the patient to
experience something new or different. Rather, the analyst behaves in a genuine and authentic manner that is also formulated to provide an interaction in which maladaptive schemas
can be altered or more adaptive schemas formed.

The analyst can, for example, help a patient who has difficulty organizing or regulating a particular emotional state develop better self-organizing and regulating skills by allowing
himself to experience the difficult emotion along with the patient and then communicate to the patient, through his vocal
tones and rhythms and facial expressions, his more mature organization and regulation of that state. This technique relies
on the patient's inherent tendency to match emotional states.
In matching the analyst's emotional state, the patient alters
the self-organizing and self-regulating schemas that define that
state. Other types of interventions can help patients with problems in containing, tolerating, transiting between, and integrating emotional states; coordinating defensively dissociated
feelings and thoughts; and in repairing disrupted emotional
connections with the analyst.

When a patient is assessing his beliefs about himself and
others in treatment, he requires the analyst to intervene in a
fashion that is optimally responsive to the beliefs being tested.
The patient communicates these beliefs and the expected response in the types of interactions he forms with the analyst,
the kinds of feelings he expresses and engenders in the analyst,
and in the stories, dreams, and images he creates to convey the
meanings he has attributed to the interaction.

For example, a patient who threatened to quit treatment
to test his fear of abandonment required the analyst to disagree
with his plan to terminate. He communicated the desired response by interacting with the analyst in a way that caused the
analyst to feel so anxious that the analyst felt compelled to
protest his leaving. A second patient, also concerned about
abandonment, did not want the analyst to be threatened by the

potential termination. In a dream he reported on the day that he raised the issue of leaving treatment, the patient describes how he responded with calm and patience to the news that his son wanted to enlist in the army to fight in Vietnam. The analyst inferred from the dream that he was to calmly wait for the patient to decide what he wanted to do.

In these illustrations the analyst's interventions were his genuine responses to what the patient communicated about himself and what he expected and needed from the analyst. The analyst's interventions created an interaction that enabled the patient to reformulate his schemas in a manner that accommodated the analyst's emotional reactions, attitudes, and beliefs. These optimally responsive interventions create for the patient a *corrective emotional experience*. The corrective emotional experience is the principal way in which patients alter their organizing and conceptual schemas.

INTERPRETATIONS

We adhere to the traditional psychoanalytic concept of an interpretation which is to make the unconscious conscious (Greenson, 1967). Interpretations facilitate the process of changing schemas by making the patient conscious of the unconscious experiences and beliefs that are determining her behavior, especially with the analyst. Interpretations *explain* a particular aspect of the patient's immediate, here-and-now experience. They are most effective when her schema-based expectations are violated or her connection to the analyst is disrupted. The patient can then consciously test the adaptive adequacy of these schemas; experiment with new ways of organizing and interpreting experience and of relating to the analyst; and change those schemas that she determines to be maladaptive.

The analyst infers a patient's unconscious experience and beliefs from the types of interactions that the patient forms with the analyst and the meanings that the patient attributes to these interactions. After experiencing multiple instances of a particular type of interaction or story theme in the patient's material, the analyst constructs hypotheses about the patient's organizing and conceptual schemas that he formulates into interpretations that account for a specific aspect of their here-and-now interaction.

Mr. P, for example, complained of not being able to experience joyous feelings. The analyst observed over and over again in their time together that Mr. P would experience grief, sadness, and depression with the analyst, but he would sever his ties to the analyst whenever the analyst would be happy for him or express joyous feelings. The analyst inferred from these interchanges that Mr. P was so upset by positive arousal that he would sever his connection to the analyst. The analyst made this interpretation to Mr. P when Mr. P became mute after the analyst acknowledged positively Mr. P's long awaited promotion. After hearing a story Mr. P told about his relationship to his mother, which was in response to the analyst's empathic understanding of Mr. P's loss when his wife miscarried, the analyst revised his hypothesis about the schema underlying Mr. P's aversion to positive arousal. In the story, Mr. P described his mother as a depressed woman who shunned him whenever he was happy. When his father left her for another woman, Mr. P's mother reached out to Mr. P for comfort, holding and caressing him while they cried. The analyst then explained to Mr. P that his story suggested that he only permits himself to have sad feelings with the analyst, because he believes that the analyst, like his mother, cannot tolerate his happy feelings and will abandon him if Mr. P were to share these feelings.

CASE VIGNETTE

An excerpt from the analysis of Mr. K, a married professional man, will be used to illustrate our approach to psychoanalytic treatment.

Mr. K   (looking hesitantly at the analyst as he lies on the couch, and in a very soft voice): Hi. How was your weekend?

Analyst   (feeling tight in his stomach at the question about his personal life and conflicted about rebuffing the patient, responds in a business-like tone): Fine, thank you. And yours?

Mr. K   (without emotion in his voice): Mondays are like returning from a vacation. I have mixed feelings. I want to take charge and make things happen, but I also want to retreat to the good feelings of the weekend. I feel tight now behind my neck and ears. I feel self-conscious.

Analyst   (tension and discomfort still in his voice as he reflects on his countertransference experience of Mr. K mentally represented in the image of a needy and intrusive child): I noticed when you asked about my weekend a reticence in your voice and glance.

After the weekend break, Mr. K attempts to establish a closer emotional connection with the analyst by asking him about his weekend. Mr. K's question together with his enticing soft voice filled the analyst with tension and conflict. The analyst assimilated the patient's question and tone of voice to schemas that depicted Mr. K as a needy person asking an inappropriately intrusive question. The analyst's defensive, curt response and business-like tone of voice signaled to the patient his desire for distance. In response to these signals Mr. K extinguished his feelings. Mr. K's flat emotional state conveyed to the analyst that his distancing maneuver was successful, but at the cost of his emotional ties to Mr. K. The analyst's reflection on Mr. K's hesitant manner of asking about his weekend conveyed the analyst's desire for the focus to be on Mr. K's experience, while the tension in the analyst's voice expressed his continued discomfort with the interaction.

This opening dialogue of Mr. K's Monday hour illustrates very well how the form and content of the therapeutic interaction are the result of the patient and the analyst influencing one another to respond in a particular manner and to accept the meaning that they each attributed to the interaction. The vignette also demonstrates how the patient and the analyst apprehend one another's experience by listening not only to what they each say, but importantly, by attending to their nonverbal signals. In this example, the patient's and analyst's vocal tone and rhythm were important communications about how each of them was experiencing the interaction and what they each wanted from the other.

Mr. K   (with an edge of irritability in his voice): Yes, a reticence. Today is just going to be a repeat of last week with my clients. At my client meetings I'm the one at the marker board, leading the discussion. I'm invariably frustrated by these people because they're so stupid. They're simply not intelligent enough to understand what I'm doing for them. They can't even ask questions about it. I look at them and they look blankly back at me, no response, no acknowledgment, no connection, no nothing! I just want to throw up my hands and leave. No matter how good I am or what I do, I'm ignored. There is no place for me there, so why go to work?

Analyst   (with understanding and in a calm voice): Your feelings about your interactions with your clients may also reflect your experience of our interaction when you asked me about my weekend. You took the lead to make a connection with me and my response left you feeling empty, ignored, as if I didn't get the message.

Mr. K's response to the analyst's interpretation of Mr. K's reticence illustrates the use of a narrative story about events in the patient's current life to unconsciously express the meanings that the patient attributes to the therapeutic interaction. The analyst surmised that Mr. K's story about his interactions with his clients was also about their interaction because the event that Mr. K described was similar to their interaction from Mr. K's perspective. The analyst therefore inferred that the feelings and beliefs that Mr. K described in his interaction with his clients were also the emotions and meanings he was attributing to his interaction with the analyst. By interpreting Mr. K's story as a representation of Mr. K's experience of their interaction, the analyst has identified and interpreted Mr. K's transference to him. The analyst also accounts for his influence on the therapeutic process by acknowledging that his behavior is the subject of Mr. K's transference, specifically his nonemotional response to Mr. K at the beginning of the hour. And, importantly, he communicates his emotional acceptance of Mr. K's position in the calm, soothing voice absent any irritation or distress.

Mr. K (some uneasiness in his voice): I want to be let in, but I'm not sure if I'm not being asked in or if I'm not allowing anyone in. Either way I feel alone and that there is something wrong with me. I have this image of my getting up and walking out of the session. (Mr. K sits up, faces away, and begins to cry.) I need to feel safe. I'm having this image of my mother and I. I feel a pressure like I did when I was 9 or 10. I'm with my mother, going over my history lessons with her, and she's just not there. She just didn't care, not about my feelings or what I thought. It wasn't safe to have feelings at all. So I don't. I have this image now of you becoming my mother and my mother becoming you, back and forth. I'm angry, alone, and confused.

The analyst's first impression of Mr. K's response to the analyst's interpretively linking the experience he had with his clients to his experience of the analyst that day, was to question the correctness of the interpretation. Mr. K's stating that there is something wrong with him, that he wants to leave the session, and that his mother is just not there, all suggest that the analyst's interpretation had further alienated Mr. K. However, Mr. K did not employ any defensive communication styles. He continued to relate to the analyst in an emotionally meaningful manner using stories and images to convey his meanings to the analyst. And, although very emotional, the coherence of Mr. K's communication indicated that there was no disruption of his sense of self. He knew who he is and who the analyst is, where they are, and the purpose of their interaction. So the analyst entertained a second hypothesis. He reckoned that the interpretation was correct and that the patient felt understood. In feeling understood Mr. K also felt safe to experience the hitherto defended against memories of how he and his mother formed the schema that causes him to feel emotionally alienated from others. The analyst opined that Mr. K's confusion, especially the image of his mother becoming the analyst and vice-versa, was indicative of Mr. K's comparing the analyst's empathic behavior with his mother's nonempathic behavior. In other words Mr. K was trying to make the analyst's behavior fit the old schema, which of course it could not. So, the analyst formulated the following intervention to base on his second hypothesis:

Analyst   (with a caring, soft tone in his voice): Today, you've experienced me as unavailable emotionally to you as was your mother. Without an emotional connection to me you feel unsafe and cut off from you own feelings. Without feelings you believe that there is something missing inside of you, something that you don't have to make me interested in you, to make our relationship work.

Mr. K   (crying now but less intensely): Yes, you understand. I want to be wanted here, but I get scared and shut down, turning off my feelings. I know when I do that it sends a message: don't get close, stay away. I don't need you.

Mr. K's last response indicates that the analyst's second hypothesis was correct. Not only did Mr. K confirm the intervention, he added material. He sketched out the defensive schema he constructed with his mother to protect himself and her from the terrible feelings he was experiencing. Mr. K also noted the interpersonal consequences of his behavior: "Don't get close, stay away."

The analyst's last intervention is constructed out of the information that Mr. K provided in the images, feelings, and memories that characterized the history lesson with his mother. The analyst identified himself with mother, as had the patient, but this time told the story from the patient's perspective of the analyst's behavior with him. The object of the intervention was to continue the corrective emotional experience of being emotionally understood and responded to by the analyst. Indeed, the emotional reciprocity between Mr. K and the analyst invited Mr. K to join the analyst in understanding their interaction, which, importantly, included the analyst's contribution to making Mr. K feel alienated. Of equal if not more importance is the emotional context in which this intervention occurred. The analyst maintained his calm, soothing, and understanding voice. His invitation to Mr. K to express his feelings, even after his intense outburst of hurt and anger, communicated to Mr. K that the analyst could contain Mr. K's feelings and that his feelings do not always destroy relationships. This experience ran counter to Mr. K's experiences with his mother and his clients, thereby requiring Mr. K to revise his schemas to account for this interaction with the analyst.

CONCLUDING REMARKS

Interactional theory illuminates the organization and content of a patient's mind through understanding the types of relationships he forms with the analyst and others and the meaning he attributes to these relationships. Interactional technique posits that it is through the creation of new experiences with the analyst that the patient is empowered to change maladaptive ways of organizing and interpreting his experience of himself and the world.

REFERENCES

Bacal, H. A. (1985), Optimal responsiveness and the therapeutic process. In: *Progress in Self Psychology*, ed. A. Goldberg. New York: Guilford, pp. 202–226.

Beebe, B., & Lachmann, F. M. (1988), Mother–infant mutual influence and the precursors of psychic structure. In: *Frontiers in Self Psychology: Progress in Self Psychology*, ed. A. Goldberg. Hillsdale, NJ: Analytic Press, pp. 3–25.

———— ———— (1994), Representation and internalization in infancy: Three principles of salience. *Psychoanal. Psychol.*, 11:127–165.

Dorpat, T. L. (1994), On inauthentic communication and interactional modes of defense. *Psychoanal. Psychother. Rev.*, 5:25–35.

———— Miller, M. L. (1992), *Clinical Interaction and the Analysis of Meaning: A New Psychoanalytic Theory.* Hillsdale, NJ: Analytic Press.

———— ———— (1994), Primary process meaning analysis. *Contemp. Psychoanal.*, 30:201–212.

Greenson, R. (1967), *The Technique and Practice of Psychoanalysis.* New York: International Universities Press.

Greenwald, A. G., & Banaji, M. R. (1995), Implicit social cognition: Attitudes, self-esteem, and stereotypes. *Psycholog. Rev.*, 102:4–27.

Horowitz, M. J. (1988), *Introduction to Psychodynamics.* New York: Basic Books.

Langs, R. (1978), *The Listening Process.* New York: Jason Aronson.

Lichtenberg, J. D., Lachmann, F. M., & Fosshage, J. L. (1992), *Self and Motivational Systems.* Hillsdale, NJ: Analytic Press.

Mandler, G. (1984), *Mind and Body.* New York: Norton.

Miller, M. L. (1996), Validation, interpretation, and corrective emotional experience in psychoanalytic treatment. *Contemp. Psychoanal.*, 32:385–410.

———— Dorpat, T. L. (1996), Meaning analysis: An interactional approach to psychoanalytic theory and practice. *Psychoanal. Rev.*, 83:219–245.

Nisbett, R., & Ross, L. (1980), *Human Inference.* Englewood Cliffs, NJ: Prentice-Hall.

Piaget, J. (1970), *Structuralism.* New York: Basic Books.

Sander, L. W. (1988), The event-structure of regulation in neonate-caregiver system as a biological background for early organization of psychic structure. In: *Progress in Self Psychology,* ed. A. Goldberg. Hillsdale, NJ: Analytic Press.

Sandler, J. (1960), The background of safety. *Internat. Rev. Psycho-Anal.*, 41:352–356.

Shore, A. N. (1994), *Affect Regulation and the Origin of the Self: The Neurobiology of Emotional Development.* Hillsdale, NJ: Lawrence Erlbaum.

Stern, D. N. (1985), *The Interpersonal World of the Infant.* New York: Basic Books.

Stolorow, R. D. (1994), The nature and therapeutic action of psychoanalytic interpretation. In: *The Intersubjective Perspective,* ed. R. D. Stolorow, G. E. Atwood, & B. Brandchaft. Northvale, NJ: Jason Aronson.

────── Brandchaft, B., & Atwood, G. E. (1987), *Psychoanalytic Treatment: An Intersubjective Approach.* Hillsdale, NJ: Analytic Press.

Weiss, J., & Sampson, H. (1986), *The Psychoanalytic Process.* New York: Guilford Press.

Werner, H., & Kaplan, B. (1963), *Symbol Formation.* New York: Wiley.

2.

Relational Psychoanalysis

Robert M. Gordon with Lewis Aron, Stephen A. Mitchell, Jody Messler Davies

Relational psychoanalysis is a distinctive contemporary school of psychoanalysis. It developed from a convergence of several major currents of psychoanalytic theory, including British school object relations, American interpersonal psychoanalysis, self psychology, and infant developmental research (Mitchell, 1988). The much encompassing term *relational* includes interactions between the individual and the social world, internal and external interpersonal relations, as well as self-regulation and mutual regulation, thus building the bridge between the interpersonal and intrapsychic realms (Aron, 1996). Relational psychoanalysis also highlights interactions between physical, temperamental, motivational, and psychological processes, emphasizing context and meaning (Ghent, 1992).

The relational model views the operations of the mind as fundamentally dyadic and interactive in nature. Experience emerges in an interactive field between people. The analytic situation is understood in relational psychoanalysis to be shaped by the continual participation of both the analysand and the analyst, as well as by the coconstruction of meaning, authenticity, and new relational experiences. Old relational patterns are inevitably repeated, but it is hoped that each analyst and patient dyad can discover unique ways to move beyond

31

this embeddedness in the past and construct and negotiate new and creative ways of being with each other. Relational analysis suggests that it is not objective truth that the analyst and patient pursue, so much as the meaning that they mutually construct.

SIGNIFICANT CONTRIBUTIONS TO CONTEMPORARY RELATIONAL PSYCHOANALYSIS

Contemporary views of relational psychoanalysis have been influenced by the writings of Aron, Benjamin, Bromberg, Davies, Frawley, Greenberg, Hoffman, and Mitchell, whose ideas will be more fully described throughout the chapter. A theme involving the mutual contributions of both the analyst and patient to all clinical phenomenon is noted.

In 1983 Greenberg and Mitchell published *Object Relations in Psychoanalytic Theory,* a landmark in the delineation of relational psychoanalysis that has had a dramatic impact on all subsequent theorizing in the field. Object relations "refers to individuals' interactions with external and internal (real and imagined) other people, and to the relationship between their internal and object worlds" (Greenberg and Mitchell, 1983, pp. 13–14). The authors delineated two mutually exclusive models of the mind: the drive–structure and relational–structure models. The drive model, originally developed by Freud (1915), stated that relations with significant others—so called object relations—and the individual's internal representations of these relations are vicissitudes of the drives themselves. Freud comprehended the role of objects (i.e., others) largely in relation to the discharge of drives: objects facilitate or inhibit discharge. Drive theory is derived from a philosophy that views humans as essentially individualistic. Human goals and desires are seen as predominantly personal in nature.

The second method of understanding object relations holds that relations with others as opposed to internal drives constitute the basic motivational force in human behavior. This relational model views men and women as social individuals, with human satisfactions realizable within the tapestry of relationships, past and present.

During the past decade there has been a proliferation of books and articles on relational psychoanalysis reflecting both the interpersonalizing of many theoretical constructs and a shift from a one- to a two-person perspective on the analytic situation (Ghent, 1989). In a later book, Mitchell (1988) crystallized a distinct relational trend, describing the clinical application of the relational-conflict model. In a later work Mitchell (1993) articulated the mutual wishes, needs, and fears of both the analyst and patient as they enter into a new relationship. Other writers have stressed the importance of experiencing others as having their own inner subjective world and separate centers of initiative, of the attainment of mutual recognition as a vital aspect of health (Benjamin, 1988), and of refinements in the concept of analytic neutrality (Greenberg, 1991).

Relational psychoanalysis also has been strongly influenced by Hoffman's writings on the social–constructivistic model (1991, 1992a, 1993, 1994), which emphasized the analyst's inevitable and continual participation in the creation of the transference. The constructivistic model maintains that the observer plays a critical role in shaping, constructing, and organizing what is being observed. Extending this idea the relational model stresses the ambiguity of reality: each individual has his or her plausible view; all knowledge is perspectival; and there are perspectives and centers of subjectivity other than one's own (Aron, 1996).

Bromberg's writings (1991, 1993, 1994, 1996) reflected a discernible shift with regard to the understanding of the human mind and unconscious processes. He viewed the self as multiple and lacking in cohesion. The clinical relevance of his perspective on dissociation and the self were further developed by Davies and Frawley (1994) who see dissociation as resulting from the need to integrate overwhelming anxiety and the need to integrate contradictory images of significant others.

More recently Aron (1996) provided a detailed description of the implications of a relational model that includes viewing transference, countertransference, resistance, and interpretation in an intersubjective context. Intersubjectivity refers to the ability to recognize others as having a separate center of initiative and feelings and with whom feeling states can be shared.

He viewed the analyst and patient as mutually constructing their relationship and mutually regulating their interaction, as well as their experiences of their interaction.

These contributions to the contemporary field of relational psychoanalysis consistently stress that the analyst needs to be sensitively aware and accept the responsibility that it is their own character and subjectivity that shapes the values, theoretical convictions, and forms the foundation for clinical interventions (Aron, 1996).

HISTORICAL PERSPECTIVE

As is true of all important developments in the history of ideas, psychoanalytic models arise in an intellectual, cultural, and social context and are fashioned in the context of dialectical tension between differently oriented clinicians (Berman, 1996). The relational perspective emerged from the dialectical tensions between several groups of innovative individuals, that included the Freud–Ferenczi relationship; the interpersonal writings of Sullivan, Thompson, Fromm, and Fromm-Reichmann (which developed in response to classical psychoanalysis and American Pragmatism); the British school object relations' ideas of Fairbairn and Winnicott (which emerged in response to Klein's theories); and Kohut's self psychology (which was a reaction to the limitations of American ego psychology).

Ferenczi's Contribution to Theory and Technique

Ferenczi's innovative work (1932, 1933) was largely concerned with the heart of the analytic situation: the relationship between patient and analyst. His discoveries about trauma, transference, and countertransference were in precisely those areas that are now receiving much attention among current psychoanalytic theorists and practitioners. One of Ferenczi's most important contributions was a statement of the inevitability of the analyst's repetition of the patient's original trauma, with the analyst now in the role of abuser. This clinical observation anticipated the discovery, some forty to fifty years later, of the probability of the analyst's actualizing the patient's transference expectations in that the patient pulls the analyst in as a participant in his or her reexperiencing of an early trauma, after which the patient perceives and reacts to this dynamic.

Along with his elucidation of the role of trauma, it was through his understanding and technical management of transference that he made his most radical contribution. Transference was seen as the patient's unconscious expectations of the analyst, while countertransference was viewed as the analyst's emotional responses to the patient. From early on, Ferenczi emphasized the analyst as a real person. The patient is aware of and reacts to subtle nuances in the analyst's behavior. Thus, the patient's transference does not arise solely from within the patient, but is influenced by and created in response to the analyst's behaviors and interventions. In short, the transference is induced conjointly by the analyst and patient.

This line of thought was the first conceptualization of transference as cocreated between patient and analyst. Ferenczi also stressed the influence of the analyst's character traits in the inducement of transference and countertransference. Ferenczi was the first psychoanalyst to notice ways in which the patient becomes the "interpreter" of the analyst's countertransference experience (Hoffman, 1983; Aron, 1996). He encouraged patients to express their perceptions of his countertransference reactions and conflicts.

It was Ferenczi, then, who made the first and most important shift that moved psychoanalytic theory from Freud's exclusively one-person model of the patient's development, psychopathology, and treatment toward a two-person or relational model. Transference arises in the context of countertransference; resistance arises in response to the analyst's empathic failures; dreams and acting out are attempts at communication. For Ferenczi, the intrapsychic was not replaced by the interpersonal; it was in essence an interpersonal concept (Aron and Harris, 1993).

The Impact of Interpersonal Psychoanalysis

Interpersonal psychoanalysis was developed by Harry Stack Sullivan, Clara Thompson, Erich Fromm, and Frieda Fromm-Reichmann in response to classical psychoanalysis and its intrapsychic tradition. In the development and elaboration of the dual instinct theory and the structural model, Freud (1923) stated that drives arise spontaneously, press for gratification, become conflictual, and underlie the complex structures of the psychic apparatus. The early interpersonalists felt that this intrapsychic tradition did not sufficiently address what they felt to be more important in treating psychopathology: real interactions with significant others, past and present.

Sullivan's (1953) interpersonal model was not fashioned around speculations about what was taking place in the patient's psyche, but rather on a detailed inquiry into historical events and what was currently taking place in the patient's relationships with important other people, including the analyst. Through the work of Levenson (1972, 1983) and Wolstein (1983, 1988) psychoanalysis increasingly emphasized the here-and-now features of the transference and countertransference interaction.

But there were problems with the interpersonal approach, both clinically and conceptually. Sullivan put great emphasis on language—using words to ask questions and using words to clarify and understand. This approach is helpful with many patients, but at times words can be used defensively and drive experiences further away. Furthermore, working with patients' current, here-and-now experience typically leads to an appreciation of their addictive attachments to, and identifications with, early significant others. Interpersonal psychoanalysis had no satisfactory way of describing or explaining these important self and object identifications. What mediates between past and present? The patient brings his or her interpersonal dynamics into the analytic relationship and they shape that relationship in the here-and-now. But how are those patterns stored *inside* the patient? What form do they take? How can the patient experience and access them? (Stern, 1995).

British Object Relations Theorists

The British school object relations theorists provided a corrective for these missing pieces and an exciting complement to the American interpersonal tradition. As distinct from Freud, Fairbairn (1952) maintained that everything that is to be found *inside* the patient's mind has actually taken place between the child and significant others. Fairbairn's theory is not only compatible with interpersonal psychoanalysis, it also extends the implications of Sullivan's work into areas that Sullivan had avoided.

According to Fairbairn (1952), the fundamental motivational thrust in human beings is the need to seek connections with others. Each individual shapes his or her relationships according to the patterns of relatedness that are internalized from the earliest significant relationships. The modes of connection with these early objects become the preferred and expected ways of relating to new people. New love objects are chosen for their similarity to past satisfying or unsatisfying objects, and interactions with new partners provoke the old, expected behaviors. New experiences are processed and interpreted according to old expectations. In Fairbairn's understanding of the analytic interaction, the patient experiences the analyst in the transference as an old, potentially unsatisfying object notwithstanding hopes for a new and enriching relationship. According to Fairbairn, patients cannot give up addictive ties to old objects unless they believe and trust that new ways of relating are possible, that, in fact, they can be heard and seen. He defined analytic progress as the result of a changed capacity to relate to others (Mitchell and Black, 1995).

Winnicott was a pediatrician before he became a psychoanalyst and his understanding of the types of mothering that facilitate or impede healthy development was a significant component of his theories (Mitchell and Black, 1995). At the heart of Winnicott's work was a concern with the quality of subjective experience. The importance of personal meaning and of the image of oneself as a distinct and creative center of one's own experience were core themes. Winnicott (1969) saw the patient as powerfully self-restorative and as shaping and creating the analytic relationship to provide the environmental experiences missed in childhood. It is the experience of self in relation to other that ultimately is most curative. Winnicott saw the patient as an active participant in analysis, who takes what the analyst has to offer and reshapes it according to his or her needs. He radically shifted the view of the analyst as active and in control (as the interpreter) to one in which the patient actively creates and shapes what the analyst provides in order for the patient to discover a more authentic sense of self. Winnicott encouraged analysts to tolerate uncertainty and offer spontaneous and authentic emotional responsiveness in response to the patient's needs for dependency and nurturance (Mitchell and Black, 1995; Aron, 1996).

In Argentina, Racker (1968) integrated Freudian, Kleinian, and Fairbairnian ideas into a model of countertransference. Racker viewed the analyst's countertransference as a meaningful and therapeutically invaluable tool that provides him or her with access to unconscious and otherwise inexplicable aspects of the patient's inner world. He saw transference and countertransference as inseparable entities—the coming together and intermingling of two different systems of internalized self and object representations. In a remarkably contemporary turn, Racker went so far as to include in the patient's transference real aspects of the analyst's personality, accurately perceived, which may or may not be consciously available to the analyst. Racker (1968) portrayed the analyst as struggling with internal conflicts similar to those of the patient and criticized "the myth" of the analytic situation that "analysis is an encounter between a sick person and a healthy one" (p. 132). He emphasized the analyst's continual embeddedness and active participation in the analytic process.

Two neo-Kleinian analysts, Bion (1962) and Ogden (1979) made significant contributions to relational psychoanalysis by interpersonalizing Klein's (1946) concept of projective identification. Klein viewed projective identification using a one-person psychology as a fantasy in the mind of the infant or patient that was unconsciously placed into the mother or analyst. Projective identification differs from pure projection in that it not only expels outward aspects of the self, but also induces the object of the projection to experience the projective. Bion (1962) believed that the patient's projections are processed through the analyst's own anxieties, conflicts and dynamics. Ogden (1979) further transformed the concept into an interactional construct by describing projective identification as a process in which a group of fantasies and accompanying self representations are deposited into the analyst to be returned in a modified and less dangerous version.

Intersubjective Contributions

Stolorow and Brandchaft (1994) described the interplay between the patient's and analyst's subjective realities in the analytic encounter. Ogden (1994) emphasized the dialectical nature of intersubjectivity. He stressed that although the mother–infant dyad exists in unity, they are definitely separate entities with their own physical and psychological subjectivities. The moments of synchrony that occur between the mother and infant or between analyst and patient are what Ogden refers to as intersubjectivity, whereas their separate realities represent their subjectivities. Benjamin (1988) stated that one of the critical goals of relational psychoanalysis is for the patient and analyst to mutually recognize their separate subjectivities and centers of initiative.

CONCEPTUAL PILLARS OF THE ANALYTIC SITUATION REVISITED

The conceptual shift from a one-person to a field or dyadic approach to the operations of the mind has enormous implications for understanding the analytic situation. Within relational model theory, many aspects of the psychoanalytic process have been reconceptualized.

The classical psychoanalytic model is based on the premise that psychoanalysis provides a very unique kind of experience for the patient through the establishment of a carefully controlled analytic situation. The couch, the frequency of meeting four or five times per week, the fundamental rule of free association, the largely silent analyst who remains shrouded in anonymity—these structural and technical factors make it possible for the patient to undergo an experience that activates early childhood memories and passions. While these intense feelings are experienced as directed toward the analyst, they are, in actuality, long buried oedipal feelings and wishes from early childhood (Freud, 1912, 1913, 1933).

The centerpiece of this vision is the premise that the experiences of the patient in analysis derive from *inside* the patient, experiences that uncoil in the carefully designed analytic space provided by classical technique. It is this premise that makes the classical model so fundamentally a one-person perspective. The analytic encounter is like a time machine, in which the patient, through the temporal displacements of the transference, returns back to his or her past. The analyst as a person is not particularly important. He or she performs the functionary role of operator of the time machine. As long as the analyst is competent, he or she will provide a generic function that enables the patient to experience, explore, and understand his or her past more fully.

Transference and Countertransference

In the classical model, transference and countertransference are viewed as temporal displacements. In the former, the patient experiences something from the past, displaced onto the person of the analyst. Freud (1912, 1913) viewed the patient's transference feelings toward the analyst as representing the emergence of repressed feelings toward significant childhood figures displaced onto the person of the analyst. He viewed countertransference as an obstacle or impediment to treatment that the analyst had to overcome through self-analysis or further psychoanalysis. Recent writers who follow the classical model, such as Jacobs (1986, 1991, 1995) and Renik (1993a,b), have stressed the therapeutic value of countertransference.

In the relational model, transference and countertransference define the global, interactive experience of the analysand

and analyst respectively. Each is assumed to respond to the *actual* participation of the other, shaped by internal dynamics and the personal past of both. Thus, neither transference nor countertransference need to be distortions. The patient's transference is an expression of his or her effort to reach the analyst, to protect themselves, and to regulate their interactions with the analyst. Conversely, the analyst's countertransference is an expression of his or her efforts toward self-protection, reaching, and regulating his or her interactions with the patient.

In relational psychoanalysis, transference and countertransference are seen as mutual creations by patient and analyst. Transference reactions are revealed in and inevitably shape the analyst's countertransference. Hoffman (1983) believed that transference operates like a "Geiger counter," with past experiences sensitizing patients to selectively attend to or notice meanings that might be unimportant to others (see also Mitchell, 1988, 1993; Fiscalini, 1995a,b; Gabbard, 1995; Aron, 1996).

Transference–countertransference interactions are the central focus of the psychoanalytic process. The patient's psychopathology is viewed in terms of adhesive ties to old relationships and patterns. These pathological relationships, including internal object relationships, manifest themselves in the interaction with the analyst. The analyst is inevitably and usefully drawn into the patient's repetitive patterns of experience and action. The analyst invariably will behave according to the patient's design and eventually become a participant in his or her patient's transference. Levenson (1972, 1983) stated that the therapist must become trapped, immersed, and participate fully in the system and then work his or her way out by increasing the patient's awareness of these patterns of interaction.

Resistance

In traditional psychoanalytic thinking, resistance to the analytic process derives from the *internal* battle between the patient's impulses and defenses (Greenson, 1967). In the relational model, resistance reflects the patient's struggle between old and new relational patterns, between adhesive ties to unsatisfying objects (reanimated in the transference–countertransference integrations with the analyst) and the possibility of new forms of relatedness that patient and analyst struggle to discover. Because the analyst is necessarily deeply and conflictually responsive to the patient's transference anxieties, there is always a complementary *counterresistance* in the analyst and patient to finding new ways of engaging each other.

Conflict

Relational approaches view the mind as inherently conflicted in nature. The relational-conflict model emphasizes that problems in living are a function of the patient's loyalty to internalized loved ones of the past and the difficulties in separating from the familiar and familial. Consistent with Fairbairn's (1952) clinical observations, the more depriving or harmful the internalized figures from the past, the stronger the connectedness to the past. For example, living in an emotionally deprived family environment often leads to greater fearfulness of exploration and the pursuit of new experiences. Patients are viewed as striving to achieve new and enriching experiences, while simultaneously repeating internalized and familiar patterns (Mitchell, 1988; Hirsch, 1994). Mitchell (1997) stated that the fundamental human conflicts rest on the "need for a grounding that feels completely known and predictable, a reliable anchoring, a framework, . . . and, on the other hand, a longing to break out of established patterns, stepping over boundaries, encountering something unpredictable" (p. 28).

Enactment

The term *enactment,* as described by Jacobs (1986, 1991), was intended to delineate the ways in which analyst and patient verbally and nonverbally act upon each other. Jacobs viewed enactment as a form of ongoing unconscious communication, interpersonal influence, and persuasion between analyst and patient. Enactments are initiated by both participants. Renik (1993a,b) stated that countertransference enactments always precede countertransference awareness. Thus, analysts will enact their countertransference before they become aware of the specific meanings of these actions.

Model of the Mind: Views on Trauma and Dissociation

The relational model of the mind views the psyche as developmentally organized. It rests on the fundamental assumption that the basic units of psychic structure are composed of early interactive experiences as they come to form a template and perceptual filter through which all later experience is viewed and meaningfully encoded and organized. Thus, the mind is organized around representations of mutually interactive dyadic engagements, both satisfying and frustrating. Within these relationships of mutual influence the infant learns to self-regulate intense affect states by learning to control and modulate the behavior of significant others (Beebe, 1985; Beebe and Lachmann, 1991). Stern (1985) has demonstrated how these dyadic experiences come to be mentally represented and then organized into more broadly defined categories, necessitating a certain amount of generalization across separate events. Though closely related to actual lived experience, these internal representations are not veridical reconstructions in memory but are changed via generalization and categorization. These encoded memories will be shaped and colored by both powerful affective cross currents and the intense, mutually interactive systems of object related fantasy that infuses the interpersonal situation.

Trauma

Analysts often discover that irreconcilable interpersonal schemata are separately maintained in subsystems of organized self-other impressions, subsystems which coexist in intricately organized psychodynamic patterns of relative clarity (Davies,

1996a). One of the clearest examples of such irreconcilable
subsystems of self and object representation is captured in the
mental organization of events secondary to severe parental
abuse. Davies and Frawley (1994) described how the abused
child is called upon to integrate impossibly different represen-
tational schemas. One system involves organizing instances of
an evil, toxic, abused child self with an infantile or sadistic,
out-of-control parent abuser. This includes intense emotions
of rage, terror, shame, and guilt organized around fantasies of
mutual destruction, penetration, betrayal, omnipotent seduc-
tion, hyperarousal, etc. The other system incorporates instances of self with other in which nurturance, caretaking,
protection, and warm affection predominate along with moments of relative safety, bodily sensations of quiescence and
soothing. These representations of self and other are dramatically incompatible as are the intense affective linkages and organizing fantasies that unite them. It is not that one system
becomes conscious and the other system unconscious. Both
subsystems alternate in consciousness as each is called forth
by a particular evocative charge of an interpersonal present
(Davies, 1996a).

Dissociation

According to Bromberg (1994) and Davies (1996b), trauma
creates affects and thoughts that cannot be integrated by the
victim. Bromberg stated that the mechanism of dissociation is
a defense against overwhelming anxiety that would result in
fragmentation. It provides an escape where dramatically incompatible emotions or perceptions are needed to be cognitively
processed in the same relationship. The traumatic experience
that is causing the incompatible perception and emotion is
removed from the cognitive processing system and remains in
an unformulated and unsymbolized state (Van der Kolk, 1987).
Bromberg (1994), Davies and Frawley (1994), and Stern (1996)
emphasized that dissociative self-states cannot be put directly
into words and can only be known through the impact on the
analyst–patient interaction.

RELATIONAL MODEL TECHNIQUE

There is a basic problem in attempting to establish technical principles within a relational perspective. If each analytic dyad is assumed to be unique, if the meaning of the analyst's actions are not determined by what the analyst thinks they are but by what the analyst and patient together decide they are, and if the analyst cannot know how to be the patient's analyst at the start of the process but discovers it only in the struggle that emerges through transference-countertransference patterns—if all this is assumed, how can there be any prescribed technical principles? On what basis could one possibly decide that any specific intervention is more therapeutic than any other action? Does anything go?

From a relational perspective, the analyst should make clinical decisions based on self-reflection. People interact with each other in many different ways; various forms of interaction differ in terms of the kinds of constraints they place on the expressiveness of the other. The analyst should find a way to participate with each patient that allows that patient the fewest constraints, the greatest freedom to explore their own experience, past and present. For some patients, a relative silence on the part of the analyst allows them the greatest freedom. For other patients, the analyst's silence is experienced as malevolent and withholding. For some patients, the couch provides emancipatory possibilities; for some patients the couch is deadly. The meaning of the analyst's participation is created between the two participants and the analyst must try to do the right thing—to facilitate for the patient the greatest possible self-expression and self-understanding.

THERAPEUTIC ACTION

Therapeutic action within the relational model depends upon the establishment of a safe environment in which both the patient and analyst contribute unique perceptions of their shared experience. As the patient's early relational patterns are reenacted within the analytic space, adhesive, pathological ties to old objects will be highlighted and held in stark contrast against the new and one hopes more adaptive and flexible relationship that the patient and analyst struggle to negotiate in the present.

Imagine the consequences of living in a house with only one window. For all intents and purposes the view from that one window will define that person's reality. Only by experiencing the view from a new window, built perhaps on the other side of the house, will that individual gradually internalize a degree of perspective and relativity, a sense that vision and meaning involve choice and agency. Through the process of contrasting, integrating, and appreciating the nuances of alternative perspectives and subjectivities other than one's own, the patient and analyst will develop more richly textured and complex self and other representations. The patient and analyst will coconstruct a shared vision from two different perspectives of the world existing beyond the walls of the self.

Maintaining an optimal tension between the recreated past and the interpersonally negotiated, new analytic relationship becomes one of the critical functions of the analyst. Indeed, this is Greenberg's (1991) reformulation of analytic neutrality. In both behavior and attitude the analyst strives to create an atmosphere of neutrality. In essence, an analyst's neutrality is intended to communicate a supportive stance without an expressed predilection for a particular aspect of the patient's personality. Greenberg advocated the need for optimal tension as reflected in the patient's experience of the analyst as both a safe and as a threatening presence.

In a therapeutic model that stresses the reenactment of maladaptive interpersonal patterns, the analyst's very presence and ability to provide certain holding, soothing, containing functions can highlight the boundaries between old and new relational experience. Both active participation and clinical observation are essential analytic tools. The analyst observes and participates in the patient's relational world and knows the patient "from the inside out" (Bromberg, 1991). The analyst must fully enter the patient's relational world to freely engage in transference–countertransference reenactments and then disengage sufficiently to observe, contain, process, and interpret with the patient what has occurred between them. The analyst's ability to maintain the rhythm of active participation and observation as well as engagement and disengagement from the passionate undercurrent of countertransference pressure remains indispensable to analytic success.

CLINICAL VIGNETTE

The following clinical vignette is a modified version of the case presented by Mitchell and Black (1995). Harvey, an artist of considerable skill but limited accomplishments, had sought treatment for a variety of problems involving inhibitions in his ability to commit himself to work and intimate personal relationships. His first analyst, who seemed to have an ego psychology orientation, had seen him for five years and then retired from practice. Harvey took about one year to mourn the loss of his therapist then decided to seek treatment again. Because he wanted to be in analysis several times a week, which he would have difficulty affording on a private basis, he applied to a clinic of a psychoanalytic training institute, where he would be seen by a candidate in training.

The candidate who began seeing Harvey quickly assumed that he was an ideal patient. Harvey was deeply committed to psychoanalysis and had clear ideas about what it had offered and might continue to provide him in the future. Harvey's first analysis provided insights into the complex relationship he had with his mother, a bright, creative woman who had a longstanding history of depression. Following the birth of Harvey's immediately older brother, she had become paralyzed with depression and was hospitalized for several years during which she was essentially immobile and nonverbal. She then decided to have another child and was reanimated and finally returned home from the hospital. Giving birth to and caring for Harvey was the central focus of her existence. As a child, Harvey was unaware of the family secret concerning his mother's psychiatric history and lengthy hospitalization. Nevertheless, he sensed in her an extreme fragility. He became a very loyal and dedicated son, surrendering himself to her overprotective, anxious care.

Harvey's relationship with his first analyst was understood by the two of them as involving a father transference: he often felt abandoned and neglected by the analyst in ways he had experienced with his own father, and he sometimes enjoyed fantasies about being the analyst's favorite patient, a position he had never experienced with his own father. Harvey's relationship with his second analyst also appeared to organize around a sense of the analyst as a longed-for, idealized father figure, who was sometimes experienced as abandoning, sometimes as bestowing a precious attention.

Approximately three years into treatment, Harvey's second analysis took a sudden and dramatic turn, bringing to the forefront issues that bear directly on many of the major controversies regarding analytic technique and therapeutic action. The analyst began to realize that the feeling of great competence and wisdom he generally experienced when working with Harvey had a great deal to do with the way Harvey operated in the sessions. As the analyst became more interested in the subtleties of their interaction, he began to realize that there was a consistent and soothing rhythm to the way in which Harvey presented material. He would tell a dream and provide interesting associations; then he would pause, cueing the analyst that it was time for him to respond. Whatever the analyst said was enthusiastically received and elaborated upon. The analyst understandably felt much more talented and competent with Harvey than with his other patients.

One day Harvey suddenly began talking in an extremely pressured, anxious fashion. It was clear that something dramatic had happened to change his mood—he seemed quite frightened. The analyst noted the shift and asked what had happened. Although Harvey initially denied that anything had occurred, he eventually stated that something indeed had taken place, but that he was not going to talk about it. It took several weeks for the two of them to sufficiently examine Harvey's fears so that he could safely discuss his anxieties in greater depth. Eventually the analyst was able to elicit an explanation.

In one of the analyst's brief comments he had used a word that Harvey had never used before. Harvey was afraid that the analyst had made up this word (a schizophrenic "neologism"), that it did not really exist. This absolutely terrified him because Harvey had privately harbored concerns about his analyst's emotional stability for a significant period of time. Harvey, who felt quite protective of the analyst, was convinced that the analyst would be horrified to have his instability visible to Harvey.

Harvey believed that the analyst suffered from severe emotional difficulties, which he compensated for by helping others. At the same time, Harvey felt certain he was the analyst's favorite patient, the one who helped him feel most competent, most professional, least crazy. This in turn enabled Harvey to feel special. Only Harvey knew the analyst's secret, and the very fact that he concealed this secret was, in part, how Harvey demonstrated his love and support for the analyst. What was most important to the analyst, Harvey believed, was the certainty that his problems were hidden and that he be perceived as competent and professional.

When Harvey eventually expressed these perceptions and convictions about the analyst's deepest and darkest secrets, he feared that this would destroy the analyst's confidence and that the analyst would retaliate through emotional withdrawal and physical abandonment.

As the two of them worked through this therapeutic crisis, Harvey kept telling the analyst that this whole story must have nothing to do with the analyst, but was transference based on his experiences with his crazy mother. His mother had been a kind of impostor as a mother, using her helping role to keep herself organized and cohesive. Through his deep devotion to her and his terror of abandonment, he had kept her together by being her loyal son. All of these ideas and feelings that were experienced toward the analyst must be transferred from his experience of his mother.

The heart of the therapeutic action took place through the analysis of the transference–countertransference matrix. Transference and countertransference were viewed as mutual creations, rather than as initiated solely by the patient or analyst. Harvey was encouraged to express his perceptions of the analyst's craziness and fragility, as well as his understanding of his analyst's central conflicts. Like Harvey, many patients grow up convinced of the danger in expressing negative perceptions, which results in feelings of mystification and passivity. In this case, the analyst and patient explored the impact of Harvey's protective manner toward his analyst. They further examined the benefits and psychological price this behavior held for Harvey.

In supervision, the analyst worked through his particular contribution to this impasse in treatment. He focused on the narcissistic benefits he experienced in being idealized, which enabled him to inhibit the patient's negative reactions and aggression. It was rather difficult for Harvey to imagine himself as important to the analyst in ways other than as protector and rescuer. If the analyst did not need Harvey for these purposes, what possible significance could he have for the analyst? During an extended exploration, the analyst at times felt quite moved by Harvey's dedication and disclosed this to him. He found it touching that Harvey wanted to help him to the point of sacrificing his own future if he felt it would enable the analyst to feel competent and whole. In fact, Harvey deeply resented this protective role, but believed that he had no choice. Later in the analysis, Harvey suggested that there was something confirming and liberating in knowing of his emotional impact and significance to the analyst. This enabled him to increase his level of trust, hope, and safety about renegotiating their relationship in ways that allowed less merger and more autonomy and spontaneity.

According to the relational perspective, it was critical that Harvey's analyst endorsed Harvey's observations about the analyst's anxieties and depression as reality based. Had they been labeled as transferential distortions, Harvey's sense of reality would have been undermined. Harvey might have again abandoned his own perspective and compliantly surrendered to the analyst's presumably superior vision. The relational model also assumes that Harvey had developed particular sensitivities that allowed him to perceive qualities in others, including the analyst, that others might not see. Were the analyst to insist or even agree with Harvey that his experience of him as crazy was a distortion, displaced from his experience of his mother, ironically it would be a way of behaving much like her. It would communicate a closed attitude toward Harvey's perceptions and concerns. The analyst's reluctance to explore these reactions may have confirmed Harvey's suspicions that the analyst was, indeed, fragile and in need of careful protection. Harvey eventually learned that the analyst was not without craziness, but that whatever craziness the analyst experienced was different from Harvey's mother and did not require the loving and hateful sacrifice of Harvey's own authentic experience to maintain a connection.

Relational analysts believe that the most crucial factor in therapeutic progress is enabling the patient to have a new experience rooted in a new relationship. Old relational patterns are inevitably repeated. It is hoped, nonetheless, that the patient and the analyst can find new and more flexible ways to move beyond these repetitions, to free up their relationship, and to construct and negotiate new ways of being with each other (Pizer, 1992, 1996). Greenberg (1991) stated that the analyst needs to achieve a dialectical balance between being too similar to the original objects and being radically different from them. Hoffman (1992b) pointed out that what appears to be part of something old (repetition) may actually turn out to be part of a new experience and that what seems like a new experience may turn out to be a repetition of an old pattern. Even when the analyst is reenacting with the patient an aspect of an old relational pattern, the repetition in all likelihood is not an exact replica of the old experience; it is, in all probability, analogous to it instead. On the other hand, when the analyst is a new object, providing a "corrective emotional experience" for the analysand, it is unlikely that the analyst is literally the opposite of the old object; rather, the analyst is likely to provide a healthy variation of the old experience.

CURRENT CONTROVERSIES IN RELATIONAL PSYCHOANALYSIS

The major controversies in relational psychoanalytic technique include the therapeutic use of self-disclosure, while major new perspectives on the conceptual level pertain to the understanding of self and gender.

Self-Disclosure

The issue of the degree and nature of an analyst's deliberate and purposeful self-disclosure is one of the most controversial in contemporary relational psychoanalysis. Self-disclosure can be divided into inevitable and unintentional events and more purposeful and intentional acts. Purposeful self-disclosure includes the sharing of countertransference reactions and revealing one's thinking and feelings regarding an interaction between the analyst and patient (Aron, 1996). The arguments against making deliberate self-disclosures include: it complicates the treatment unnecessarily; it deflects attention away from the patient's subjective experience; it obscures the nature of the patient's transference; and it may provide a great deal of information about the analyst, which may impede the elaboration of the patient's fantasies about the analyst. In contrast, Gorkin (1987) suggested that judicious disclosures of countertransference reactions can have the positive therapeutic effect of: establishing the therapist's honesty and genuineness; confirming the patient's sense that the analyst is similar to the patient and has conflicts and transferences; clarifying the nature of the patient's interpersonal impact on the analyst and others in general; and breaking through deeply entrenched impasses in treatment. The selective sharing of countertransference reactions facilitates more intensive affective interpersonal interactions (Aron, 1996). Ehrenberg (1995) suggested that carefully considered self-disclosure encourages patients to collaborate more deeply in the mutual exploration of the immediate, here-and-now analytic encounter. Jacobs (1995) stated that self-disclosure sometimes allows the patient to experience the analyst's communication as more authentic and personal resulting in a stronger impact on the patient.

There are no technical guidelines as to what self-disclosures are correct that are independent of the particular analyst–patient relationship, of the stage of treatment, and of the patient's and analyst's character. A detailed exploration is needed of the meaning of the self-revelation for both the patient and analyst (Aron, 1996). Cooper (1996) advocated a greater clinical focus on exploring what takes place after a self-disclosure is made.

Views of Self: Singularity versus Multiplicity

Discernible differences are noted in contemporary relational psychoanalysts' descriptions of the self. Is self an integrated, internally coherent entity, or is the self a configuration of fluid, nonlinear, discontinuous states of consciousness? (Bromberg, 1994; Davies, 1996b).

Proponents of the multiple view of the self believe that psychological health occurs when an individual is able to experience their own sense of multiplicity and integrity, allowing for both a sense of internal consistency and continuity, while simultaneously being receptive to novel experience, contradiction, and ambiguity (Aron, 1996; Mitchell, 1993). A multiple view of the self stresses that individuals present different and unique selves in different social contexts. In contrast, self psychologists promote a view of self as a singular focus on the individual's striving for an integrated sense of self. Lachmann (1996) articulated that the advantages claimed for viewing the self as multiple are totally consistent with a process model of a singular self. He views the principal functions of the self as initiating, organizing, and integrating experiences.

Gender

One of the most controversial and debated topics in relational psychoanalysis is whether gender, which is defined as a person's experience of being a man or woman, is a fixed and unitary developmental achievement, or more of a fluid concept that is subject to change over the course of time? Sweetnam (1996) argued that the complex and dialectical nature of gender is an experience that at times feels coherent and fixed and at other times is more receptive to flux and change. She incorporated the dialectical formulations of the psychological positions described by Klein (1940, 1946) and Ogden (1986, 1994) to conceptualize gender as having either a fixed or fluid quality depending on which psychological position is contextualizing the experience. Each position provides a specific context with particular anxieties, quality of interpersonal relationship, symbolic capacity, and imaginative flexibility that significantly impacts on how masculinity and femininity is experienced.

CONCLUSION

The history and development of relational psychoanalysis highlights that "psychoanalytic tradition ... is best served by a framework that balances continuities with discontinuities, preservation with change, gratitude with an openness to moving on" (Mitchell, 1993, p. 8).

REFERENCES

*Aron, L. (1996), *A Meeting of Minds: Mutuality in Psychoanalysis.* Hillsdale, NJ: Analytic Press.
———— Harris, A., Eds. (1993), *The Legacy of Sandor Ferenczi.* Hillsdale, NJ: Analytic Press.
Beebe, B. (1985), Mother–infant mutual influence and precursors of self and object representations. In: *Empirical Studies of Psychoanalytic Studies,* Vol. 2, ed. J. Masling. Hillsdale, NJ: Analytic Press, pp. 27–48.
———— Lachmann, F. (1991), *The Organization of Representation in Fantasy: Three Principles.* Typescript.
Benjamin, J. (1988), *The Bonds of Love.* New York: Pantheon.
Berman, E. (1996), Relational psychoanalysis: A historical background. Paper presented at the 20th Annual Conference of the Israel Association of Psychotherapy. Zichron Yaakov, Israel, May 2.
Bion, W. R. (1962), *Learning from Experience.* New York: Basic Books.

---

*Recommended reading.

Bromberg, P. (1991), On knowing one's patient inside out. *Psychoanal. Dial.*, 1:399–422.

—— (1993), Shadow and substance. *Psychoanal. Dial.*, 10:147–168.

—— (1994), "Speak! That I may see you": Some reflections on dissociation, reality and psychoanalytic listening. *Psychoanal. Dial.*, 4:517–548.

—— (1996), Standing in the spaces: The multiplicity of self and the psychoanalytic relationship. *Contemp. Psychoanal.*, 32:509–535.

Cooper, S. (1996), The thin blue line of the interpersonal-intrapsychic dialectic: Commentary on papers by Gerson and Spezzano. *Psychoanal. Dial.*, 6:647–669.

Davies, J. M. (1996a), Dissociation, repression and reality in the countertransference. *Psychoanal. Dial.*, 6:189–218.

—— (1996b), Linking the "pre-analytical" with the postclassical. *Contemp. Psychoanal.*, 32:553–576.

*—— Frawley, M. (1994), *Treating Adult Survivors of Childhood Sexual Abuse*. New York: Basic Books.

Ehrenberg, D. B. (1995), Self-disclosure: Therapeutic tool or indulgence? *Contemp. Psychoanal.*, 31:213–228.

Fairbairn, W. R. D. (1952), *An Object-Relations Theory of the Personality*. New York: Basic Books.

Ferenczi, S. (1932), *The Clinical Diary of Sandor Ferenczi*, ed. M. Balint & N. Z. Jackson. Cambridge, MA: Harvard University Press, 1988.

—— (1933), Confusion of tongues between adults and the child. In: *Final Contributions to the Problems and Methods of Psycho-Analysis*. London: Karnac Books, 1980, pp. 156–167.

Fiscalini, J. (1995a), The clinical analysis of transference. In: *The Handbook of Interpersonal Psychoanalysis*, ed. M. Lionells, J. Fiscalini, C. H. Mann, & D. B. Stern. Hillsdale, NJ: Analytic Press, pp. 617–642.

—— (1995b), Transference and countertransference as interpersonal phenomenon. In: *The Handbook of Interpersonal Psychoanalysis*, ed. M. Lionells, J. Fiscalini, C. H. Mann, & D. B. Stern. Hillsdale, NJ: Analytic Press, pp. 603–616.

Freud, S. (1912), The dynamics of transference. *Standard Edition*, 12:99–108. London: Hogarth Press, 1958.

—— (1913), On beginning the treatment (Further recommendations on the technique of psychoanalysis). *Standard Edition*, 12:121–144. London: Hogarth Press, 1958.

—— (1915), Instincts and their vicissitudes. *Standard Edition*, 14:117–140. London: Hogarth Press, 1958.

—— (1923), The Ego and the Id. *Standard Edition,* 19:1–66. London: Hogarth Press, 1961.

—— (1933), New Introductory Lectures on Psycho-Analysis. *Standard Edition,* 22:1–182. London: Hogarth Press, 1964.

Gabbard, G. O. (1995), Countertransference: The emerging ground. *Internat. J. Psycho-Anal.,* 76:475–485.

Ghent, E. (1989), Credo: The dialectics of one-person and two-person psychologies. *Contemp. Psychoanal.,* 25:169–211.

—— (1992), Foreword. In: *Relational Perspectives in Psychoanalysis,* ed. N. J. Skolnick & S. C. Warshaw. Hillsdale, NJ: Analytic Press, pp. xiii–xxii.

Gorkin, M. (1987), *The Uses of Countertransference.* Northvale, NJ: Jason Aronson.

*Greenberg, J. (1991), *Oedipus and Beyond: A Clinical Theory.* Cambridge, MA: Harvard University Press.

*—— Mitchell, S. (1983), *Object Relations in Psychoanalytic Theory.* Cambridge, MA: Harvard University Press.

Greenson, R. R. (1967), *The Technique and Practice of Psychoanalysis.* New York: International Universities Press.

Hirsch, I. (1994), Countertransference love and theoretical model. *Psychoanal. Dial.,* 4:171–192.

Hoffman, I. Z. (1983), The patient as interpreter of the analyst's experience. *Contemp. Psychoanal.,* 19:389–422.

—— (1991), Discussion: Toward a social-constructivistic view of the psychoanalytic situation. *Psychoanal. Dial.,* 1:74–105.

—— (1992a), Some practical implications of a social-constructivistic view of the analytic situation. *Psychoanal. Dial.,* 2:287–304.

—— (1992b), Expressive participation and psychoanalytic discipline. *Contemp. Psychoanal.,* 28:1–15.

—— (1993), The intimate authority of the psychoanalyst's presence. *Psychol. Psychoanal.,* 13:15–23.

—— (1994), Dialectical thinking and therapeutic action in the psychoanalytic process. *Psychoanal. Quart.,* 63:187–218.

Jacobs, T. J. (1986), On countertransference enactments. *J. Amer. Psychoanal. Assn.,* 34:289–307.

—— (1991), *The Use of the Self.* New York: International Universities Press.

—— (1995), Discussion of Jay Greenberg's paper. *Contemp. Psychoanal.,* 31:237–245.

Klein, M. (1940), Mourning and its relation to manic-depressive states. *Internat. J. Psycho-Anal.,* 21:125–153.

—— (1946), Notes on some schizoid mechanisms. *Internat. J. Psycho-Anal.,* 27:99–110.

Lachmann, F. M. (1996), How many selves make a person? *Contemp. Psychoanal.*, 32:595–614.

Levenson, E. (1972), *The Fallacy of Understanding.* New York: Basic Books.

——— (1983), *The Ambiguity of Change.* New York: Basic Books.

*Mitchell, S. (1988), *Relational Concepts in Psychoanalysis.* Cambridge, MA: Harvard University Press.

*——— (1993), *Hope and Dread in Psychoanalysis.* New York: Basic Books.

——— (1997), Psychoanalysis and the degradation of romance. *Psychoanal. Dial.*, 7:23–41.

——— Black, M. J. (1995), *Freud and Beyond.* New York: Basic Books.

Ogden, T. (1979), On projective identification. *Internat. J. Psycho-Anal.*, 60:357–373.

——— (1986), *The Matrix of the Mind.* Northvale, NJ: Jason Aronson.

——— (1994), *Subjects of Analysis.* Northvale, NJ: Jason Aronson.

Pizer, S. (1992), The negotiation of paradox in the analytic patient. *Psychoanal. Dial.*, 2:215–240.

——— (1996), Negotiating potential space: Illusion, play, metaphor and the subjective. *Psychoanal. Dial.*, 6:689–712.

Racker, H. (1968), *Transference and Countertransference.* New York: International Universities Press.

Renik, O. (1993a), Countertransference enactment and the analytic process. In: *Psychic Structure and Psychic Change,* ed. M. Horowitz, O. Kernberg, & E. Weinshel. Madison, CT: International Universities Press, pp. 137–160.

——— (1993b), Analytic interaction: Conceptualizing technique in light of the analyst's irreducible subjectivity. *Psychoanal. Quart.*, 62:553–571.

Stern, D. (1985), *The Interpersonal World of the Infant.* New York: Basic Books.

Stern, D. B. (1995), Cognition and language. In: *The Handbook of Interpersonal Psychoanalysis,* ed. M. Lionells, J. Fiscalini, C. H. Mann, & D. B. Stern. Hillsdale, NJ: Analytic Press, pp. 79–138.

——— (1996), Dissociation and constructivism: Commentary on papers by Davies and Harris. *Psychoanal. Dial.*, 6:252–266.

Stolorow, R. & Brandchaft, B. (1994), *The Intersubjective Perspective.* Northvale, NJ: Jason Aronson.

Sullivan, H. S. (1953), *The Interpersonal Theory of Psychiatry.* New York: W. W. Norton.

Sweetnam, A. (1996), The changing contexts of gender: Between fixed and fluid experience. *Psychoanal. Dial.*, 6:437–459.

Van der Kolk, B. A. (1987), *Psychological Trauma.* Washington, DC:
    American Psychiatric Press.
Winnicott, D. W. (1969), The use of an object. *Internat. J. Psycho-
    Anal.,* 50:711–716.
———— (1971), *Playing and Reality.* Middlesex, U.K.: Penguin.
Wolstein, B. (1983), The pluralism of perspectives on countertrans-
    ference. *Contemp. Psychoanal.,* 19:506–521.
———— (1988), Introduction. In: *Essential Papers on Countertransfer-
    ence,* ed. B. Wolstein. New York: New York University Press,
    pp. 1–15.

3.

Intersubjectivity Theory

Donna M. Orange, Ph.D., Psy.D.

HISTORY OF THE THEORY

Intersubjectivity theory refers broadly to the psychoanalytic theory originally articulated by Atwood and Stolorow (1984), and developed in Stolorow, Brandchaft, and Atwood (1987), in Stolorow and Atwood (1992), in Orange (1995), and in Orange, Atwood, and Stolorow (1997). By *intersubjective* we mean a perspective from which each individual's experience and action are seen as embedded in a constitutive interplay with others' differently organized worlds of experience. For Atwood and Stolorow (1984):

> [P]sychoanalysis seeks to illuminate phenomena that emerge within a specific psychological field constituted by the intersection of two subjectivities—that of the patient and that of the analyst. . . . [Psychoanalysis is] a science of the *intersubjective,* focused on the interplay between the differently organized subjective worlds of the observer and the observed . . . [pp. 41–42].
>
> Patient and analyst together form an indissoluble psychological system, and it is this system that constitutes the empirical domain of psychoanalytic inquiry [p. 64].

The intersubjective perspective is a general view about psychoanalysis, not a metapsychology or a clinical theory. It is a basis
for exploring the developing field—two subjectivities and the
field they create together and from which they emerge—in any
form of psychoanalytic treatment, relational or drive based.
With its focus on the field, intersubjectivity theory also carries
a view of development and of pathogenesis:

> [P]sychological development and pathogenesis are best concep-
> tualized in terms of the specific intersubjective contexts that
> shape the developmental process and that facilitate or obstruct
> the child's negotiation of critical developmental tasks and suc-
> cessful passage through developmental phases. The observa-
> tional focus is the evolving psychological field constituted by
> the interplay between the differently organized subjectivities of
> child and caretakers . . . [Atwood and Stolorow, 1984, p. 65].

Intersubjectivity theory describes the emergence and modification of subjectivity, and defines these processes as irreduc-
ibly relational.

It is important to distinguish these theorists' use of the
terms *intersubjective* and *intersubjectivity* from several related
ideas. First, intersubjectivity theory describes relatedness that
exists between any two people to the extent that they have
become subjects or experiencers. Thus, these terms do not refer primarily to the developmental achievement as characterized by Stern (1985) and Benjamin (1988). These authors
describe a stage of recognition of another's subjectivity as connected and responsive to one's own. This mutual recognition
may be a late achievement in the intersubjective field of an
analysis and is not required for the constitution of an intersubjective system.

Second, intersubjectivity theory differs from family systems
theory, as represented by Bowen and his collaborators (Kerr
and Bowen, 1988). Our intersubjective viewpoint requires subjectivity, or rather two or more subjectivities, and retains its
focus on the interplay between differently organized subjectivities. It cannot work within the intersubjective field and simultaneously step outside the field to describe it, as family systems

theorists attempt to do. We are always involved in, affecting, and affected by, whatever we attempt to describe.

This impossibility may also account for what appears as psychoanalytic disinterest in empirical research. Positivist philosophers like Grünbaum (1984) and psychoanalysts like "closet empiricist" Spence (Bruner, 1993) find psychoanalysis unscientific—inadequately interested in the experimental verification or falsification of hypotheses, and in the replication of experiments—but they have misunderstood the essential nature of the intersubjective field. Psychoanalytic work is not replicable because each person involved, and each analytic pair, develops idioms and meanings that are completely context-dependent. Even the best case studies can only feebly attempt to capture the sense of a particular intersubjective field, or of an analytic couple. We must examine the theories, prejudices, and assumptions that form our own subjectivity, but we can work psychoanalytically and understand psychoanalytically only from within a particular intersubjective field.

Third, for similar reasons, intersubjectivity theory differs from the interpersonal psychoanalysis described in another chapter in this volume. Interpersonalists tend to focus on the here-and-now interactions between patient and analyst. Because intersubjectivity theorists, like self psychologists, emphasize subjective experience, we also differ from interpersonalists who locate difficulties in living in the patient's desire for control, in repetitive enactments of earlier relational patterns, or in disavowal of responsibility. Intersubjectivity theory concerns itself little with such interpersonalist concerns as who is doing what to whom, with gambits, control, and agency. Such "participant observation" requires maintaining an external perspective that interferes with "undergoing the situation" with the patient (Gadamer, 1975). Our intersubjective perspective—though interested in the *experience* of interaction and agency—resembles more closely those currents in relational thinking that emphasize development (Winnicott, 1958; Bollas, 1987; Ghent, 1992), emotional experience (Socarides and Stolorow, 1984–1985; Orange, 1995) and conversation between differently organized and inevitably subjective perspectives, (Orange, 1995; Aron, 1996).

On the other hand, intersubjectivity theory transcends the Freudian view of human beings. In classical theory, human beings are seen as self-contained bundles of well or poorly harnessed sexual and aggressive instincts, some directed at "objects." Intersubjectivity theory conceives humans as organizers of experience, as subjects. It views psychoanalytic therapy as the dialogic attempt of two people together to understand one person's organization of emotional experience by making sense together of their shared experience (Orange, 1995).

BASIC THEORETICAL IDEAS AND PROPOSITIONS

Although intersubjectivity theory is a recent arrival on the psychoanalytic scene, its roots appear in early phenomenology. Like Freud, Husserl studied with the philosopher Brentano, who unrelentingly emphasized the experience of the intentional subject. Unlike Freud, who—at least intermittently—embraced scientific empiricism, Husserl (1931) and later philosophers of subjectivity insisted that all experience was subjective experience and therefore not accessible to objective measurement and causal explanation. It could only be described and understood.

The original authors of psychoanalytic intersubjectivity theory, influenced as well by personology theory (Murray, 1938) and by their own researches into the subjective origins of personality theories (Atwood and Stolorow, 1993), recognized in Kohut's work the radical perspective needed. Though he welcomed and promoted exchange between psychoanalysis and the other humanistic disciplines, Kohut (1959) insisted that the entire domain of psychoanalytic inquiry was that of subjective experience. He implicitly rejected drive theory, along with metapsychological constructs generally. The only data for psychoanalytic understanding, Kohut believed, were those that were accessible by introspection and empathy (vicarious introspection). Although intersubjectivists criticize particular aspects of self psychological theory, such as transmuting internalization of psychological structure via optimal frustration (cf. chapter 7) and a preexisting nuclear self, they completely accept its most fundamental tenet, its definition of the sources of psychoanalytic inquiry and understanding.

In the early 1980s, however, Atwood and Stolorow began to work with Bernard Brandchaft, who brought to the collaboration extensive and intensive understanding of British relational theories, especially of their view that emotional life is always constituted in attachment contexts. Now their "psychoanalytic phenomenology" with its thoroughgoing emphasis on the development and maintenance of the subjective organization of experience moved toward a fully intersubjective conception. In this view, all self experience—including enduring patterns of personality and pathology—develops and maintains itself within, and as a function of, the interplay between or among subjective worlds of organized and organizing experience. Conversely the field itself consists of the relatedness between subjectivities. The two people may be parent and child, siblings, analyst and patient, spouses, and so on. We see pathologies, from phobias through psychoses, in these terms, and refuse to place the origins or the continuance of psychopathology solely within the patient. This point of view, therefore, differs with drive theory in all its variants. Instead, intersubjectivists study the intersubjective conditions, or emotional environment, in which particular subjective configurations arise and continue.

The fundamental structures of subjectivity, in our view, are the organizing principles, whether automatic and rigid, or reflective and flexible. These principles, often unconscious, are the emotional conclusions a person has drawn from lifelong experience of the emotional environment, especially the complex mutual connections with early caretakers. These conclusions also function as expectancies for future experience, for example, "I will always be a failure," or "No one could ever love such a disgusting creature as I am." Until these principles become available for conscious reflection, and until new emotional experiences lead a person to envision and expect new forms of emotional connection, these old inferences will constitute the sense of self. This sense of self includes convictions about the predictive nature of various forms of relatedness. A person may feel, for example, that any kind of self-articulation or differentiation will invite ridicule or sarcasm. An adult who thinks of undertaking some new task may hear (internally) "What do you know, wet-behind-the-ears?"

Within this perspective, intersubjectivity theorists have attempted to rethink such fundamental psychoanalytic ideas as the unconscious. Stolorow and Atwood (1992) have identified three realms of unconsciousness. The "prereflective unconscious" is comprised of those organizing principles, or emotional convictions, that operate automatically and out of awareness. They arise as emotional inferences a child draws from intersubjective experience in the family of origin. These beliefs-expectancies may concern relatedness, as in, "I must adapt to others' needs (moods, expectations, and so on) if I am to retain significant emotional ties." They may also consist of a fundamental sense of self, still intersubjectively configured: "I will never amount to anything," "I am always a burden," "I am worthless and a good-for-nothing." Such organizing principles are sometimes direct quotations from parents who nickname their children "Mad Mary" or "Terrible Theresa," or "good-for-nothing." More often, these principles are emotional inferences drawn as the child attempts to organize some sense of self out of chaotic, traumatic, or more subtly confusing early and later relational experience.

Stolorow and Atwood (1992) have also described what they call the dynamic unconscious. This consists of emotional information, once consciously known, that had to be "sequestered," or forgotten, because it created conflict for the subject. In particular, these memories would have threatened the tie to caretakers on whom the child needed to depend. Such unawareness is dynamic, as in Freudian theory, because the effects of these early experiences, unavailable for reflection, continue to appear as repetitive patterns of distress or dysfunction in an adult's life. Memories of parental cruelty are common examples.

Finally, the "unvalidated unconscious" describes those aspects of relational and self experience that could never fully become experience (Orange, 1995) because they found no validating response in the emotional environment. Often aspects of one's talents, one's interests, one's character, or one's emotional life have never found the recognition they need to become fully real for the person.

In short, our intersubjective perspective on psychopathology and unconsciousness views all psychological phenomena as coconstituted and codetermined, both in childhood and in analysis. In childhood, personality, pathology, and boundaries between conscious and unconscious experience develop within the mutually regulated contexts of attachment to caregivers. In treatment, we analysts are always implicated in the phenomena we observe, a persecutory delusion, for example. There is no isolated mind, no single or predictable unconscious content, only persons developing in contexts of relatedness.

THERAPEUTIC TECHNIQUE AND THERAPEUTIC ACTION

An intersubjective understanding of psychopathology and of various forms of unconsciousness has important consequences for psychoanalytic practice. Psychoanalysis will be understood to consist in the cocreation of an emotional environment, an intersubjective field, in which it is safe to explore together these "regions" of unconsciousness that make up the problematic aspects of subjectivity. Transference (the patient's experience of the analytic process) and countertransference (the analyst's experience of the analytic process—my term is *cotransference* [Orange, 1995]), the organizing activity of both patient and analyst within the analytic experience, make up the intersubjective field of the analysis. The joint effort to understand both past and present organizing activities as a function of the experience of particular intersubjective fields creates a comfortable flow between the venues of past and present.

The intersubjective field of the analysis, made possible by the emotional availability of both analyst and patient, becomes a developmental second chance for the patient (Orange, 1995). New, more flexible organizing principles can emerge, now accessible to reflection, so that the patient's experiential repertoire becomes enlarged, enriched, and more complex. Under severe stress, old organizations of experience may return, but now a person can recognize them and relativize them by reference to their origins in past relational experience.

CLINICAL ILLUSTRATION

Intersubjective fields may involve conjunction (similarity) or disjunction (dissimilarity) between the subjective worlds of experience involved. Some impasses in treatment develop because the organizing principles of patient and analyst are too different for them to find or maintain a common ground of understanding. A patient's difficult experiences in analysis do *not* arise *solely* out of some pathological constellation inside of her, but rather they take form in the interplay between her world and her analyst's world. This interplay may be characterized by mutual, reciprocal invalidation, misunderstanding, and objectification. Other treatment problems develop when analyst and patient are too similar in their emotional organization (Stolorow, Brandchaft, and Atwood, 1987). This situation, termed intersubjective conjunction, can make it difficult for the analyst to recognize what is going wrong or why treatment seems not to be progressing.

A 40-year-old woman, for example, came for treatment because of intense anxiety and growing depression, with an alarming wish to be dead that she related to her failing marriage. She had, out of deference to her parents' wishes, married a wealthy man and had become a very competent servant, managing the home, and providing excellent care for their two daughters, now adolescents. She reminded me of Stevens the butler in the film *The Remains of the Day.* With no sense of a life, preferences, opinions, or purposes of her own, her primary function was to make sure things ran smoothly for her nuclear and extended families. In the cultures of both extended families—hers and her husband's—this was the only role for a woman, even an extremely intelligent one.

For many years, by her initial account, the system had run smoothly. Her family of origin had been "wonderful" and her marriage "okay." Only now, when she had developed a friendship with another married woman, had she begun to feel anxious and depressed. The company of this friend made her feel important in her own right, and comfortable and safe in ways she could never remember having felt before. Soon she began to realize that she had been missing these experiences before and during her marriage. In addition, the contrast between her marriage and that of her friend brought despair over her own present situation and future life prospects, and anxiety at the almost inconceivable thought of her own freedom. In treatment she preferred not to discuss the loneliness of her own marriage, nor the anger she sometimes momentarily felt when her husband berated her or failed to volunteer to help at times when she was obviously overburdened. From me she simply wanted help with feeling better, with putting options out of her mind, and with accepting the conditions of her life.

My original sense was that I was very different from her. She seemed to feel entirely trapped in her marriage while I had, after all, left one that had been troubled. If she could just come to understand what I had come to understand and feel, she could be just fine. I, of course, thought I knew what would be best for her, and apparently I communicated my attitude in some way. The intersubjective field formed by my agenda and sense of things, with her very strong tendency to comply with others' expectations of her, only heightened her anxiety. Torn between complying with her parents' expectations, her husband's demands, and now my agenda, she felt bound to lose someone. For all sorts of practical reasons—her daughter's soccer matches, for example—she became unable to keep regular appointments. The needs of others always intervened.

I had to shift gears, to find another perspective on the situation. To do this, I needed to become aware of my own emotional organizing principles and needs, to see how similar these were to hers in spite of the apparent differences, and to recognize the nature of my impact on the treatment. What helped me was noticing this patient's ways of taking care of me in the sessions—telling me she was fine, asking about my well-being, watching the clock—and remembering how I had been like that with my own analyst. This patient and I were very alike in our compulsive caretaking and in our assumption that our only value as persons lay in our capacity and skill as caretakers. So I was taking care of her, trying to fix her life, and she was taking care of me, trying to establish her value in my eyes and to maintain her fragile sense of worth in her own eyes.

When we reflected together on our caretaking patterns, we both began to change. The need to be helpful and caretaking loosened its grip on me, and her freedom in relation to me very gradually increased. Our tie no longer depended on her divining and complying with my hopes for her. We began to talk more about the complexity of compliance, caretaking, and loss of selfhood required to maintain ties in her family of origin. I began to be more able to feel my way into her emotional predicament. Simultaneously she began to report more sustained frustration with her marriage and her family role, along with some efforts to tell her husband and children that she expected respectful treatment. She also began to ask them for help occasionally, and was surprised that they protested less than she had expected. She is working at perceiving and following her own feelings and interests, and is just beginning to sense that these will lead her wherever she needs to go. As a result, she feels less trapped. She does feel a new kind of sadness—less despairing, but full of mourning for the person she never had a chance to become.

DISCUSSION

Intersubjectivity theorists see transference—earlier viewed as displacement of emotion from early caregivers to the analyst—as an organizing activity, as the attempt to make sense of the relational experience of a particular psychotherapy or analysis. We assume that both patient and analyst, historically and relationally situated, are always attempting to make sense together, to organize experience. We often distinguish between the selfobject aspect of transference, in which the analyst functions as support for the self-development and cohesion of the patient, and a repetitive dimension of transference. In this repetitive dimension, the patient, who brings a particular relational history to the treatment, may experience the analyst as the failing or abusive early caretaker. The analyst, no blank screen but a person with a history and emotional organization, may unwittingly recreate with the patient the intersubjective field of childhood. The memory of the pathogenic intersubjective field returns as transference. Selfobject transferences, or what Freud called the unobjectionable positive transferences, recede into the background, and can seem completely inaccessible. Depending, however, on the strength and reliability of the analytic bond, and on the analyst's capacity to reflect on her own contribution to the repetitive intersubjective impasse, the process of working on the impasse may restore the selfobject transference to the foreground. It may even contribute to the therapeutic effectiveness of the analytic bond.

RECENT ADVANCES AND DIRECTIONS

Intersubjectivity theory has several leading edges. One is the effort, pioneered by its creators' work on psychosis and borderline pathology, to reconceptualize all pathogenesis in intersubjective terms. We see psychotic delusions as concretizing particular relational experiences, including experiences in treatment, and automatic expectancies (Orange, Atwood, and Stolorow, 1997). Similarly, intersubjectivists are attempting to understand anxieties, affective disorders, narcissistic disorders, dissociation, the classical neuroses, sexual compulsions, and symptom formation in terms of a person's formative relational experiences.

A second continuing direction in the development of psychoanalytic intersubjectivity theory will continue to study the psychoanalytic situation itself. In particular, we are studying the influence of our own theories and personal emotional organizing activity on the psychoanalytic field. A recent contribution by Bacal and Thomson (1993) examines a particular kind of countertransference arising from the analyst's emotional needs for validation and a sense of worth. They show how frustration of these needs affects the intersubjective field of the treatment and suggest that the analyst's unawareness of these needs is an underlying factor in many treatment failures. In another contribution, Orange (1995) has studied the contribution of the analyst's emotional availability or presence to the intersubjective field of treatment.

Intersubjectivists are in a position to contribute a new perspective to many old and new questions in psychoanalytic theory and practice. For example, a current area of interest just begging for an intersubjectivist inquiry, for example, is the intersubjective genesis of the experiences of gender and sexual orientation in personal development and in psychoanalytic treatment (cf. for example, Kiersky, 1996). Another leading edge, already developed in a series of papers (Brandchaft, 1988, 1993, 1994) studies the structures of pathological accommodation originating in the intersubjectively determined requirement to give up a sense of internally centered selfhood to retain crucial emotional ties. First Brandchaft (1988) presented his case of intractable depression. The patient felt he must give up any hope for artistic success in the face of parental predictions and needs dictating that he should and would come to nothing. The battle for his soul was joined on the turf between his artistic achievement and his tie to a parent who needed him to fail.

In a later paper, Brandchaft (1993) used the evocative metaphor of a spirit imprisoned to describe similar struggles between emotional ties and liberation. The implication, of course, is that no one should have to make such a choice, but that in some families the authentic self has no place to grow. Most recently, Brandchaft (1994) has articulated what he calls the structures of pathological accommodation. He explains that many of us develop organized, and seemingly intractable, patterns of living that accommodate to the emotional needs of parental figures. In this process they lose any access to an internal reference point for feeling and living. Overall, Brandchaft is articulating the intersubjective sources of deeply entrenched psychopathology.

I think our intersubjective perspective will develop as a psychoanalytic approach to understanding emotional development, as a clinical sensibility to the embeddedness of all psychological life in constitutive intersubjective contexts, and as a contextualist psychoanalytic epistemology, that points to the influence of any general or clinical theory on the field. In the words of its creators, "[psychoanalysis] is a science of the *intersubjective,* focused on the interplay between the differently organized subjective worlds of the observer and the observed" (Atwood and Stolorow, 1984, pp. 41–42).

REFERENCES

Aron, L. (1996), *A Meeting of Minds: Mutuality in Psychoanalysis.* Hillsdale, NJ: Analytic Press.
———— Harris, A., Eds. (1994), *The Legacy of Sandor Ferenczi.* Hillsdale, NJ: Analytic Press.
*Atwood, G., & Stolorow, R. (1984), *Structures of Subjectivity: Explorations in Psychoanalytic Phenomenology.* Hillsdale, NJ: Analytic Press.
*———— ———— (1993), *Faces in a Cloud: Intersubjectivity in Personality Theory,* 2nd ed. Northvale, NJ: Jason Aronson.
Bacal, H., & Thomson, P. (1993), The psychoanalyst's needs and the effect of their frustration on the treatment: A new view of countertransference. Paper presented at the sixteenth Annual Conference on the Psychology of the Self, Toronto, Canada.
Benjamin, J. (1988), *Bonds of Love: Psychoanalysis, Feminism, and the Problem of Domination.* New York: Pantheon.
Bollas, C. (1987), *The Shadow of the Object: Psychoanalysis of the Unthought Known.* London: Free Association.
*Brandchaft, B. (1988), A case of intractable depression. In: *Learning from Kohut: Progress in Self Psychology,* ed. A. Goldberg. Hillsdale, NJ: Analytic Press, pp. 133–154.
*———— (1993), To free the spirit from its cell. In: *The Widening Scope of Self Psychology,* ed. A. Goldberg. Hillsdale, NJ: Analytic Press.
*———— (1994), Structures of pathological accommodation and change in analysis. Paper presented to the Association for Psychoanalytic Self Psychology, New York City.

*Recommended reading.

Bruner, J. (1993), Loyal opposition and the clarity of dissent. *Psychoanal. Dial.*, 3:11–20.

Gadamer, H. (1975), *Truth and Method*, tr. J. Weinsheimer & D. Marshall, 2nd ed. New York: Crossroads, 1991.

Ghent, E. (1992), Paradox and process. *Psychoanal. Dial.*, 2:135–159.

Grünbaum, A. (1984), *The Foundations of Psychoanalysis, A Philosophical Critique.* Berkeley: University of California Press.

Husserl, E. (1931), *Ideas: An Introduction to Pure Phenomenology.* New York: Macmillan.

Ivory, J. (1993), *The Remains of the Day.* (Film.)

Kerr, M., & Bowen, M. (1988), *Family Evaluation.* New York: W. W. Norton.

Kiersky, S. (1996), Exiled desire: The problem of reality in psychoanalysis and lesbian experience. *Psychoanal. & Psychother.*, 13:130–141.

Kohut, H. (1959), Introspection, empathy, and psychoanalysis: An examination of the relationship between mode of observation and theory. In: *The Search for the Self*, ed. P. Ornstein. New York: International Universities Press, 1978, pp. 205–232.

Murray, H. (1938), *Explorations in Personality.* New York: Science Editions, 1962.

*Orange, D. (1995), *Emotional Understanding: Essays in Psychoanalytic Epistemology.* New York: Guilford.

*———— Atwood, G., & Stolorow, R. (1997), *Working Intersubjectively: Contextualism in Clinical Practice.* Hillsdale, NJ: Analytic Press.

Socarides, D., & Stolorow, R. (1984–1985), Affects and selfobjects. *The Annual of Psychoanalysis*, 12:105–120.

Stern, D. N. (1985), *The Interpersonal World of the Infant.* New York: Basic Books.

*Stolorow, R., & Atwood, G. (1992), *Contexts of Being: The Intersubjective Foundations of Psychological Life.* Hillsdale, NJ: Analytic Press.

*———— Brandchaft, B., & Atwood, G. (1987), *Psychoanalytic Treatment: An Intersubjective Approach.* Hillsdale, NJ: Analytic Press.

Winnicott, D. (1958), *Through Paediatrics to Psycho-Analysis.* New York: Basic Books, 1975.

4.

The Interpersonal Approach to Psychoanalysis

Eric Singer, Ph.D.

INTERPERSONAL PSYCHOANALYSIS

Interpersonal psychoanalysis often seems puzzling to many for whom it represents a new approach to thinking about psychoanalysis and psychoanalytic psychotherapy. Repeatedly, one confronts confusion regarding the constituents of interpersonal psychoanalysis. Lack of understanding often has led to the misperception that there really is no such entity. This assertion is usually grounded in the false premise that interpersonal psychoanalysis has no body of metapsychology, no concept of an internal world, no genetic underpinnings, and no systematized method of treatment. While all of this is decidedly untrue, there are indeed discernible reasons why such confusion and ignorance have grown up around this version of psychoanalysis.

Harry Stack Sullivan (1940, 1953, 1956, 1964) is generally credited with being both the founder of the school of interpersonal psychoanalysis and the initial articulator of the concepts and principles around which it has developed. Sullivan was both a pragmatist by nature and an operationalist in thought, and he spent his earliest years as a psychiatrist working with

severely disturbed patients. This combination made it difficult
for him to see the utility in such rudimentary concepts as the
unconscious. The stubborn prickliness of his character often
led him to make sarcastic and derogatory sounding remarks
about analytic practice and theory while positing his more op-
erationally oriented ideas. He did this despite the fact that,
as we shall see, many of the formulations that comprise the
metapsychology of interpersonal psychoanalysis are not significantly different epistemologically from those of other psychoanalytic schools. Nevertheless, his penchant for tweaking those
constructs that he believed strayed too far from the objective
data of life, particularly as manifested in therapy, led him to
make comments that often appeared antianalytic, despite his
acknowledged reverence for Freud's genius (Sullivan, 1964).

But this is only one of several reasons why interpersonal
psychoanalysis has remained confusing to many; another is the
very nature of Sullivan's writings themselves. The fact that Sullivan was a poor writer who often made up his own words has
further complicated the task of understanding the essential
theoretical and clinical points he made about what has become
known as *interpersonal psychoanalysis.*

Beyond Sullivan's idiosyncrasies, however, there are other
critical factors that make it difficult to fully comprehend the
breadth of interpersonal thinking. Interpersonal theory as well
as its clinical technique eschews formulaic approaches. Training, in light of this particular viewpoint, leads one away from
attempts at systemization. Thus, without a compilation such as
The Standard Edition to serve as a referent, interpersonal writings have often seemed discrete, unconnected, and individualistic, rather than being parts of a larger body of knowledge. In
fact, another difficulty in "knowing" interpersonal psychoanalysis, paradoxically enough, is its very richness. So many interpersonal   concepts   have   been   subsumed   by   various
contemporary theories and ways of approaching clinical material, that many students fail to associate them at all with interpersonal thinking. Thus, for instance, Sullivan's pioneering
work with regard to the importance of the analytic relationship
and the analyst's use of countertransference often goes unrecognized. It is only recently that an attempt has been made to

put together such a compendium (Fiscalini, Lionells, Mann, and Stern, 1995).

THE INTERNAL WORLD

The concept of an internal world is a difficult one under any circumstance. For interpersonalists, this is especially true because the concept relates directly to a single individual, and interpersonalists do not believe in a one-person psychology, as it has come to be called, but rather a two-person psychology. This is the topic that Sullivan (1953, 1964) addressed directly when he asserted his belief that outside of an interpersonal environment one has only a human animal, not a human person. By this he meant that while personhood potential exists at birth, it is only actualized in the presence of others. In theory, then, if an organism were to be born and never encounter a person, that organism would forever remain an animal, not a person. Of course, this hypothetical extremity is an impossibility, but it makes the point—there is no human person, and, consequently, no internal world, outside of an interpersonal context. The question therefore becomes how best to represent this phenomenon, while respecting the fact that individuals do, in fact, move about in the world as single entities.

Ultimately, all theories have had to grapple with this issue. It is worth noting that Freud (1905) dealt with this matter by positing endogenous drives (instincts). This allowed him to speak of individuals cathecting objects with libido, thereby internalizing them to develop an internal world. Klein (1975) followed a similar path, as did her disciples, although her ideas about the nature of the drives continued to change from those formulated by Freud. But interpersonalists do not believe in a theory of endogenous drive energy, the satisfaction of which compels the organism to act and engage with the world. How then to account for the experience of others and the ensuing development of an internal world?

It is at this point that Sullivan becomes obscure and difficult to follow. In truth, he never really articulated and developed this matter sufficiently. He spoke of a need for *tenderness* and the anxiety that may be engendered in the pursuit of that need. From infancy, the development of the internal world is shaped by the wish to avoid this anxiety. The *self-system* is the resultant, anxiety-avoiding *dynamism*. (Sullivan chose to speak of *dynamisms* rather than *structures* because he wished to avoid what he felt was a static quality associated with the latter term.)

Recognizing Sullivan's vagueness around this issue, subsequent interpersonal theorists have tried to articulate their views more precisely. Thus, Levenson (1984) claimed that Sullivan actually implied a *drive to avoid anxiety,* meaning that the avoidance of anxiety is the primary motivating force in life. More recently, Singer (1989, 1993, 1996) has suggested that what really underlies interpersonal theory is a *drive for tenderness,* and that the anxiety about which Sullivan and Levenson spoke is not primary, but a secondary artifact that stems from unsuccessful attempts to secure tenderness.

This is an area of debate that involves metatheoretical questions that remain very much unanswered at this point in contemporary interpersonal theory. Nevertheless, whatever position one takes on this issue, it is clear that the anxiety engendered in interpersonal engagements or integrations is critical in the development of the individual's internal world. All interpersonalists would agree with that statement, and would further agree that this process begins during infancy and proceeds throughout the course of life in a similar although increasingly complex manner as begun in infancy. Thus, interpersonal theory should be thought of as both a genetic and deterministic theory—each earlier stage of development directly influences the manner in which subsequent stages are handled. However, despite the deterministic aspect of the theory, interpersonal theory also posits a built-in reparative stage of development (see below).

It is instructive to examine the rudimentary development of the internal world during infancy, since the developmental paradigm of infancy remains the same throughout life but is most simply described during this era. This is because the stage of infancy involves the least number of integrations with different significant others and the least number of interpersonal tasks. Therefore, while actually quite complex, the development of the internal world during infancy can be most easily schematized.

The concept most central to the interpersonal view of the internal world is that of personifications. There are essentially two types of personifications—*self* and *other*, or *me* and *you*. A personification is simply the organism's experience of that which is being represented. While this sounds simple enough, it is indeed a complicated concept which needs elaboration. The key term in this definition is *experience*, which implies that the personification need bear no resemblance to reality. It is a personal, idiosyncratic phenomenological representation, that often bears only superficial resemblance to what would be called *consensually validated reality* or reality as most observers would describe it. Thus, the infant may perceive and experience the mother in ways that are quite at odds not only with how the mother views herself, but, in fact, how others would view her. This would then constitute the infant's personification of mother, or, more accurately stated, at this point in development, the mothering one. The nature of the infant's experience of himself or herself in relation to this mothering one is the infant's personification of him/herself. This too may bear little objective resemblance to how others would view the infant.

The critical point is that the personification is a matter of the personifier's experience. While it is rare that the personification bears no relationship to objective reality, it is frequently the case that it is distorted in some significant way. While it is tempting to think of these personifications as self-image and other-image, the danger in doing so involves the tendency to forget that the concept of personification refers to the experience of the self in conjunction with the other, or the other in conjunction with the self, rather than some static "image." This is a critical concept which permeates interpersonal thinking, and refers to the interpersonal idea that self and other representations are multifaceted and continually dependent on the nature of the ongoing interpersonal integration in which the individual is involved.

To further elaborate on the nature of these rudimentary personifications, let us turn to some early examples of infant–mother interactions to illustrate what actually transpires. I will use the interpersonal situation of nursing, be it breast or bottle, because it is an essential experience for all infants, and one that is relatively easily schematized.

If we assume that the infant's first prehension, or organization of experience, will be that of the nipple, since feeding is arguably the first interpersonal engagement of life, the first personification will be of either good nipple or bad nipple. From this initial dichotomy, an increasingly complex schematization will follow. That is, good nipple comes to represent the infant's experience of the presented nipple that leads to *satisfaction*. (In interpersonal language this term refers to the alleviation of physiochemical tensions, such as hunger.) Barring organic or mechanical complications, the only thing that can interfere with the infant's attaining such satisfaction is the presence of anxiety. Thus, in the absence of anxiety, the infant will suck, receive the satisfying nutrient, and the interpersonal integration (the nursing situation between infant and mothering one) will cease when the infant's hunger and/or need to suck is sated, that is, when the infant is satisfied.

The repetition of this process will eventually lead to the intrapsychic representation of this nipple—the one that satisfies—as the good nipple. As the organism matures and develops increased capacity to perceive and prehend, the nipple will become integrated into the experience of the larger organism organized as "mother," namely, that person or object who brings to the infant the good nipple. This experience will then be organized around the personification of good mother, who need not be the actual mother at all. The personification is of the experience of a satisfying mothering. Thus, the father, a nanny, an older sibling, or anyone else who participates with the infant in the interpersonal integration surrounding the experience of satisfying nursing will become represented within the personification of good mother.

The nipple that does not satisfy will become personified as bad nipple, and, as in the good nipple scenario, subsequent

experiences in a nonsatisfying feeding situation with a pre-
hended carrier of this bad nipple will be personified as bad
mother. Again, this certainly need not, as noted, always involve
the actual mother. The personification relates to the interpersonal integrative experience in a mothering situation. It is to
be stressed that in this most rudimentary situation what is personified is, in fact, experience with the other, not the other
per se. This is the basic paradigm for the development of the
internal world throughout life, and is the primary consideration from which distortion and subsequent pathology are to
be understood.

We have now elaborated one half of the personified dyad,
namely the "other" personification. We have, however, thus
far failed to consider a most important question—what makes
the nipple nonsatisfying or bad? Again, barring organic or mechanical considerations, the answer is anxiety. But what is anxiety, and to whose anxiety are we referring?

Here we have reached a watershed for interpersonal theory. Anxiety per se is not definable! There is no fortuitous
endogenous drive seeking release and coming into conflict with
an external prohibition and causing anxiety, as is argued in the
Freudian model. Rather, anxiety is thought of as a reduction
in the feeling of well-being about oneself, brought about by
experiences that conflict with one's internal representations of
oneself as "good." In effect, anxiety is an outgrowth of the
experience of what will become personified as bad me. But,
since in our example, the infant does not as yet have such an
internal representation, the anxiety in this very early nursing
situation to which we are referring must be inherent to the
mothering one. And indeed it is, although not exclusively.

Anxiety is a phenomenological state, an affective experience, and one that interpersonalists posit is transmissible, or
contagious, if you will. Consequently, anxiety in the mothering
one makes the infant feel anxious. Sullivan (1953) called this
process empathic contagion. Here is where some of the vision-
ary status we earlier accorded Sullivan can be seen. Although
he had no way of demonstrating this phenomenon, and insisted
one had to simply take it on faith, modern technology has
allowed for the empirical demonstration and verification of the

concept. Stern (1985), among many others (e.g., Beebe and Lachmann, 1994), has addressed this phenomenon at great length. Consequently, we may take it as a given that this kind of mothering-to-infant transmission of anxiety may occur. It is, in fact, this very process that leads to the nipple being unsatisfying, and becoming personified as the bad nipple. As was the case with the personified good mother, the personified bad mother is the organization of experience in an interpersonal integration of the other that brings with it this unpleasant experience of anxiety.

But, ultimately, the experience of anxiety is an internal, personal one. How then, in interpersonal theory, can we account for the internalization of this experience? Here, finally, we have arrived at the development of the self-personifications, and at what is in many ways at the heart of interpersonal theory. I will continue with my example of the nursing infant to illustrate this point.

Remember that the nonanxious mothering one, good mother brings the satisfying nipple to the infant. In the absence of anxiety, the infant sucks, is sated, and the interpersonal integration ceases satisfactorily. The infant's experience is clearly "good," and so the infant's participation in this satisfying dyad becomes personified as good me. What exactly does this mean, and what is its significance?

We are considering a stage in development when the organism does not have an appreciation of others as separate, discrete individuals. Infants at this stage of life have neither the neurological, psychological, nor cognitive ability to make such discriminations. Furthermore, infants are highly egocentric. Thus, the infant assumes that it is something about his or her participation in the dyad that has evoked the good mother personification. The good me personification is, therefore, the primitive organization of what the infant "thinks" he or she has done to bring forth the satisfying, nonanxiety inducing nipple. Similarly, bad me is the primitive organization of the infant's experience of what he has done to evoke bad mother in our example in the form of the nonsatisfying, anxiety-arousing bad nipple. Interpersonal theory posits that the heart of the matter involves what may, in effect, be thought of as an exaggerated, egocentric and grandiose sense of responsibility on the part of the infant!

This paradigm is, albeit rudimentary, the basic model by which interpersonalists believe that the internal world develops. In any interpersonal integration, good and bad self personifications arise corresponding to good and bad other personifications. The accrued self-personifications eventually constitute what would be called the individual's internal world and sense of self.

There is, however, a third self-personification that develops, called the "not me." This personification arises from experiences with another that are so anxiety-laden that the individual cannot fully organize them. The anxiety is so overwhelming that they remain at best only dimly grasped, reflecting the sense that the organism has done something so dreadful that this behavior is best banished to the realm of not me. The presence of numerous not me experiences bespeaks of severe psychopathology and is the theoretical underpinning for the process known as dissociation and potentially psychotic states. It should be evident that development in an environment where there is a preponderance of not me experiences speaks to the presence of severely disturbed parents or caretakers.

Several points need to be stressed here. First, what makes all this possible is the infant's need for contact and human tenderness—in our example in the form of feeding. But there are many more complex interpersonal integrations, both in infancy, and throughout the course of development and life. As these become more complicated, so too does the nature of the personifications. But since this is a deterministic theory, what has transpired and developed earlier, will surely form a part of the later integrations. Recalling that bad me personifications reflect the organization of experiences that evoke anxiety, and that the organism seeks to avoid such states, certain poorly understood interactions—misperceptions by the infant of his or her role in the transaction—may never get rectified in the service of avoiding the anxious state. This self-protection is a function of the aforementioned self-system, which Sullivan saw as highly resistant to education. Thus, what starts out as a simple nursing experience has enormous future ramifications.

A second point involves the process of cognition. Infants do not think in the way we commonly understand that process. The kind of organizing of experience we have been discussing is based on a very primitive form of logic. Interpersonalists call this kind of thought process *parataxic thought*. It is, in effect, a kind of illogical logic, often based on coincidental temporal or spatial sequencing to which the infant erroneously attributes meaning. A simple example of this might be as follows: The sun shines in the infant's eyes and hurts. The infant cries. Simultaneously, a cloud passes across the sun, ending the pain to the infant. Unaware of the concepts of sun and clouds, the infant attributes the cessation of pain to the act of crying.

Similarly to the infant or young child's inability to conceptualize "sun" and "clouds," the inability to discriminate others as separate organisms with needs and wants of their own gives rise to the assumption of overresponsibility about whatever happens to them in conjunction with others. This is the basis of what interpersonalists call *parataxic distortions* of which transference phenomena are essentially a later, more developed form. And once these distortions lead to the development of bad me self-personifications, they become very difficult to change.

A final point involves the confusion surrounding the development of the personification of others and consequently of self. In regard to nursing, for example, many different others interact with the infant. Since it is not the person per se but the experience with the other that gets codified, there are a myriad of types of exchanges and integrations that the infant, in his or her primitive way, must sift through. It should be clear that this greatly increases the potential for the development of parataxic distortions, since different people are made anxious by different things at different times. This fact is, of course, something about which the infant has no awareness, and so the organizing of this kaleidoscope of experiences into something approaching a consistent whole is truly one of the wonders of psychic development. It is not at all surprising that individuals come through this period of life with skewed impressions of themselves. What is remarkable is that they manage to integrate all of this as well as they do!

With this basic model of how interactions between individuals in interpersonal integrations leads to internal world self-representations, let us now turn to examine the basic developmental epoches that interpersonalists posit. We will find that our basic model of the development of personifications will be at play in each of the interpersonal tasks that the individual confronts as he or she grows and matures into a human person.

THE DEVELOPMENTAL SCHEMA

Every psychoanalytic theory has a developmental schema, a sequencing of stages through which the organism is believed to pass in the process of maturing into a viable, functioning person. In Freud's (1905) classical model, for instance, this process was schematized in the form of the well-known oral, anal, phallic, latency, and genital stages. In part because of his training, Freud patterned his sequence roughly after the neurological ontogeny of the fetus.

Sullivan's (1953) schema, and the one generally adhered to by most interpersonalists, is defined through very different parameters. Rather than a neurophysiological substrate, Sullivan's thinking reflected what he viewed to be the basic interpersonal issues and tasks confronting the growing organism at each stage of life. Furthermore, consistent with his interest in the operational and knowable, he chose a very different kind of terminology for his sequence. Thus, the interpersonal scheme of human development consists of the following life eras: infancy, childhood, juvenile, preadolescence, early adolescence, late adolescence, and adulthood.

While there is useful information and thinking related to all of these stages, it is generally conceded that the first five are the richest, and I shall focus on them. I will also follow Sullivan's lead in avoiding specific age determinants regarding the onset and conclusion of each stage. Rather than age, each stage is demarcated by the specific interpersonal task to be mastered during that epoch. Quite naturally, during each of the eras we will survey, personifications are continuing to develop, consistent with and based upon those already organized from preceding eras.

We begin, of course, with infancy, a stage we have already touched on in our example of the development of the earliest personifications. Central among the issues confronting the infant during this period are the establishment of sense of self, and recognition that one exists separate from others. Coincident with this process is the matter of the establishment of a basic sense of trust and security in the world. As was suggested in the preceding section, to a great degree the relative success or failure of this process depends on the relative psychological health of the infant's caretakers, including, but not restricted to, the parents. The greater the caretakers' difficulties in dealing with issues of infant autonomy (separateness from the caretaker) and dependency (reliance on the caretaker), the more anxious the caretakers will be, in general, and, most importantly, in the presence of the infant. This will lead to the infant's increased personifications of bad me and not me. The more developed these personifications become, the more restricted the infant's world will be, because he or she will limit behavior and interactions to realms that do not evoke the anxious or bad mother personification. In severe cases, where the infant believes many forms of his participation evoke this personification, only a very limited range of behavior and integration will be possible. Any variation from these circumscribed realms will begin to produce anxiety in the infant, which will persist in the growing individual as he or she moves through the subsequent life stages. One will then find an individual who sooner or later will not be able to comfortably engage the world in a manner that more successfully developed individuals are able to do.

Interpersonal theory is consistent with all psychoanalytic theories in that it posits that intense early experiences of a negative nature with parenting figures cause the most severe psychological damage to the organism. Indeed, one would expect that in the most severely damaged individuals—schizophrenic patients, for instance—the period of infancy would be where one would find the earliest evidence of repeated psychological assault by the caretakers.

To demonstrate the kind of extreme phenomenon to which we are referring, we may ask how, for instance, an infant begins to develop a sense of itself as distinct from its environment; that is, how it begins to define itself as separate from the other physical objects and persons in its world. One of the primary ways is through the process of *self-sentience,* the experience of knowing about one's own body. As the infant matures both neurologically and motorically, he or she is able to perform more complex operations which help with this initial, primitive self-delineation. A good example of this phenomenon is thumb-sucking. Once the infant is able to get the thumb into his or her mouth and suck it, an extraordinary discovery is made. While in previous sucking experiences, sensation was limited to the oral cavity and alimentary canal, now a whole new situation arises. Not only does the infant experience the sucking process in the mouth, but now the thumb itself feels sucked! This is, of course, radically different from earlier sucking experiences, wherein the nipple did not feel sucked to the infant. Viewed in this light, one begins to appreciate the power of self-sentience in the formation of a sense of body integrity and power to affect some experience.

Self-sentience becomes an increasingly important aspect of all bodily experience. Thus, for instance, a similar experience occurs as the infant discovers its genitals. Not only do the fingers feel something, but the perineal region feels a sensation when touched by the fingers. To illustrate, consider a male infant who has just discovered that touching his genitals produces two interesting sensations (in his hand/arm and genitals). He is observed in the process by his mother. For her own reasons, this greatly disturbs the mothering one, and she becomes highly anxious, to the point where she physically restrains the infant from this process.

If this is the case with the mother, it may also be true of the father, and other caretakers who are around the infant, since families often tend to be homogeneous in matters regarding the arousal of anxiety and its avoidance. Consequently, the infant will likely have the repeated experience of being made

anxious whenever he touches himself in this manner. He will
have no sense that this problem is not really of his making, but
inherent to the psychology of the caretakers. He will assume
that it is his behavior which evokes the bad mother, and in one
respect he is absolutely right. But the infant will not know that
it is not *his* problem. Repeated experiences of this nature will
teach the infant that he has a problem with an infusion of
anxiety and unpleasantness when he touches his genital area.
The infant will conclude, eventually, that this behavior is best
personified as bad me, or, even more problematically, as not
me, and he will cease the behavior.

Now, this experience will not necessarily be a problem for
some time. Assuming that his parents are not overtly psychotic,
the infant will learn that touching his genitals is permissible
behavior in private, in connection with such matters as dressing
or urinating. But with the subsequent onset of puberty, when
at times there is no ostensible rationale for touching the genitals other than the production of sensation, the inclination to
touch will evoke the earlier organized bad me personification,
bringing with it an infusion of anxiety. Unless the youngster is
fortunate in a way we shall address later, he will be faced with
great conflict, the origins of which will not be understood. He
will not know why he feels anxious when he does what others
do; only the experience of feeling anxious will be known. The
old personification will have lain dormant, since there will not
have been reason to touch himself in this way—namely, for
the production of sexual pleasure—prior to puberty; the early
experiences from childhood will have long since been forgotten or dissociated if the anxiety engendered was extreme. The
young man will be a confused and conflicted young adolescent
who will have to find a circuitous route to avoid a human behavior that somehow seems alien to him.

I have chosen an extreme example to illustrate how the
seeds of severe pathology can be sown in infancy. But the situation need not be so dramatic, nor need it be ubiquitous. Any
consistent interference from anxiety-laden caretakers will impact on the infant's growing sense of autonomy, power, and
body awareness—all components of a basic sense of self, and

of ease and security in the world. The severity and pervasiveness of these intrusions and assaults will determine the degree to which compensatory and subliminatory means are available to the developing individual for dealing with these areas of difficulty in the ensuing stages of his development.

CHILDHOOD

Infancy is followed by the era of childhood, of which the great hallmark is the acquisition of speech and therefore a major means of interpersonal communication. The task of childhood is cooperation. By this is meant that the growing individual learns that he or she no longer will be treated favorably simply for being who he or she is. In order to secure favor, the young child learns he or she must cooperate, that is, do what the other wants, in return for something. This, then, marks the end of the era of unconditional love, a time when the infant is loved and accepted no matter what he or she does. Of course, for many individuals, such as the infant described in our previous example, that experience may not have been much in evidence. But for the majority of individuals, infants are generally treated tenderly just for being who they are.

All this changes in childhood. Now, for reasons unknown to the youngster, he must do certain things mother wants done. This is the era of beginning socialization, and it is important to parents that their children be viewed as good. Thus, the child learns to do certain things because behaving in certain ways will bring rewards. This is called *cooperation* and is not to be confused with *collaboration,* a much later developmental phenomenon that foreshadows intimacy. The significance of this distinction lies in the fact that during the childhood stage in life there is little appreciation of the other as a separate individual with needs of his or her own. Rather, the cooperative mode is highly egocentric, and is far from reflecting an interpersonal integration in any way based on a wish to please the other. The child learns to do things so he or she will get what he or she wants.

By the same token, the child learns for the first time to conceal things he or she knows will bring anxiety, displeasure, and will not bring what the child wants. And in this endeavor, speech and language become an important means to an end. Interpersonalists speak of this era as the time when dramatizations and "as if performances" make their appearance. These are both verbal and nonverbal in nature, and often form the basis around which personifications get organized representing the experience of a seemingly "magical" quality of obsessional thoughts and compulsive behaviors. A simple example of what this means might be the child who learns that, regardless of what he or she is really feeling or thinking, the use of the word "please" prevents the experience of anxiety. Since there is no understanding by the child of why this happens, it seems like "magic." The amount of self-experience that the child learns to conceal in the service of socialization will, of course, accumulate on top of what he or she has already learned during infancy. The more disastrous that earlier period has been, the less freedom the child will now have to find ways to cooperate. In such cases, the newly developing forms of childhood concealment will be especially severe, extreme, and limiting.

If we think about this process in terms of internal world development, we can begin to understand the concept of *sub-personifications*—that is, ways in which one learns to disguise what one really feels in certain situations. Essentially, this amounts to the masking of what one experiences as bad me, substituting in its place an unintegrated or unreal good me personification. But by the very nature of the process, while one does not feel anxious, one also does not feel real, and often feels angry, resentful, and false. These latter feelings, however, invariably cannot be expressed or shown, leading to the pyramiding of more and more sub-personifications as specific situations demand. Parenthetically, a byproduct of this is an increasing sense of exhaustion, because the self-system is taxed more and more to keep developing and using sub-personifications.

While there are significant differences, it is not completely misleading to think of some of this last process as analogous to what Winnicott (1965) describes as the development of "false selves." Interpersonal metapsychology demands a different conceptualization regarding how and why these personas arise, but the notions of something false or "as if" are similar. Furthermore, the phenomenon described as splitting in other theoretical models, referring to the failure to integrate good and bad aspects of an experience into a unitary whole, would be located by interpersonalists in the early childhood era. Here language reinforces and codifies the nonintegration of aspects of self (good and bad me personifications) that began to develop during infancy. Interpersonal theory, consistent with other psychoanalytic thinking, ascribes the mechanisms of splitting to a developmentally later epoch than psychotic processes. Nevertheless, interpersonalists uniquely view splitting as a function of the need for the child to develop cooperative skills. The extent to which the individual has been hampered during infancy with respect to the organization of a significant degree of good me personifications—that is, how comfortable and free from anxiety the experience of expressing his or her feelings has been—will determine the extent to which the process of the use of dramatizations and as-if performances will be required by the child to learn how to cooperate.

JUVENILE ERA

Similarly, the extent to which the developing individual must resort to these childhood coping mechanisms will greatly affect the manner in which he or she handles the issues and tasks that arise during the ensuing juvenile era. Here the interpersonal hallmark of the epoch involves the developing need for compeers, while the interpersonal tasks demanded of the juvenile revolve around the learning of compromise and accommodation. It is during this period that affects such as jealousy and envy make their appearance, as the juvenile begins to compare him- or herself to others. While true object-relatedness, involving an awareness of the other as a person with his or her own needs, still is lacking, there is an increasing awareness of others.

As is true of the entire developmental sequencing in interpersonal theory, the more adequately earlier issues from prior stages have been resolved, the greater chance the individual has of successfully negotiating this turbulent stage. Thus, the more comfortable the juvenile is with him- or herself—that is, the less anxious he has been made to feel about aspects of personal experience, and, therefore, the less hidden he has had to become through the development of malignant sub-personifications—the more he will be able to appropriately deal with the issues of competition and accommodation. This latter process is, in effect, an extension of the childhood issue of cooperation into the world outside the family.

Several possibilities exist for the juvenile. The most healthy one is the increasing development toward a well-integrated adult stage of life, in which issues of competition and compromise predominate life's challenges. A potential salutary effect of this period is the opportunity, if the individual is still intact enough at this time, to appreciate that the world and people are more varied than he or she has been exposed to at home. This may lead not only to an increased awareness of the richness of life in general, but to a sense that there are things about him or her that may not be so different from others, even if that is not the experience within his personal family. Thus, for instance, a youngster may learn that laughter, something he or she does, is not an unusual experience, even if in the child's own home it seems to be an alien phenomenon.

There are also, however, serious potential pitfalls for the less fortunate juvenile. The individual who brings home stories about teachers and compeers that are at odds with the mores of easily threatened parental figures (including such things as values, expressed needs, self-images, etc.) may once again find that these fresh outlooks generate anxiety in the parents. A frequent method by which adults handle such feelings within themselves is through disparagement. The unfortunate juvenile may then learn that the way to approach differences between people is not to grasp the potential richness they may offer, but rather to disparage them. This, of course, makes future integrations in the search for tenderness even more difficult and likely to be less rewarding.

An even more disastrous outcome for the juvenile is the development of what interpersonalists call a *malevolent transformation*. This is a very complicated process that involves an interpersonal orientation in life based on the notion that the world is full of enemies and one can never expect tenderness in life. While this may sound like a paranoid position, insofar as it implies people are against the individual, it is different from that entity, and is, in most respects, even more insidious and destructive than the paranoid outlook. While the paranoid generally localizes the danger around certain discrete issues, and even individuals, which are often avoidable, people who employ malevolent transformation as a way of life are convinced there is no place to obtain tenderness. Thus, the process impacts on a basic human need, and pervades virtually all of life.

The juvenile period corresponds roughly to the classical period of latency. However, while the latency concept implies quiescence and solidification of the already established internal world, the interpersonal concept of the juvenile epoch posits a much more active period, with the opportunity for new and more complex internal organizations. Rather than stressing consolidation, interpersonalists see this period as an expanding time for the developing person.

PREADOLESCENCE

This is even more the case during the ensuing stage, which is referred to as *preadolescence*. This period is the time leading up to puberty, roughly equivalent to the latter stages of latency in the Freudian schema. Interpersonalists think of this epoch as a particularly critical period in personality development, for the critical issue at this time is the development of collaboration. Collaboration is the sine qua non for true object relatedness, intimacy, and love. In contrast to the more primitive means of relating via cooperation, collaboration embodies the notion of awareness of the other as a separate individual, with needs and concerns of his or her own.

The collaborative preadolescent begins to develop an early form of intimacy and love, in which concern for the other is motivated not only by a sense of what one needs to do in order to secure what one wants for oneself, but also out of concern with what is important to the other. This is most often played out through the establishment of a "chumship," a special relationship with a special compeer, the person usually referred to as "my best friend." Chums are generally, although not necessarily, of the same sex, and often appear so intertwined with each other as to seem to be lovers. They do everything together and conjointly explore all sorts of new phenomena, including sex. Mutual masturbation is often a frequent isophilic or same-sex activity during this period. It is often through this special attachment that one individual is brought into contact with a third compeer, leading to the development of a chain of friendships, something that Sullivan (1953) referred to as the creation of "gangs." He used the term without its latter-day perjorative connotation to suggest the establishment of a community of friends.

Another important aspect of this period that Sullivan (1953) stressed, and that most interpersonalists still consider valid and important, is the potential for reparative experiences during this period. If a child has been relatively unfortunate thus far in his or her development, but is lucky enough to find a "chum"—perhaps in the form of another outcast—the youngster has a chance to secure tenderness not previously obtained for being "who one is." This, then, is a potential opportunity to rectify some of the earlier developed bad me and not me personifications, through the loving eyes of the "chum." Again, this is a complex process that includes the potential for the development of sexual orientation. The period is so rich and critical that during an investigatory clinical interview, questions about this epoch and the presence, absence, and nature of the "chum"/"best friend" are usually pursued and explored.

LATER STAGES

While Sullivan's interpersonalist developmental schema continues on with the further stages of early adolescence, adolescence, and adulthood, I will conclude our discussion at this point. These later stages are each important in their own right, and each has important interpersonal issues that must be confronted and resolved. Early adolescents, for instance, must grapple with early pubescence, and the turning of what Sullivan (1953) referred to as the "lust dynamism" toward others. Later adolescents must integrate these feelings with those of intimacy and love.

My purpose has been to demonstrate the kinds of developmental issues interpersonalists envisage as critical to an individual's developmental path, and to indicate how the way with which these issues are dealt reflects itself and leads to changes in the internal world. The path itself is, of course, viewed as a sequential one, with active choices inherent to each stage. The freedom to choose one way or another is contingent on choices made earlier, and based on internal self and other personifications. Each new choice alters or reifies the personifications already in existence. It is most important to bear in mind that interpersonalists view development as an ongoing and active process, fraught with the issue of choice.

CLINICAL WORK

We have now examined, albeit briefly, some of the basic interpersonal postulates as to what is involved in the psychological makeup of an individual, and what has contributed to his or her development. Let us now consider how these viewpoints manifest themselves in the clinical situation. How do interpersonal psychoanalysts translate these theoretical considerations into clinical technique? What, in the interpersonal perspective, constitutes "cure," and how does a therapist work toward this end?

Interpersonal psychoanalysts rarely think or talk specifically in terms of cure, believing that the term has too discrete and concrete a connotation. Since pathology from this perspective is viewed as representing problems in living within the human condition, the more appropriately raised questions revolve around the kinds of problems an individual has, how they developed, what keeps the individual locked into his or her nonproductive stance in life, and what can be done to change these patterns.

It should not be surprising that interpersonalists view the problems in living to be manifested through interpersonal operations and integrations with others. Though internalized and represented by the personifications of the internal world, problems in living are reflected in the failure to achieve satisfaction and security in the outside world in one's dealings with one's fellow humans.

At the heart of interpersonal theory is the concept that individuals develop in a manner designed to secure the most tenderness with the least anxiety. Thus, essential questions are where and when significant experiences in early life gave rise to intolerable anxiety, what misunderstandings and distortions attended these situations, and what compromises were instituted to deal with them. Interpersonal theory respects the fact that the young individual is not cognitively capable of assimilating and evaluating data in a syntactic and truly logical manner. As a result, he or she has undoubtedly made the mistake of generalizing to others from specific integrations with specific objects in an effort to avoid anxiety. The resultant distortions, of which transference (the erroneous attribution of qualities to a person) is a highly specialized form (Singer, 1993), are called *parataxic distortions,* and are the basis on which the personality and its attendant pathology develop. Consequently, interpersonal analysts are most interested in identifying these distortions and the larger patternings to which they lead, and then in helping the individual find a new way of forming secure or anxiety-free interpersonal integrations. This process involves identifying the areas and sources of the distortions and exploring new kinds of integrations, both with the therapist and individuals in the outside world, not contingent on the earlier distortion-filled model of avoiding anxiety. The result is the disappearance of specific symptomatology and freedom for the individual to lead a more productive and satisfying life.

Since misconceptions play such a central role in the development of pathology, and because they arise initially in an effort to avoid anxiety, the individual works very hard, through the dynamism of the self-system, to avoid attending to phenomena believed to evoke anxiety. This is accomplished primarily via the operation of selective inattention and its "big brother," dissociation. These two processes are designed to keep anxiety provoking situations out of awareness, and they do so by limiting the individual's conscious awareness of situations that have been construed as leading to the experience of anxiety. The self-system is an ever-vigilant dynamism designed precisely for this monitoring function. A hallmark of interpersonal technique therefore involves extremely careful scrutinizing of the material of the therapy session—whether it be data the patient reports from his or her experiences in life or transactions within the therapy session itself between patient and therapist. The therapist listens for the gaps in the patient's presentation, for those places where there are omissions that make the entire sequence seem awkward or incongruous, especially in regard to the conclusions the patient has reached, which explain his or her behavior. The more the analyst and patient are able to attend to these gaps in the reporting of various material, the better they are able to increasingly locate where the perceived sources of anxiety must lie. So the interpersonal analyst is always listening to the material a patient presents with an ear toward this phenomenon. The simplest way to schematize this process is to think of a patient reporting "A then C." The analyst will want to know "What happened to B?" and the exploration will proceed from there.

Coincident with this reporting of material is the fact that the patient is having an ongoing relationship with the analyst. The same kinds of misconceptions and distortions evidenced in the reported material will play themselves out in the interpersonal dyad between patient and analyst. This is the basis of transference which is, as earlier suggested, a very special form of parataxic distortion. It is important to realize that what makes transference so special is not that it occurs in the analytic setting, but rather that it is object-related (Singer, 1993). Interpersonalists believe that it is particularly crucial to the understanding of transference to understand that the analyst is an active participant in the engagement with the patient, not simply a neutral figure onto whom distortions are projected. In this view, the analyst brings to the therapeutic engagement his or her personality, replete with all its human foibles. This dictum is a sine qua non of interpersonal psychoanalysis.

The transference, therefore, can only be understood in the context of an interplay between two mutually engaged individuals. The analyst constantly monitors the interplay between the two participants, looking for the same kinds of distortions the patient reports in encountering the outside world. But the analyst also continuously monitors his or her participation, and must understand and know himself or herself, so as not to confuse accurate perceptions of less than wonderful attributes of the analyst with patient distortion. To do so, or to deliberately fail to acknowledge accurate perceptions because of his or her own security needs, would lead the patient down the same mystifying route that the patient has earlier experienced, wherein his or her own perceptions and experiences must be compromised in the service of avoiding the induction of anxiety—in this instance, anxiety induced in the analyst! The more aware the analyst is of these countertransference tendencies (idiosyncratic reactions based on security needs), the more exciting, illuminating, demystifying, and richer will the engagement between analyst and patient become.

Interpersonal thinking, however, has taken this notion of the interplay between transference and countertransference phenomena a step further. Interpersonal theory posits that the power of the patient's distortions and the manner in which they lead to engagement is so strong that the analyst will inevitably be forced into the position that the patient expects from others in the world at large. This is the concept of transformation, a notion first promulgated and then developed by Levenson (1972), and subsequently by many others (Epstein and Feiner, 1979; Gill, 1983; Singer, 1989; and Ehrenberg, 1992, to name just a few). This is a critical concept for contemporary interpersonal psychoanalysis.

Although an oversimplification, the essence of this idea is that at some point the analyst catches himself or herself engaging the patient in a manner that is coincident with the patient's expectations but at odds with the analyst's essential self-experience. This use of the analyst's experience leads the analyst and patient into a mutual exploration of how the two of them arrived at this position, leading to a further illumination of how the patient engages others and forces what often is a self-fulfilling outcome of the patient's distorted notions of how others will treat him. The continued elucidation of these experiences, and interpretation of the ongoing as well as historical aspects of these dyadic configurations is what constitutes the heart of the working through phase of an interpersonal analysis. Thus, for instance, repeated attention to a kind of suspiciousness, based on earlier derived parataxic cues, with which the patient engages the analyst, and the analyst's recurring reaction to this process, will likely lead to new awareness on the part of the patient as to how unproductive interpersonal situations arise in his or her life. This process, repeated across all areas of the patient's life, allows for the reconfiguring of the internal self and other personifications, permitting the patient to carry a different sense of both self and other, and therefore to engage the world in a different fashion. The result of this phase is termination and "cure."

While this is a highly condensed and schematized version of how interpersonal analysts operate, it contains most of the essential elements of interpersonal thinking. It is, however, important to briefly mention one other critical issue. Early in the course of the treatment, the analyst will have ascertained the developmental level at which the patient operates, which is a complex process in and of itself. This is because all individuals operate differently in different settings. Nevertheless, the skilled analyst will be aware of the developmental level of his or her patients within different contexts. As a function of this understanding, the analyst will try to shape the nature of his or her analytic interventions so as to meet the level of the patient's emotional development. Just as one cannot teach algebra to someone who has not yet mastered addition, so, for instance, one cannot talk about collaboration to a person who has not yet comprehended the psychological essentials of cooperation. To do so only confuses and mystifies the patient, and often leads to experiences of humiliation and anxiety. In fact, it is in this way (by analysts misjudging what the patient is capable of accurately hearing and processing) that transformations, and strong transference and countertransference exchanges often arise. It is, however, the increasing ability of the patient to grasp new and more object-related forms of intervention, involving an increased appreciation of the other as a separate individual with needs of his or her own, that is the basis for the phenomenon of the "deepening" of an analysis as it moves along.

The following vignette, versions of which have appeared elsewhere (Singer, 1989, 1993), is a brief sketch designed to highlight some of these principles.

> The patient, a provocative young actor who was being seen at a reduced fee, regularly berated his therapist with respect to his requests for fee increases. He would rationally acknowledge his own increased standard of living, that the treatment had been useful to him, and that he was aware that the therapist's expenses were continually escalating with the cost of living. Nevertheless, he would invariably end each such engagement with a sullen, submissive agreement to pay the fee increase, claiming that he "had no choice," declaring that the therapist was exploitative, and that he and everyone else should be entitled to free care. After the patient had secured a financially advantageous position for himself, and the therapist had again raised the issue of a fee increase, the patient reacted similarly as in the past, although with somewhat less vituperativeness and more resignation. This time the therapist intervened by saying that he understood the patient's feeling of deprivation and that the notion of "should" was designed to disguise the patient's own desires, wants, and disappointments. The therapist added that, while he did not think of himself as a money-hungry or exploitative person, if the patient was remarking on his observation that the therapist was someone interested in furthering himself and his own life, that was an accurate perception. This was in marked contradistinction to the earlier efforts on the part of the therapist to get the patient to recognize and sanction the reasonableness of the therapist's requests for fee increases. This time the therapist's intervention led to an increase in the patient's friendliness toward and interest in the therapist, as well as to the introduction of material about the patient's feeling of having done damage to his younger sister by what he experienced as his "greedy" desire to have his parents to himself.

Note first of all that the episode involves an active interpersonal integration between the two participants, and is far more than a projection by one onto the other. It is a repeated patterning, which in prior instances had led to a transformation of the therapist—the therapist had, in fact, begun to experience himself as "greedy" and had tried to get the patient to understand the therapist's needs. The transformation was broken and therapeutic movement occurred when the therapist caught this in himself and returned to his predominant perception of himself.

Note also that the analyst's concern about his own "greediness" arose because of his attempts at intervening in a manner beyond the patient's developmental ability to grasp. This was a man dealing with early issues of deprivation, unconditional love, and magical thinking in the form of "shoulds." The attempt to get him to recognize another's needs when he was not yet able to acknowledge his own needs was doomed to failure, but was typical of the kind of engagement that the patient regularly orchestrated.

A final noteworthy aspect of the episode involves the development of new data. Although the therapist had taken a complete history, and had learned much additional information in the course of the analysis, the material involving the patient's feelings regarding his sister had never come to the fore. It was only through this engagement with the analyst that the heretofore dissociated material was brought into the open and was available for examination and analysis.

CONCLUSION

Interpersonal theory continues to move in new and fruitful directions. Much attention is still being paid to the nature of the interplay between patient and analyst. Concepts, such as "deconstruction," "linguistics," and "chaos theory" are being explored with regard to their utility for enhancing the scope of how interpersonal analysts think about patient–therapist interactions. The work of infant researchers continues to provide new data from which to theorize about human development. Beyond confirming many of Sullivan's early observations and hypotheses, new techniques of study add much to the understanding of how "human animals" become human persons through their interaction with significant others. The growing interest in what has been termed *relational thinking* has brought a new set of theorists and clinicians, with new clinical data and fresh ideas into an arena in which interpersonalists can further develop their thinking regarding not only clinical interactions but also the structure of the internal world.

REFERENCES

*Beebe, B., & Lachmann, F. M. (1994), Representation and internalization in infancy: Three principles of salience. *Psychoanal. Psychol.*, 11:127–165.
*Ehrenberg, D. B. (1992), *The Intimate Edge.* New York: W. W. Norton.
*Epstein, L., & Feiner, A. (1979), *Countertransference.* New York: Jason Aronson.
*Fiscalini, J., Lionells, M., Mann, C., & Stern, D. (1995), *The Handbook of Interpersonal Psychoanalysis.* Hillsdale, NJ: Analytic Press.
*Freud, S. (1905), Three essays on the theory of sexuality. *Standard Edition*, 7:123–243. London: Hogarth Press, 1953.
*Gill, M. (1983), The interpersonal paradigm and the degree of the therapist's involvement. *Contemp. Psychoanal.*, 19:200–237.
*Klein, M. (1975), *Envy & Gratitude and Other Works.* New York: Delacorte Press.
*Levenson, E. A. (1972), *The Fallacy of Understanding: An Inquiry into the Changing Structure of Psychoanalysis.* New York: Basic Books.
*——— (1984), Harry Stack Sullivan: The web and the spider. *Contemp. Psychoanal.*, 20:174–187.
*Singer, Eric (1989), Illusion, awareness, and validation. Paper presented to W. A. White Clinical Services, May.
*——— (1993), Transference and parataxic distortion. *Contemp. Psychoanal.*, 29:418–440.
*——— (1996), The drive for tenderness. Typescript.
*Singer, Erwin (1970), *Key Concepts in Psychotherapy.* New York: Basic Books.

───────────
*Recommended reading.

*Stern, D. (1985), *The Interpersonal World of the Infant.* New York: Basic Books.

*Sullivan, H. S. (1940), *Conceptions of Modern Psychiatry.* New York: W. W. Norton.

*———— (1953), *The Interpersonal Theory of Psychiatry.* New York: W. W. Norton.

*———— (1956), *Clinical Studies in Psychiatry.* New York: W. W. Norton.

*———— (1964), *The Fusion of Psychiatry and Social Science.* New York: W. W. Norton.

*Winnicott, D. W. (1965), *The Maturational Processes and the Facilitating Environment.* New York: International Universities Press.

5.

Constructivist Accounts of Psychoanalysis

Richard Loewus

The nature of psychoanalytic knowledge has been the subject of controversy throughout the history of the field. Challenges to the validity of psychoanalytic ideas stem from a fundamental question regarding knowledge in general: How can we come to trust what we believe to be real?

Positivism-empiricism, the philosophy of knowledge into which Freud was born, in which he trained, and within which he developed his theory of mind, holds truth as absolute. For the positivist, reality is independent of the descriptions, formulations, and laws we create in our attempts to know the one true world. Reality is unitary and discoverable. Science is the discipline that searches for the true nature of the world through its systematic methodology.

Fearing that his new discipline might not be regarded as a science, and that it would then be disrespected, devalued, and ultimately rejected, Freud unwaveringly insisted that psychoanalysis was a new natural science of the mind. Thus, challenges to the validity of psychoanalytic knowledge, commonly framed in terms of whether psychoanalysis is or is not a science, may be understood as ways of challenging Freud's epistemological claims, his intellectual heritage, and the nineteenth century scientific zeitgeist. These challenges have focused on three general areas: (1) Challenges to the validity of clinical interpretation—understanding offered within the clinical enterprise. (2) Challenges to the validity of psychoanalytic metapsychology—psychoanalysis as a general theory of human psychology. (3) Challenges regarding whether clinical "data" can be held as validation of the general theoretical tenets of psychoanalysis—the validity of psychoanalytic methodology.

Over the past twenty-five years, psychoanalysts and philosophers have offered reformulations of psychoanalysis that rest on current trends in epistemology that involve some form of relativism—the proposition that reality is not absolute. In this view what we hold to be true is significantly influenced by the methods, assumptions, and perspectives that we employ to arrive at what we claim to know (e.g., Protter, 1985, 1988; *Psychoanalytic Dialogues,* 1992).

The difference between positivism and relativism is most often, but not most usefully, stated in its most extreme form by pitting absolute positivism against radical relativism: Either there is one given, ready-made world to which we must appeal to establish the truth of our views, formulations, and ideas (*absolutism*), or, if not, anything goes, and these views, formulations, and ideas dissolve into stories or myths that answer to nothing (*radical relativism*).

Constructivism offers an alternative to these mutually exclusive positions. Its assertions regarding the nature of knowledge are counterintuitive and difficult. It will be useful to present a brief review of some its basic tenets before discussing their use in current psychoanalytic theorizing and practice.

In concert with radical relativism, constructivism holds that there is no one, given, real world to which all our ideas must answer. Constructivism holds there are innumerable versions of the world, many of which are contradictory. All of our formulations, scientific or otherwise, are constructions which answer to our own purposes, rather than to some ready-made world. Unlike radical relativism, however, constructivism asserts that not every version qualifies as equally right. We do not have free rein to construct anything we please and claim it as equally correct or valid as any other construction. The constructivist assertion that there are many versions of the world in no way disarms said versions of their relative usefulness or power. Nor does it relieve the constructivist from the responsibility to provide standards by which the relative rightness of any construction can be assessed. A practitioner or theorist who subscribes to a constructivist epistemology is challenged to provide these standards of relative rightness for his or her given field of study.

Constructivism holds that our descriptions, formulations, and laws are products of our own minds, accomplished through the creation and manipulation of the symbols and the systems we invent to use them to express understanding. Symbols are not transparent tools for the description of a ready-made world, but actively participate in the versions we create through their definition and use. Understanding consists of the processes we use to create versions of the world, and the considerations that go into the judgments we make regarding their relative rightness (see below). The theory asserts that human understanding is not limited to any one area of inquiry or given system of representation, and that epistemology must include a philosophy of both art and science. Hence, the concepts and variables generally used to define the nature of knowledge and knowing require reconsideration and expansion in order to include both realms.

Truth, for example, is a measure of the convergence of discourse with the real world. As such, truth is limited to verbal statements. The concept of *rightness* subsumes that of truth in constructivism. While truth is absolute, rightness is relative. Rightness refers to a set of standards that helps determine the acceptability of a given idea. It depends on goodness of fit with these standards, and the degree to which the idea is useful and works to a desired end. Such fitting does not refer to a match with what exists independently, because for the constructivist nothing exists independently of its symbolic construction.

Relative rightness is not limited to constructions formulated in language. Systems of reference other than linguistic descriptions can be considered. Whereas a musical passage, a verbal question, or a glance may not be considered in terms of their truth value, all may be considered in terms of relative rightness. This opens epistemology to what is shown through the whole variety of referential media, as well as to what is stated or written in language.

Constructivism replaces the concept of knowledge with that of understanding which encompasses a wider range of phenomena than does knowledge. We may understand regardless of truth value or credibility. We can understand art, facial expressions, gestures, and behaviors. Understanding does not involve closure or finality; it opens epistemology to emotional experience as well as rational thought.

THE UTILITY OF A CONSTRUCTIVIST APPROACH TO CLINICAL PSYCHOANALYSIS

For the constructivist analyst each of us lives in a world of our own making, a world constructed of individual, characteristic processes we select and apply to construct subjective experience. As a student of such constructions and processes, the analyst endeavors to psychoanalytically understand, unravel, and reconstruct (1) the particular world the patient has constructed of subjective experience, and (2) the individual processes, in conflict and synthesis, that a patient has developed to continually recreate, and thereby sustain, his or her previously created world. The purpose of analytic inquiry is to help the patient realize the nature of their subjective understanding of the world, to understand the processes by which they have previously and continue in the present to construct this world, and to allow for the development of a wider, more psychoanalytically complete set of meaning making processes.

In the analytic dialogue selective instances of a patient's productions, narrative or otherwise, are taken by the analyst to be samples of psychoanalytically salient clinical principles, rather than as proofs of psychoanalytic laws. A given production is analytically relevant to the degree that it exemplifies an analytic principle, and the analyst's bringing it into the clinical interaction is therapeutically powerful to the degree that the patient can see how it fits into their experience and can use it to expand their self-understanding.

Hence, the clinical dialogue requires examination and respect for both participants' subjective experience. From the analyst's perspective there are two fundamental interrelated contexts which organize their understanding. One is the context of the psychoanalytic world view, what Schafer (1983) calls its master narratives, or psychoanalytic theory. The other is the context of the particular analysis at a given time between particular individuals.

From the perspective of constructivist theory, when an analyst takes some clinical occurrence as interpretable, he or she is asserting that it is an example of an accepted psychoanalytic principle. Psychoanalytic interpretation is a choice by the analyst within the context of their understanding. Which of the two above contexts that is the more pertinent at a given moment is also an important matter of choice.

Hence, constructivism has important implications for the relevance and utility of the concept of truth in psychoanalytic interpretation. The analyst is no longer concerned with whether an interpretation is factual or true in the positivist sense, but focuses instead on the degree to which it fits and works in the two contexts mentioned above. Does it fit and work with the master narratives; that is, is it theoretically coherent? Does it fit and work in this analysis at this time with this patient; that is, is it technically coherent, well timed, and tactful? Can the patient accept the idea that their actions reflect the qualities that the analyst has suggested? Does the interpretation organize in a psychoanalytic way other parts of the patient's story and contribute to a more comprehensive narrative? Is the interpretation coherent in the bridge it makes between these two basic contexts? The measure here is constructivist rightness, the ongoing fitting and working into contexts, a dialectic between master narrative and singular analysis.

Fitting and working does not mean that any interpretation is as right as any other, of course. Stern (1989) points out that should an analyst interpret a patient's silence as angry when the patient is assured that it is not, the patient can often tell the analyst they are wrong, even if the patient cannot yet offer a more precise description of the nature of the silence and its explanation: "It is like watching a figure emerge from a dense fog.There is a shape there, but it is fuzzy. It could be a person. It could even be a dancing bear. But it couldn't be an elephant" (Stern, 1989, p. 11). Hence, one standard of good fit is a sense by the patient that the analyst is onto something authentic about the patient's experience.

Within psychoanalysis there have been two basic approaches to the use of constructivism: *Hermeneutic/Narrative Psychoanalysis* and *Social Constructivist Psychoanalysis*.

Hermeneutics is the art or science of interpretation. Etymologically, hermeneutics derives from Hermes, the name of the Greek god assigned to deliver the gods' messages to mortals. Originally, hermeneutics was proposed as a methodology for interpreting the meanings of the *geisteswissenschaften*, the products of human affairs, as opposed to the *naturwissenschaften*, the natural sciences. Proponents of modern hermeneutics assert that their discipline provides an epistemological foundation for all descriptions of understanding and is not limited to human productions.

Since interpretation has traditionally held a central place in psychoanalytic therapy, the nature of interpretation is crucial to its epistemological status. The clinical dialogue centers on interpretation, both theoretically and technically. Historically, interpretation is the medium through which the beneficial changes of psychoanalytic therapy are said to be delivered. Hence, many modern analysts have been attracted to a hermeneutic framework for psychoanalytic interpretations (e.g., Ricoeur, 1970; Habermas, 1971; Gadamer, 1975; see also Grünbaum, 1984; Sass, 1988).

In 1982 Spence offered an important hermeneutic reformulation of psychoanalysis. He asserted that because psychoanalysis confuses "narrative truth" with "historical truth" it cannot lay claim to scientific status. The aim of historical truth is to come as close as possible to a description of "what really happened." Hence, since historical truth seeks the one true account of a patient's past, it is essentially a positivist variable. Narrative truth, on the other hand, is "the criterion we use to decide when a certain experience has been captured to our satisfaction; it depends on continuity and closure and the extent to which the fit of the pieces takes on an aesthetic finality. Narrative truth is what we have in mind when we say that such and such is a good story" (Spence, 1982, p. 31).

For Spence, it is not possible to support the view that psychoanalysis is a method for uncovering repressed memories of historical personal experiences in order to arrive at the one final true version of a patient's life history. Rather, Spence asserted that the life history constructed through psychoanalytic treatment is strongly shaped by narrative influences such as coherence, continuity, sequence, and comprehensiveness—the elements of a good story. Further, the narrative elements that provide the structure for psychoanalytic treatment are supplied by the analyst's theory. As a result, the picture of the analyst as a passive receiver of the patient's unconscious meanings is untenable, because the analyst is instead actively listening for gaps, inconsistencies, and discontinuities from a specifically psychoanalytic perspective. The result is not an objective, historically true account, but a particularly psychoanalytic version of a life story, a psychoanalytically constructed narrative.

ROY SCHAFER'S NARRATIONAL PSYCHOANALYSIS

Roy Schafer (1976, 1983, 1992) has offered a reformulation of psychoanalytic theory and clinical understanding based on constructivist and hermeneutic principles. His emphasis is on the use of constructivist epistemology to understand the analyst's use of his or her particular theory in understanding the patient's experience. His psychoanalytic heritage is classically Freudian with an emphasis on ego psychology. He characterizes psychoanalysis as "a way of constructing the world it tells about through application of its master narratives and the storylines they generate" (Schafer, 1992, p. 272). The master narratives of psychoanalysis are its theory. Within the context of these master narratives, analysts listen in order to arrive at a coconstructed autobiography that constitutes, at the termination of analysis, a psychoanalytic version of the patient's life. The classical characterization of the analyst as objectively and passively receiving the patient's unconscious meanings through the reciprocal processes of the analyst's evenly hovering attention and the patient's free association, is replaced with a view in which the analyst and patient actively construct personal meaning from their combined experiences within the specific context of psychoanalytic master narratives.

A given psychoanalytic biography is only one of many possible accounts of a life. Schafer recognizes that we cannot check the truthfulness of analytic life historical constructions against "what really happened." Furthermore, all constructions will be subject to changes as analysis progresses, because as the analysis deepens, new understandings will be refocused on former versions of the same events.

Psychoanalytic master narratives guide the analyst in selecting from the patient's narratives, behaviors, and other material what is relevant to the analysis. They guide the analyst in identifying gaps and inconsistencies to explore in the patient's reports. These master narratives set important limits on what is held as valid and acceptable within a psychoanalytic context. This is one meaning of Schafer's assertion, "The facts are what the analyst makes them out to be" (Schafer, 1983, p. 255).

For Schafer, narration constitutes experience. When a patient speaks to an analyst about his life, he is giving a current narrative version of his experience. As analysis progresses, the analyst joins the narrational activity of the patient to psychoanalytically revise the patient's version of his or her life. As a result, not only the patient's narrative changes; by definition, so will his or her experience. Schafer (1992, pp. 156–160) credits Freud with having created a new kind of dialogue—the transformational dialogue—in which words change worlds: What the patient presents originally as the facts of his or her life "become *psychoanalytic* facts . . . only after they have been systematically retold by the analyst . . . " (Schafer, 1983, p. 189).

This version of psychoanalysis holds that the analyst "takes everything in the analytic situation as a text that requires interpretation" (Schafer, 1992, p. 176). In considering Freud's writings on psychoanalysis, Schafer likens himself to a literary critic.

He regards Freud's work as texts open to interpretation, rather than as fixed theoretical laws or prescribed, inflexible rules for clinical practice. Hence, hermeneutics informs the analyst's understanding of both his or her theory and the patient's reports in the clinical hours.

In the clinical arena, Schafer asserts that the analyst is "an influential co-author . . . [who] . . . cohabits" (Schafer, 1992, p. 177) the text with the patient. As such, any claim to a stance of objective observationalism or empirical science is untenable. Rather, the idea of a cohabited, coauthored text "accord[s] to constructivism and its corollary, perspectivism, an essential place in psychoanalysis" (p. 177).

Schafer (1983b) includes the processes of redescribing, reinterpreting, recontextualizing, and reducing, as formats for psychoanalytic interpretation. The analyst may, for example, take the patient's description of himself as powerless in his relationship to a superior and *redescribe* it as not voicing his opinions. The analyst may further *reinterpret* the patient's passivity as a defense against acting aggressively, or describe the patient's withdrawal from confronting his superior as fear of retribution by a castrating father figure, thus *recontextualizing* a current action in the setting of a psychoanalytically relevant childhood danger situation. The effect of these processes is *reduction* of the patient's description of his experience to analytically relevant terms.

Discussing Freud's transformational dialogue, Schafer (1992) adds the processes of destabilizing, defamiliarizing, and deconstructing the patient's presentation of self and history as fundamental psychoanalytic narrational procedures. Destabilization, for example, may address the analysis of defenses—the various ways in which the patient strives to keep disturbing thoughts and feelings from conscious experience—in order to arrive at a richer narrative that reflects the more complex analytic visions of irony and tragedy (Schafer, 1976). Defamiliarization refers to enriching the patient's narrative by adding new psychoanalytic meanings, revising it, for example, by placing greater emphasis on unconscious modes of experience. Deconstruction revises unidimensional versions of self and others by relocating the patient's assumed positions on dimensions of psychoanalytic relevance to relatively more complex and inclusive positions (e.g., heterosexual-homosexual; sadism-masochism; wish-defense).

The analyst may suggest that a patient's repeated expression of disdain for her lover's retreat from conflict reflects her own fear of acting angrily and, hence, destructively (destabilization). Adding to this interpretation, the analyst may suggest that her fear of acting destructively speaks to guilt over wishing to defeat her lover (defamiliarization). The patient may begin to accept an enriched view of herself as not simply reasonably responding to her lover's withdrawal, and come to understand her feelings regarding aggressive attacks as both pleasurable and painful (deconstruction). All of this may then be understood in the context of early experiences with, and reactions to, parental authority. As a result, her more complex view of herself and her lover—that he is in part responding to her unconscious wish to attack him aggressively—enriches her understanding of their interaction.

In developing his narrational version of psychoanalysis, Schafer identifies characteristics and requirements of psychoanalytic master narratives. The first and most important characteristic is a focus on psychic reality, a term that emphasizes the ubiquity and power of the influence of unconscious experience on everyday life. Psychic reality represents a reality that extends beyond the conventional world. It is the focus of psychoanalytic activity, the realm of transference and defense. It is a world of " . . . unrecognized symbols, concretized metaphors, reductive allegories, or repressed storylines of childhood" (Schafer, 1983a, p. 257).

A second defining characteristic of the psychoanalytic dialogue is the attention the analyst pays to the dialogue itself. Clinical psychoanalysis focuses on the evolution of meanings within the analytic dialogue. "The analyst's highest priority must be to attempt to understand *in a psychoanalytic fashion* the construction and communication of experience in the here and now of the analytic session" (Schafer, 1983a, p. 252).

As such, the most important historical construction within the treatment is the history of the analysis itself. Meanings captured in the here-and-now of the clinical dialogue are taken as models for structuring interpretations of the past, present, and future. Hence, analysis is a "set of principles for participating in, understanding, and explaining the dialogue between psychoanalyst and analysand" (Schafer, 1983a, p. 212).

One measure of the psychoanalytic rightness of interpretation, then, is the degree to which the currently constructed meanings of the patient's experience of the ongoing history of the analytic relationship itself fit and work as a structure for organizing and understanding the patient's past and present experience outside analysis.

A third characteristic of clinical analysis is the analyst's attention to the influence of an inner dialogue that includes "a multitude of voices rising from [one's] own inner world . . . that, by perception or projection or both, the analysand locates in the analyst or others in the surround" (Schafer, 1992, p. 160). Psychoanalysis includes both narration between others in the here-and-now as well as the patient's inner dialogue with voices from the past. Through this principle, Schafer embraces the intrapsychic aspect of psychoanalytic understanding.

SOCIAL CONSTRUCTIVISM—THE PSYCHOANALYTIC RELATIONSHIP UNDER THE CONSTRUCTIVIST LENS

With its heritage of participant observation (Sullivan, 1953, 1954), interpersonal psychoanalysis has been a fertile ground for a constructivist reformulation of psychoanalysis.[1] Opposed to the classical position of the analyst as a detached observer, participant observation underscores the participation of the analyst in creating the phenomena he or she simultaneously observes.

Generally, the social constructivist movement emphasizes the influence of culture and social variables in the construction of understanding. Within psychoanalysis, the central focus of the social constructivist analyst is on his or her moment to

---

[1] Harry Stack Sullivan, the first interpersonal psychoanalyst, would not have supported the constructivist position. Sullivan himself was a strict empiricist.

moment subjective experience in developing clinical under-standing. Within this view, analytic work is a function of the analyst's current perspective, both conscious and unconscious. Importantly, the analyst's current perspective is a function of the analyst's participation in the analysis. This current perspective is affected not only by the analyst's training and theoretical orientation, but by the analyst's personal experience in and out of the analysis. The analyst now is a "participant constructivist" (Hoffman, 1991, p. 78), an epistemologically evolved partici-pant observer. The analyst constructs understanding by partici-pating with the patient in the psychoanalytic interaction, and this participation within the analytic dyad is the primary data for the social constructivist psychoanalyst.

A fundamental assumption of social constructivist analytic work is that the analyst cannot know the meaning of his or her participation while he or she is embedded in the analytic field. One of the social constructivist analyst's most important func-tions is to identify and articulate the nature of his or her unwit-ting involvement with the patient which reenacts the patient's characteristic relational assumptions.

Hoffman (1983) offers a critical review of the evolution of the concept of the analyst as a neutral blank screen, a central tenet of classical clinical theory. He proposes that any concep-tualization that upholds a division between real and transfer-ence aspects of the analytic relationship is by definition *conservative*. The difference between real aspects versus trans-ference aspects of the analytic relationship roughly parallels that between historical and narrative truth. Hoffman points out that any psychoanalytic theory that holds that there is only one accurate, hence real, description of the psychoanalytic relation-ship, and that anything short of that is a distortion, hence trans-ference manifestation, is a conservative theory. It is conservative because it holds onto some form of the classical definition of transference as a distortion by the patient of the actual analytic relationship.

Only those reformulations that fully reject any clear "di-chotomy between transference as distortion and non-transfer-ence as reality based" (Hoffman, 1983, p. 393) can be viewed as the more complete or *radical* critique of the blank screen.

Furthermore, the radical critique requires acknowledgment that the patient can and does perceive aspects of the analyst's experience that the analyst may not see. The radical critic, asserting the fundamentally social nature of understanding, rejects what Hoffman calls the *"naive patient fallacy"* (Hoffman, 1983, p. 395), the belief that perceptions of the analyst by the patient that the analyst does not currently hold of him- or herself must be, by definition, distortions, and therefore, transference manifestations. The consulting room becomes a more democratic arena, and the analyst's authority as the arbiter of reality is rejected.

We see here the use of constructivism to fundamentally reconceptualize the nature of the psychoanalytic dialogue. The analyst cannot know from moment to moment the nature of the effects that his or her decisions, choices, and personal participation have with the patient in the ongoing interaction. As a result, social constructivism "requires that analysts embrace the uncertainty that derives from knowing that their subjectivity can never be fully transcended" (Hoffman, 1992, p. 287). From a social constructivist perspective, psychoanalysis is characterized as a dialectic action between the analyst's often unwitting unconscious involvement with the patient in the immediate interpersonal field of the clinical encounter on the one hand, and the attempt to extricate him- or herself from this entanglement so as to construct new understanding on the other. Stern (1989, 1990) refers to this aspect of social constructivism as the analyst's being embedded in the analytic field.

Social constructivism views the analyst's subjective experiences as critically important and useful clinical phenomena rather than intrusive, distorting countertransference. There is a shift from reliance on theory for authority, or what Schafer calls master narratives, to reliance on subjective experience. Although the general theories of social constructivism and hermeneutics do not demand this, the difference between social constructivism and hermeneutic versions of psychoanalysis can be understood to pertain to the relative primacy of these two contexts. For the social constructivist, the subjective experience of the analyst in the clinical interaction is the primary source of data and authority. For the hermeneuticist, it is the master narrative that carries the greater weight in guiding the analyst's interventions.

For the social constructivists, then, the analyst's authority derives from "a special kind of authenticity" (Hoffman, 1992, p. 295) comprised of the analyst's subjective experience in the moment, as well as his or her professional training and identification, theoretical understanding, and clinical experience. Importantly, the analyst's authenticity "is continually the object of psychoanalytic skepticism and critical reflection" (Hoffman, 1992, p. 296). Freed from the constraints of a positivistic requirement for the one, true interpretation, the analyst has "more leeway for a spontaneous kind of expressiveness" (Hoffman, 1992, p. 292), an expressiveness that includes personal conviction based on subjective experience.

Hence, for social constructivist analysts, there is less emphasis than is the case in more classical orientations on theoretical formulation of the patient's inner conflict exclusive of the analytic interaction. All analytic material presented is considered in the context of the clinical interaction. The focus of social constructivism is on the meanings the parties coconstruct out of their shared relational experiences in the treatment.

According to Stern (1992), constructivism indicates that the analyst cannot be considered an arbiter of truth. Rather, the analytic relationship is one of "equality and balance; patient and analyst share in the creation of what they agree is true" (Stern, 1992, p. 332). The standards for agreement are constructivist standards—conviction, coherence, goodness of fit, completeness.

Stern notes that the equality he advocates is not a requirement for unconsidered agreement with the patient. The analyst, based on his or her own analysis, training, and experience, maintains authority regarding analytic constructions. In fact, Stern asserts that the constructivist analyst is free to debate with the patient, so long as such debate is submitted to analytic curiosity. This attitude of curiosity, a continual effort to widen and further the psychoanalytic inquiry in a spirit of collaboration, is at the heart of Stern's model. The analyst attempts to "open himself as fully as possible to an awareness of the presumptions that structure his experience with the patient, but the mutative event itself, that is, the explicit awareness of these perceptions and the new kinds of interaction that such awareness makes possible, cannot be made to happen" (Stern, 1996, p. 283). Social constructivism frees analysts to include for analytic inquiry casual, seemingly nonanalytic interactions and spontaneous reactions on the analyst's part.

These considerations derive from the social constructivist position that there is nothing to behold within the patient apart from what transpires between the two parties to therapy. In the classical analytic model the analyst follows the patient's associations into the patient's unconscious to uncover material that is already there, frozen in time and waiting to be uncovered and brought to consciousness through analysis. Stern notes that Freud's associationist view of cognition held that exposure to a given reality resulted in a formed "piece" of perception that was then consciously registered and stored in memory for later retrieval, unless it was repressed. Psychoanalysis was seen as the retrieval of received but repressed experience, the remembering of historical truth, or alternatively, the excavation and reexperiencing of archaic wishes and desires. This attitude is captured in Freud's well-known original formulation, "The hysteric suffers mainly from reminiscences" (Breuer and Freud, 1893–1895, p. 7).

In Stern's social constructivism there is no unconscious material lying within the patient to be uncovered and revealed by the analyst. Stern's "unformulated experience" (Stern, 1983) is a constructivist reconceptualization of the unconscious mind and defense. This is a concept born of constructivist epistemology and modern cognitive research that suggest that experience is more actively constructed than passively received. Mental representations, including those produced through memory, are created through active processes which proceed through progressive levels of articulation. They are not imprinted on a passive receiver. Hence, memory is an active, creative construction in the present. When a patient recalls a past event in the analytic setting, the patient is, with the analyst's help, constructing meaning in the present. The contemporary analytic meaning must fit and work with what the patient feels about his or her past, and fit and work with the meaning being constructed presently in the analysis.

In this model defense is reconceptualized as the interference with, or active turning away from, the process of constructing experience through symbolic representation. Where Freudian defense mechanisms act on fully formed mental representations of experience, and do so through various distortions or repression, Stern's defense mechanisms prevent mental representation from being consciously articulated in the first place. Hence, when defense is lifted, fully formed memories, thoughts, or fantasies do not simply reappear. Rather, the lifting of defense opens the door to the "transformation of certain murky and unnoticed cognitive and affective material of the patient's into clear and convincing meaning" (Stern, 1989, p. 10). Stern likens these "murky" experiences to images seen through a fog—there but unformed, as yet unable to be articulated.

Hence, rather than interpreting unconscious experience hidden from the patient through repression, the analyst notes psychoanalytically relevant gaps and inconsistencies in the patient's construction of the world and his narrative history. The analyst shares these observations with the patient in the hope of engaging the patient's curiosity about his experience and broadening and deepening the inquiry. For Stern, "The analyst does not have a set of theoretical or 'artistic' skills by which the patient's unconscious can be reliably grasped. *An interpretation is the analyst's own experience and is treated as such*" (Stern, 1992, p. 357; italics added). The key social constructivist assertion is that the analyst's interpretations are not lawfully derived authoritative pronouncements based on theoretical laws, but instead are expressions of the analyst's particular understanding of the patient through his experience within the field of the clinical interaction.

Stern considers clinical psychoanalysis the reinstatement of the process of active formulation of experience through understanding the interactions in the therapeutic relationship: "[B]y creating between them a world of thought and curiosity, patient and analyst rescue unformulated experience from the oblivion of the familiar" (Stern, 1989, p. 96).

IMPLICATIONS OF CONSTRUCTIVISM FOR THE THEORY OF TRANSFERENCE AND THE NATURE OF THERAPEUTIC ACTION

According to classical theory, transference is specifically the "actualisation of unconscious wishes" (Laplanche and Pontalis, 1973, p. 455) within the psychoanalytic relationship. For the classical analyst, transference denotes the patient's reliving in the therapeutic encounter with the analyst unconscious wishes derived through infantile experiences with important caretakers from the patient's history. Transferences are thus seen as distortions of reality, to the degree that they are inappropriate to the current situation. In this view the patient is unconsciously behaving and feeling toward the analyst as if the analyst were a parental figure from the past. This the analyst interprets to the patient, with the goal of promoting the patient's insight into formerly repressed and/or unconscious wishes.

To the social constructivist analyst, patients are actively engaged in considering what the analyst's actions exemplify in the context of the analytic relationship. Transference, in this view, is seen as understanding and interpreting the patient's interpretations of the analyst's actions, motivations, and interpretations. It is assumed that the patient's feelings and perceptions represent a perspective on the analyst that has some basis in the way the analyst has participated in the interaction. The analyst is striving to comprehend what the patient takes the analyst's actions to mean. Hence, social constructivist analysts regard the nature of the analytic relationship bidirectional and interactive. Both participants are at times embedded in the relational field. This is an essential tenet of the social constructivist paradigm.

Under the social constructivist paradigm, a fundamental analytic phenomenon is reflected in the analyst's unformulated experiences of the patient (Stern, 1989; Hoffman, 1991). Until the analyst is able to articulate his experience, he is doomed to reenact with the patient the latter's characteristic problems. Before the analyst can articulate his or her experience with the patient, the analyst is embedded in the field of the clinical encounter. The therapeutic action of psychoanalysis is precisely the process of the analyst's escaping the grip of the field (Stern, 1989) so as to articulate to the patient previously unformulated experience within the clinical relationship.

While the analyst is no longer seen as a blank screen as suggested in classical theory, social constructivism rests on the assertion that the clinical interaction will bring out the patient's characteristic ways of relating. The patient, with the active, if at first unwitting, participation of the analyst, recreates in the relationship with the analyst his or her characteristic problems. The analyst is understood to be an active participant constructor of the analytic field, and to the degree that the analyst is embedded in the field, interpretations of transference are not yet possible.

Conservative and radical critiques of the blank screen concept notwithstanding, the essential nature of the concept of transference survives social constructivist reformulation and remains a primary psychoanalytic theorem. Social constructivism's theory of transference represents an interface between a fundamental constructivist principle and a central psychoanalytic master narrative. While multiple constructions of the analytic relationship is the rule, such constructions are constrained by the patient's characteristic problems in forming and understanding interpersonal relationships. Transference is a psychoanalytic embodiment of constructivism, a relativism with constraints. Importantly, the coherence of the concept of transference depends on the assertion that in good measure, those constraints are the patient's restricted capacity to construct relationships.

Therapeutic action, in this view, results from the process of establishing a clinical field in which the patient and analyst unwittingly reenact the patient's characteristic relational difficulties and then finding a way of articulating and formulating what has been constructed. To the degree that the analyst is unaware of the nature of his or her participation in these aspects of the patient's relational repertoire, he or she is not yet able to articulate them. Once the analyst becomes aware of the nature of his or her participation and the ways in which it reflects characteristic aspects of the patient's experience out-side the analytic setting as well as within it, the analyst can invite the patient to become interested and curious in the latter's contributions. Analysts "do their best to disembed them-selves . . . by trying to specify the patterns of relatedness tran-spiring in the consulting room. They learn the unconscious assumptions that structure the tiny culture of analyst and pa-tient" (Stern, 1996, p. 282).

A CLINICAL EXAMPLE OF SOCIAL CONSTRUCTIVISM

The following example of social constructivism is given by Stern (1989).

Due to an attractive career opportunity, a middle-aged aca-demic relocated. As a result, it was necessary to terminate the analysis in which he was successfully engaged. He reentered analysis after consultations with several analysts in the new city. The patient chose his new analyst with ambivalence. He unfa-vorably compared his new analyst to his former analyst. He worried that the new analyst was too young and inexperienced. He felt his new analyst was not appropriately formal and found evidence of this in the analyst's verbal interactions and in the style of his office. He felt his new analyst was too expensive, not flexible in rescheduling appointments, and spoke too much. All of these critiques the patient delivered to the analyst calmly, reasonably, and regretfully, at the same time pointing out that he felt warmly and positively toward the analyst in other ways.

The analyst felt the patient's complaints had some basis. The patient's former analyst was classically oriented. It was likely that his former analyst did speak less and that his office was more austere. However, the analyst wondered about the patient's focus on these issues. Although the patient often cited his concerns and questioned whether he should stay in the treatment, the analyst found evidence that the patient was com-mitted to the treatment in the patient's punctuality and regular attendance. Additionally, the analyst felt the patient to be devel-oping an attachment to him.

Six weeks or so into the treatment the patient criticized a painting in the analyst's office, and commented that while it would be "snotty" of him to characterize the analyst as shallow on the basis of his taste in art, he nonetheless worried that the analyst was not going to be able to understand him in depth. The analyst listened as the patient continued on with other matters, but felt a pressure to respond. Since, however, the analyst was unsure of the nature of this pressure, he remained silent.

The analyst found himself thinking he would like to tell the patient that the painting no longer appealed to him. He considered getting rid of the painting at the end of the session. He began to wonder why he felt pressured to appease the patient in this way. He realized he had worried more than he had thought about living up to the patient's former analyst, a senior man whose work he knew and admired. Further, he realized that the patient would know that his former analyst would be known to his new analyst, and the patient would have reason to believe that his new analyst would have these feelings. The patient was also knowledgeable regarding art, and would have reason to believe the analyst would likely respect his judgments about art. The result of this self-examination by the analyst was to make him realize that he had felt intimidated by the patient.

The analyst, now able to formulate his experience for himself, was able to reflect on the nature of the interpersonal field in which he had been participating with the patient, and no longer felt pressured to respond defensively. Considering his experience in more detail, he realized that at times he had felt contemptible to this patient, and wondered what the patient's contempt for him meant. He felt he had retreated from these feelings, probably as many other people in the patient's life had done. He wondered if the patient himself had felt intimidated and contemptible, either now in the treatment setting or historically, perhaps in relationship to a parent. Given the analyst's sense that the patient was also attached to the analyst, even while holding him in contempt, was the intimidation a defense against feeling too close, or alternatively a necessary ingredient for connection with others? These questions were "eventually productive in the detailed description of the field and the patient's character" (Stern, 1989, p. 17).

Importantly, the analyst was unaware of feeling intimidated and held in contempt by the patient for some time. The social constructivist paradigm assumes this kind of unconscious participation by the analyst is a necessary but not sufficient aspect of the therapeutic process. By formulating his experience of embeddedness within the field, the analyst finds his way out. He uses his newfound understanding of his own participation to formulate questions to explore with the patient. As a result the patient may join the analyst in regarding the patient's participation as an object of reflection and curiosity, thereby engendering a more inclusive self understanding.

REFERENCES

Breuer, J., & Freud, S. (1893–1895), Studies on Hysteria. *Standard Edition,* 2. London: Hogarth Press, 1955.

Gadamer, H. (1975), *Truth and Method,* tr. & ed. G. Barden & J. Cumming. New York: Seabury Press.

Grunbaum, A. (1984), *The Foundations of Psychoanalysis.* Berkeley: University of California Press.

Habermas, J. (1971), *Knowledge and Human Interests.,* tr. J. J. Shapiro. Boston: Beacon Press.

*Hoffman, I. Z. (1983), The patient as interpreter of the analyst's experience. *Contemp. Psychoanal.,* 19:389–422.

*——— (1991), Discussion: Toward a social-constructivist view of the psychoanalytic situation. *Psychoanal. Dial.,* 1:74–105.

*——— (1992), Some practical implications of a social-constructivist view of the psychoanalytic situation. *Psychoanal. Dial.,* 2:287–304.

Laplanche, J., & Pontalis, J.-B. (1973), *The Language of Psychoanalysis,* tr. D. Nicholson-Smith. New York: W. W. Norton.

*Protter, B. (1985), Toward an emergent psychoanalytic epistemology. *Contemp. Psychoanal.,* 21:208–277.

*——— (1988), Ways of knowing in psychoanalysis: Some epistemic considerations for an autonomous theory of psychoanalytic praxis. *Contemp. Psychoanal.,* 24:498–526.

---

*Recommended reading.

Psychoanalytic Dialogues (1992), Symposium "What does the analyst know?" 2(3):279–367.

*Ricoeur, P. (1970), *Freud and Philosophy: An Essay in Interpretation,* tr. D. Savage. New Haven, CT: Yale University Press.

*Sass, L. (1988), Humanism, hermeneutics and the concept of the human subject. In: *Hermeneutics and Psychological Theory,* ed. S. B. Messer, L. A. Sass, & R. L. Woolfolk. New Brunswick, NJ: Rutgers University Press, pp. 222–271.

Schafer, R. (1976), *A New Language for Psychoanalysis.* New Haven, CT: Yale University Press.

——— (1983), *The Analytic Attitude.* New York: Basic Books.

*——— (1992), *Retelling a Life: Narrative and Dialogue in Psychoanalysis.* New York: Basic Books.

Spence, D. (1982), *Narrative Truth and Historical Truth: Meaning and Interpretation in Psychoanalysis.* New York: W. W. Norton.

——— (1987), *The Freudian Metaphor.* New York: W. W. Norton.

*Stern, D. B. (1983), Unformulated experience. *Contemp. Psychoanal.,* 19:71–99.

——— (1989), The analyst's unformulated experience of the patient. *Contemp. Psychoanal.,* 25:1–33.

——— (1990), Courting surprise. *Contemp. Psychoanal.,* 26:452–478.

*——— (1992), Commentary on constructivism in clinical psychoanalysis. *Psychoanal. Dial.,* 2:331–363.

——— (1996), The social construction of therapeutic action. *Psychoanal. Inq.,* 16:265–293.

Sullivan, H. S. (1953), *The Psychiatric Interview.* New York: W. W. Norton.

——— (1954), *The Interpersonal Theory of Psychiatry.* New York: W. W. Norton.

6.

Control-Mastery Theory

Michael Lowenstein

INTRODUCTION AND HISTORY OF THE THEORY

Control-mastery theory was initially conceived by Dr. Joseph Weiss (1952, 1971; Weiss, Sampson, and the Mount Zion Psychotherapy Research Group, 1986). Weiss took an empirical approach in developing the theory. He studied process notes of psychoanalyses in order to develop a set of hypotheses about the psychoanalytic process and more broadly about human behavior and mental functioning. Weiss sought to explain how a patient acquires insight in treatment and how therapeutic change takes place. For many years, Weiss along with Dr. Harold Sampson studied transcripts of recorded analyses in an effort to generate testable hypotheses. After forming the Mount Zion Psychotherapy Research Group, Weiss, Sampson, and other members of this group began to subject their hypotheses to formal, empirical research methods (1986).

In control-mastery theory there is a tight linkage between the nature and functioning of the unconscious mind, a theory of motivation, and a corresponding theory of psychoanalytic technique. The theory is clear and deceptively simple. What is remarkable about the theory is its great explanatory power given this simplicity. Using the theory, a therapist is able to develop highly specific case formulations as well as understand a wide range of mental phenomena. Control-mastery theory is useful in helping the analyst understand what the patient is trying to accomplish and how the analyst may help the patient work toward his or her goals.

Another key feature of control-mastery theory is its emphasis on the relationship between the analyst's interventions and subsequent patient behavior. Specific criteria are used to evaluate whether the analyst's interventions have been useful. For example, does the patient show more insight, or recall new memories, or experience new affects, or in any other way, make psychoanalytic progress? Effective psychoanalytic technique from a control-mastery analyst's point of view is not defined as an adherence to certain prescribed rules, but rather as any technique that helps the patient make progress in overcoming his problems.

The analyst using control-mastery theory actively generates hypotheses concerning the work that the patient is trying to accomplish and the analyst's related task. Generating these hypotheses allows the analyst to be more flexible and open to modifying his efforts as problems arise in a treatment situation.

BASIC THEORETICAL CONCEPTS

Higher Mental Functioning Hypothesis

In control-mastery theory, as in all psychoanalytic theories, the functioning and content of the unconscious mind is clearly articulated. Weiss (Weiss et al., 1986; Weiss, 1990b) hypothesizes that the unconscious mind is capable of what is termed higher mental functioning, meaning that the unconscious mind performs some of the same functions as that of the conscious mind. One may unconsciously make judgments, decisions, carry out plans, and test reality. This is not to say that the unconscious mind functions in a completely organized and rational manner; only that its functioning is in part governed by familiar thought processes such as making inferences and appraisals. This lends a degree of orderliness to unconscious mental life and, as we shall see, to the analytic process.

The word *control* in the term *control-mastery* refers to a central aspect of unconscious mental functioning. Weiss asserts that all individuals exert a certain degree of regulation or control over their unconscious mental life and repressions (Weiss et al., 1986; Weiss, 1990b, 1993). This degree of control extends to all unconscious contents such as cognitions, affects, fantasies and behaviors. How, then, does the individual regulate his unconscious mental life? Weiss theorizes that the individual inherently seeks safety and avoids danger and, consequently, will not ordinarily allow himself to become aware of previously warded-off thoughts, memories, or affects until he unconsciously determines that it is safe to do so (Weiss, 1971, 1990b, 1993; Gassner, Sampson, Weiss, and Brumer, 1982; Weiss et al., 1986). However, if a particular cognition, affect, or other unconscious mental content is considered to be too dangerous to be consciously experienced, the individual will continue to repress it. For example, a person who was severely neglected in childhood may be unable to face the pain and sadness of his neglect (including specific childhood memories of neglect) until he may safely do so, i.e., when he becomes involved in a caring, accepting relationship.

According to Weiss, individuals are actively scanning and testing their environment, unconsciously assessing danger and safety (Weiss et al., 1986; Weiss, 1990b). Weiss's theory states that the individual is highly motivated to avoid situations that had previously been experienced as traumatic and therefore dangerous.

Adaptation

By emphasizing the need to seek safety and avoid danger, control-mastery theory stresses the importance of biological and psychological survival through adaptation to one's environment (Stern, 1985; Weiss, 1990a). Above all the individual is motivated to adapt to his reality in the service of self-preservation. His interpersonal world is a central component of this reality. From infancy onward the individual is actively constructing his reality and developing beliefs about his reality based upon actual experience (Sampson, 1990, 1992).

Human beings are inherently theory-builders or scientists. The more one is able to understand about one's environment, the better one is able to survive and flourish in that environment. Infant researchers such as Stern (1985) have observed that from the moment of birth, the infant is immersed in efforts to understand his or her environment. The infant struggles to determine how his or her interpersonal world functions and how to adapt to it. Given that the infant is completely dependent upon his or her parents and immediate family for survival, these important family members become the most valuable sources of information regarding the baby's interpersonal world. Learning as much as he or she can about parents and family (i.e., their attitudes, beliefs, morals) will help the baby to establish and maintain a more secure relationship with them. If the baby develops a strong relationship with caregivers, they are more likely to meet the infant's physical and emotional needs. The infant will do whatever he or she can to maintain and strengthen connections to parents.

A particularly important method through which the individual is able to maintain and strengthen connections with parents is by complying with their wishes. A person will comply with his or her parents in a number of ways in order to strengthen the relationship with them. The individual might behave in a certain way, have certain feelings, thoughts, or maintain certain attitudes if he or she feels that it would please parents or strengthen the relationship to them. This is done both consciously and unconsciously.

The following clinical example will illustrate such efforts in an adult patient: Barbara, a woman in her early twenties, began treatment during her first semester at a prestigious law school, complaining that she had been unable to study. Despite her considerable intelligence and seriousness of purpose, Barbara adamantly claimed that she only went to law school to "land a husband." She stated that she liked the way the actors on *L.A. Law* were dressed and thought that a legal career would enable her to look like them. Barbara's mother was a chronically depressed woman who spent most of her days shopping and reading gossip magazines. Whenever Barbara showed any interest in her schoolwork, her mother ignored her. Yet her mother came to life when they were engaged in conversations about shopping for clothes, cosmetics, or the latest celebrity gossip. Barbara inferred that her mother was pleased by her being superficial and materialistic and she therefore assumed that her mother wanted her to be this way. Conversely, Barbara felt that her mother was displeased by her interest in intellectual pursuits. Barbara complied with her mother's wishes by believing that she should not present herself as being intelligent or serious.

Another strategy that the individual may find useful in his efforts to maintain a connection with his parents is to identify with them. Identification is a largely unconscious process of internalization. The individual modifies his cognitions, affective states, and patterns of behavior in such a way as to experience himself as being like his parents. This is illustrated by the following example.

John began psychoanalysis with the hope of improving his relationship with his wife. He reluctantly acknowledged that he was behaving in a passive–aggressive, provocative, and teasing manner toward his wife, but could not stop himself from doing so. When she would ask him to wash the dishes, he would invariably drop and break one of her favorite pieces. When they had arranged to meet at a given place at a certain time, he would routinely arrive one hour late and claim that he had forgotten the agreed-upon time. John's father had been equally provocative and teasing, both with John and his mother. His father broke a number of John's model airplanes and claimed that he was only trying to help. John's father would "inadvertently" leave the refrigerator door open the night before each Thanksgiving and Christmas so that these dinners would be ruined. John had inferred that his father would be pleased if he behaved in an equally provocative, passive–aggressive way. As a child, whenever John behaved like his father by "accidentally" breaking something and incurring his mother's anger, John's father would smile and say, "That's my boy . . . a chip off the old block." John had identified with his father's passive-aggressiveness as a child and continued to do so as an adult in order to create and maintain a close connection to him.

Compliance and *identification*, therefore, are two distinct strategies utilized by individuals in order to adapt to their interpersonal worlds. In control-mastery theory, this adaptation to one's reality is viewed as a supraordinate motivational system. Control-mastery theory does not dismiss the importance of instinctual gratification, the development and maintenance of self-esteem, and other motivational systems. Rather, these systems are seen as being subordinated to adaptation.

Pathogenic Beliefs

The acquisition of both conscious and unconscious beliefs about oneself and one's world is deemed to be a central component of both normal development and psychopathology. Beliefs are termed *pathogenic* when they warn the person to relinquish an important goal because of some perceived danger such as a disruption in his or her connection with their parents. Examples of such goals would be the pursuit of a rewarding career or relationship; the ability to maintain separateness from others; the ability to depend on others; the capability of maintaining one's self-esteem; being able to feel proud; and the ability to know one's desires and aspirations. These are just a few examples of the large number of the goals that a person might relinquish in compliance with a pathogenic belief. When the individual is convinced that the pursuit of a goal is dangerous he represses the goal and inhibits himself from pursuing it. Pathogenic beliefs result in the formation of certain inhibitions and compulsions and thus determine the nature of one's psychopathology. Since these beliefs are inferred from one's actual experience, control-mastery theory emphasizes the importance of real experiences in psychopathology.

Several key factors, personal and environmental, affect this inference process and, in turn, the development and maintenance of pathogenic beliefs. The age of the individual when he or she acquires these beliefs is one such factor. In early childhood, the individual has a relatively limited capacity to process information. In addition, the child's egocentric mode of thinking plays a role in these developments (Weiss, 1993; Weiss et al., 1986). If the child experiences a trauma, they inevitably assume that they have thought, felt, or behaved in such a way that would cause the trauma. The young child has difficulty in understanding that the occurrence of traumatic events are independent of him or her, automatically blaming themselves for these traumas and feeling guilty about them. For example, a boy who at the age of 5 experienced the sudden death of his father due to a myocardial infarction, believed that he had caused his father's death. Shortly before his father's death, the boy had become more bold and aggressive in his "rough-housing" with his father. He subsequently inferred that it was his playfully assertive, "macho" behavior that had killed his father. As a result he relinquished his competitive and assertive strivings and developed a very anxious, passively compliant and tentative way of relating to men. Accidental occurrences can also result in the development of pathogenic beliefs. Any suffering, illness, or death in the family can result in the magical belief that one is responsible for these calamities.

Age also plays a significant role in determining which developmental goals or motives are believed to be dangerous. For instance, the boy described above was 5 years old when his father died. At this age, issues of oedipal competitive strivings affected the development of his specific pathogenic belief. The particular pathogenic belief that develops will be determined by the affects, thoughts, and behaviors of the individual at the time the trauma occurs.

Confusions of cause and effect also are the consequence of the child's limited cognitive abilities and may result in the development of pathogenic beliefs. For example, Ethan, a patient in his thirties, complained of an inability to communicate displeasure to his wife. Whenever she behaved in a way that bothered him, he would become quiet and withdrawn. Ethan's parents were very neglectful of him as a child. Ethan recalled that he always assumed that he must have been uninteresting for his parents to have such little regard for him. On one occasion when Ethan observed his parents paying more attention to one of his cousins, Ethan complained bitterly to his mother and was sent to his room. Ethan assumed his complaining had caused his parents to neglect him and had inferred that he was not supposed to complain.

In addition, age determines the intensity of pathogenic beliefs. The younger the child, the greater the danger of disruption of ties to parents. The young child is more apt to comply with parental behavior and wishes, being more dependent on the parent. He or she tends to equate their reality with morality and believes that the way they are treated is the way they should be treated. The young child also overgeneralizes his or her beliefs about the world. If the child has a parent who is critical, the child may infer that not only should they be criticized by that parent, but that everyone should criticize them. In addition to the younger child's greater dependency, he or she also has a more limited knowledge of relationships with others. The child will therefore rely upon the information obtained from observing parents. On the other hand, when compared to the younger child, the older child has access to a greater variety of sources of information in the form of other children, teachers, and coaches, for example, and is therefore in a better position to make discriminations.

Temperament is another factor that influences the acquisition of pathogenic beliefs. An individual's temperament will both affect and be affected by a caregiver's response. For example, a relatively quiet child who has a depressed, withdrawn mother, may infer that she is ignoring him because he is uninteresting. In response he may become more outgoing and engaging in an attempt to cheer up his mother. If, on the other hand, he continues to have no success in enlivening his mother, he may become even more quiet and withdrawn. The quiet child's belief that he is uninteresting can result in a diminished ability to receive outside sources of information that may provide an alternative belief about himself. Due to his pathogenic belief that he is an undesirable person, he may behave in a less friendly manner, and therefore, will be less likely to have his pathogenic belief disconfirmed by other sources.

While the preceding discussion emphasizes the existence of certain parental shortcomings and weaknesses which result in the development of pathogenic beliefs, such beliefs may also be the result of misinterpretations on the part of both parents and/or child. For example, the child may believe that their parents' involvement with them indicates that they are worried about the child. Through this the child may infer that the parents want to worry about him or her and, in order to please them, may act in worrisome ways which, in turn, would provoke worry from the parents.

Pathogenic Beliefs and Affects

Pathogenic beliefs are never simply cognitions; they are always accompanied by affects. Pathogenic beliefs that are acquired very early in childhood may be very rudimentary in nature; some of these beliefs may be dominated by one's affective experience. With other pathogenic beliefs, however, one may not be conscious of the corresponding affect and may have greater access to the cognition. In still other instances, the presence of a distressing affect may alert the patient or analyst to the presence of an underlying pathogenic belief. Affects such as anxiety, shame, guilt, envy, and sadness may all accompany a pathogenic belief.

Control-mastery theory assumes that *unconscious guilt* plays a large role in psychopathology (Weiss et al., 1986; Freedman, 1985; Bush, 1989; Weiss, 1993). While it is referred to as an affect, here, too, the guilt stems from certain beliefs that have been inferred from experience. This irrational guilt has its roots in the belief that one has done something bad to a loved one or has been hurtful or disloyal to a family member. Control-mastery's conceptualization of guilt differs from the traditional psychoanalytic view of guilt as rooted in the death wishes for the opposite sex parent that are a part of the Oedipus complex. The control-mastery theory of guilt holds that it can arise at any time in a person's life, and that it develops from a fundamental tendency for the individual to blame himself for the traumatic experiences of others. This type of guilt is not necessarily, although it may be, related to hostility toward a specific family member.

Two particularly common types of guilt, *separation guilt* and *survivor guilt,* underlie a wide range of psychopathology. Separation guilt is characterized by the belief that one's efforts to establish a separate existence result in the abandonment of and devastation to a family member. Survivor guilt is based upon the belief that one's successes and achievements are obtained at the expense of other family members and that these family members will be hurt by the individual's success. It also arises from the belief that having more of the good things of life than one's parents or siblings is a kind of disloyalty to them.

Basic Principles of Therapeutic Technique

The "mastery" part of control-mastery refers to the patient's strong motivation to master his or her problems, and therefore to disconfirm his or her pathogenic beliefs. The pathogenic beliefs acquired predominantly in childhood are constraining in a number of ways. They are a source of distressing affects such as guilt, shame, anxiety and envy; they limit the range and flexibility of adaptive responses; and they lead the individual to relinquish goals and to refrain from expressing or fulfilling his desires. A pathogenic belief derives its power to limit an individual by the particular danger that it warns against.

In psychoanalysis and psychotherapy the patient actively works to overcome his or her problems by having pathogenic beliefs disconfirmed. The patient works on this both in a conscious and an unconscious way. The patient seeks help from the analyst in two ways. The analyst provides the patient with knowledge which will aid in the patient's efforts to disconfirm his or her pathogenic beliefs and will also provide the patient with new experiences which will help him disconfirm these beliefs.

Unconscious Plan

The patient works to overcome his or her problems in a highly individualized way. As stated earlier, Weiss' higher mental functioning hypothesis assumes that the unconscious mind is capable of thinking, making decisions, and planning. The patient utilizes these capacities in the service of solving his or her psychological problems. The patient works unconsciously at overcoming these problems and prioritizes his or her work: He unconsciously decides which pathogenic beliefs he will work on first and which will be deferred for later efforts. The patient also considers particular methods of working on the problem. He considers all available information concerning himself and his analyst and makes decisions regarding how best to work with a given analyst. He carefully scans and monitors the analyst. He examines various aspects of the analyst's behavior including the analyst's interpretations, noninterpretive communications and actions, and the analyst's conscious and unconscious attitudes toward the patient and toward his or her particular pathogenic beliefs. The patient also unconsciously assesses his or her own particular strengths and weaknesses and considers their anxieties and ability to tolerate and modulate the painful affects associated with particular pathogenic beliefs, and make an assessment of their current reality. All of this information is used to determine how the patient will work to solve his or her problems.

The unconscious plan concept, which states that patients in analysis will work in an orderly, planful way is a unique feature of control-mastery theory (Weiss et al., 1986; Weiss, 1993). It allows the analyst to ask the questions, "What is my patient working on at a given moment in treatment?" and "What kinds of experiences and information is my patient looking for (and can I provide) at a given point in the analysis?" The plan concept does not imply that the patient has a fixed, rigid, or highly structured plan for his or her treatment. Rather, the patient's plans are highly modifiable depending on the manner in which treatment proceeds.

UNCONSCIOUS TESTING

How then does the patient carry out his or her unconscious plans? How does the patient work to refute pathogenic beliefs? Weiss asserts that the individual, both in and out of treatment, is actively scanning his or her environment and attempting to discover information concerning his pathogenic beliefs (Weiss et al., 1986; Weiss, 1990b, 1993). The patient has certain hypotheses about him- or herself and their interpersonal world and is constantly looking for data to support or refute these hypotheses. This testing of reality is a fundamental mode of thinking.

The analytic situation is a particularly well-suited environment for this unconscious testing and for the disconfirmation of pathogenic beliefs. The analyst and patient both have the goals of helping the patient toward self-understanding and to overcome psychological problems. Certain elements that are present in the analytic situation, including the affective constraints of the analyst, contribute to a patient's sense of safety and encourage a willingness to test his pathogenic beliefs. For example, the analyst attempts never to retaliate toward a patient. He ordinarily only communicates to the patient what he judges to be helpful to that person. The analyst also restrains himself from communicating his own wishes to the patient. The patient, on the other hand, invests a great deal of authority in the analyst and relies heavily upon the analyst's comments and interpretations.

In testing the analyst, the patient actively seeks to recreate a relationship with the analyst which is a version of a traumatic relationship from the patient's childhood. The patient cannot effectively work on pathogenic beliefs unless the childhood relationship that generated the belief is affectively experienced by both patient and analyst. The patient "invites" the analyst to participate in the old relationship while hoping for a new outcome. For example, if the patient as a boy was constantly ridiculed and humiliated by a parent, he may behave in the analytic situation in an abject way. He may flaunt his stupidity, behave in a provocative manner, and otherwise encourage the analyst to put him down.

If the analyst is able to assimilate and process the contemptuous feelings that will likely be provoked in him and refrain from acting upon them, either in the form of a critical interpretation or through other behavior and is able to act in a non-sadistic way, he will have passed the test. The patient may then begin to overcome his pathogenic belief that he is contemptible and that he deserves to be put down.

> This testing process is the patient's method of actively seeking a needed experience. A number of clinical observations support this view. 1) Except in desperate situations, patients test only beliefs they have already begun to think may be untrue; that is, they test only when they have some hope that the therapist will provide the needed experience. 2) For similar reasons, patients ordinarily carry out relatively easy or weak tests (in which they have relatively little at stake) early in treatment. They ordinarily only carry out powerful (risky) tests after having developed confidence, through previous experience with the analyst, that he will be able to master it and eventually provide the therapist with cues that will help the therapist to respond in a useful way, and they "coach" the therapist about the experience they need [Sampson, 1994a, p. 359].

The patient may test his or her pathogenic beliefs with the therapist in one of two ways: either by transference testing or by passive-into-active testing. In transference testing the patient attempts to recreate aspects of a childhood relationship in which he or she had suffered traumatic experiences. The patient expresses attitudes, feelings, or behavior toward the analyst that he or she experienced toward parents during childhood. The patient then observes the analyst, hoping that the analyst will not support the pathogenic beliefs and retraumatize him or her. In transference testing the patient invests the analyst with the authority of a parent. The patient looks to the analyst to disconfirm the patient's hypothesis that has proven maladaptive, as in the following example.

Nancy, a woman in her twenties, came to treatment because she was having difficulty with her boyfriend. She mentioned in the first hour that she thought that he was wonderful and that she really appreciated all of the advice he gave her.

He had convinced her that her desire to go to medical school was silly, and suggested that instead she be more practical and work on honing her secretarial skills. Nancy was about to quit her premedical education at the time she entered therapy. Her first goal for treatment was to develop the capacity to ignore unsolicited or unhelpful advice. Throughout her childhood and into her young adulthood, Nancy's mother had constantly given her useless advice on a wide range of matters. Nancy inferred through this that she needed advice and that it pleased others to counsel her. In the opening phase of treatment, Nancy insisted that she needed direction from her analyst and complained vigorously when he would not provide it. After many such interactions, Nancy came to believe that she was able to solve many of her own problems without input from others. She further realized that it was not necessary to comply with all of the advice she had been given.

In passive-into-active testing, the patient also recreates aspects of a childhood relationship, but in this form of testing the roles are now reversed. The patient who had passively experienced a traumatic relationship with a parent now actively inflicts aspects of this relationship onto the analyst. In this form of testing the patient is not vulnerable to retraumatization because it is he who is taking the parental role. In passive-into-active testing the patient hopes that the analyst will not be as traumatized as he was in his childhood. If the analyst passes the test, the patient will identify with the analyst's capacity to deal with the particular traumatic experience recreated in the test. Passive-into-active testing often evokes particularly strong countertransference affects in the therapist because the therapist is vulnerable to the same experiences which had traumatized the patient in childhood. These powerful countertransference affects may help the analyst to empathize with a patient who is unable to directly discuss his or her traumas, and may alert the analyst to the presence of passive-into-active testing.

> The fact that the tests most disturbing to the therapist are almost always passive-into-active tests may be understood in terms of the difference between the relationship of the child to his parent and that of the parent to his child. As I have noted

throughout this book, the child is powerfully motivated to maintain his ties to his parents; for the child to do this is a matter
of life and death. The child is so highly motivated to get along
with his parents that he will not behave outrageously unless he
does so in compliance with his parents, or through identification with parents' outrageous behavior.

However, some parents are not highly motivated to maintain their ties to their child or to get along with the child.
Sometimes a parent may abandon, beat, worry, or seduce a
child. Thus if a therapist feels quite belittled by a patient, guilty
to him, confused or humiliated by him, or helpless to treat him,
the patient is almost always behaving like a parent—and thus
turning passive into active [Weiss, 1993, p. 105].

The concept of passive-into-active testing is one way of
thinking about clinical phenomena that have been alternatively
understood as projective identification, identification with the
aggressor, or more pejoratively, as difficult behavior, or as primitive defenses of borderline personalities (acting out, splitting,
projection, externalization). Patients, who predominantly test
in a passive-into-active way, are often believed to be unanalyz-
able, untreatable or very difficult to keep. Passive-into-active
testing is a useful conceptualization because it provides a sense
of coherence to and understanding of ostensible impasses to
treatment. If an analyst keeps in mind that the powerful transference and corresponding countertransference are elicited in
part by the patient, in order to help him master his traumas,
the analyst will be in a better position to contain the powerful
countertransference affects and be better able to adhere to the
analytic process. Segments of an analysis in which the therapeutic alliance seems to be disrupted can often be understood as
periods of passive-into-active testing. The following case illustrates this concept:

Lisa was a 24-year-old elementary schoolteacher when she
presented for treatment because of a worsening depression.
She reported that she had been depressed most of her life
but had become increasingly despondent after leaving home
to teach school. Early in the treatment she mentioned that
her mother had also been depressed for as long as she could
remember. A year before Lisa was born, her mother gave birth

to a boy who died when he was two weeks old. Lisa's mother had hoped for another boy and was deeply disappointed when Lisa arrived. During Lisa's childhood, her mother complained incessantly; she constantly talked about the sacrifices she had made for her children and remarked on how ungrateful they were. Lisa described her mother as bitter and cynical. Her most vivid memory is of coming home from school and finding her mother asleep on the couch with soap operas on the television.

During childhood, Lisa had developed several crippling pathogenic beliefs. Most importantly, she believed that she was responsible for her mother's misery and that she had been unable to enliven her. She also felt that her very existence was a deep disappointment to her parents. In addition, she felt that she had no right to enjoy a better life than her mother (survivor guilt) and also felt that by establishing her own life and being psychologically separate from her mother, she would devastate her mother (separation guilt).

In her treatment Lisa predominantly employed passive-into-active testing. She was difficult, complained constantly, and was contemptuous toward her analyst. She told the analyst that she was suffering due to her analyst's incompetence and indifference. She ignored or belittled most of her interpretations which focused on her guilt and on her resistance to engaging in treatment. Her tone was consistently cynical and bitter. She would say, "You don't help me. I could do better talking to 1-800-Call the Psychic." She vociferously complained about how miserable she was and of how suicidal she felt. Nevertheless, Lisa made steady progress.

Despite her accusations that she was receiving no help and that her suffering was becoming unbearable, the analyst remained undaunted and persisted in the analytic pursuits. The analyst was able to contain her countertransference feelings related to Lisa's rejecting and hostile behavior and was able to continue to analyze the various elements of Lisa's depression. The analyst remained optimistic, confident, and encouraging. Lisa began elaborating on childhood memories of how relentlessly hostile, sarcastic, and unhappy her mother had been. She also revealed how gloomy and discouraging her mother was. After seven months of treatment Lisa became conscious of an important goal which she had relinquished. Ever since she had been briefly hospitalized at the age of 7 for asthma, she had wanted to become a doctor. She told her analyst that this wish would be impossible to achieve because, "you never get what you want." Lisa has continued to blame her analyst for all of her suffering and yet is taking the necessary steps toward achieving her goal of becoming a physician. Through passive-into-active testing Lisa has identified with several capacities of her analyst, in order to feel less blameworthy, less overly responsible and ineffectual, and less vulnerable to women who are rejecting.

Treatment with Attitudes

Patients work in various ways to overcome their pathogenic beliefs. Some patients test the therapist in a more focused, clearly defined manner, as seen in the examples of *transference testing* and *passive-into-active testing*. Some patients seek emotional experiences from the analyst which are less clearly defined, more pervasive, and which may be resistant to interpretive work. They are slowly able to disconfirm their pathogenic beliefs in a process called *treatment by attitudes* (Weiss, 1993; Sampson, 1994b).

For this type of patient, progress may be dependent solely on whether they view the analyst's attitudes toward them as confirming or disconfirming their pathogenic beliefs. For example, a man who had been subject to neglectful parents, and whose father was domineering, felt humiliated by all of his analyst's interpretations. The analyst quickly stopped making interpretations and instead maintained a warm, chatty, and attentive attitude. Over the course of several years, without the benefit of explicit interpretations, the patient made steady progress by becoming closer, more friendly, and attentive to his wife, and even developed certain insights concerning his anxieties about getting close to people. At times he spontaneously recovered memories related to feeling controlled and hurt by his father. The analyst was working by adopting certain attitudes (by being

friendly, collaborative, and nondomineering) and this helped
the patient disconfirm his pathogenic beliefs without the use
of explicit interpretations.

Interpretation

In control-mastery theory, no priority is given to the type of
intervention made. The analyst's interpretive behavior is not
assumed to be more important to the therapeutic process than
his other behaviors, for example: clarifications, confrontations,
suggestions, or maintaining the frame or the therapeutic alliance. It is assumed that all of these other "actions" carry with
them important implicit interpretations. When the interventions are deemed to be "proplan" the analyst's interpretations
or behavior support the patient's unconscious plan by refuting
his pathogenic beliefs. When the interventions are deemed
"antiplan"—they affirm the patient's pathogenic beliefs.

According to control-mastery theory, as in other current
psychoanalytic theories, the cognitive meaning of an interpretation cannot be divorced from its experiential, relational
meaning. Making an interpretation is not simply a matter of
making the unconscious conscious. Interpretations serve several other functions. While interpretations do function to bring
the patient's pathogenic beliefs into consciousness, they may
also provide the patient with a greater understanding that his
maladaptive, compulsive, or otherwise unintelligible behavior
is guided by pathogenic beliefs, borne out of childhood experiences. This may help the patient to feel more understood and
less ashamed of his or her psychopathology. Interpretations
serve to recontextualize time by identifying elements of the
patient's past which are alive in current mental life, and thus
give the patient a greater sense of continuity.

Interpretations may also help the patient feel safe in the
treatment situation. The very act of making an interpretation
may be reassuring to a patient. For instance, when a patient is
carrying out a passive-into-active test and actively inflicts his or
her traumas onto the analyst, it is quite reassuring when the

analyst, via his interpretations, demonstrates that despite this testing, he has not lost his ability to analyze. In addition, in the passive-into-active testing situation, interpretation may help the analyst to regain his bearings.

Interpretations also may serve to reassure a patient against certain dangers which he or she perceives are present in the current relationship with the analyst. For example, if a patient maintains the conviction that he or she is overly competitive and fears that the analyst will feel challenged and hurt by such feelings, the patient may be reassured when the analyst makes this conviction explicit. Of course this will only reassure the patient if in fact he or she experiences the analyst at that point as not feeling hurt. It is the analyst's affective communication which is mediated through language that is reassuring.

The act of placing feelings and thoughts into words may also be reassuring. For example a patient who is fearful of his or her ability to seduce the analyst may be reassured in two ways when the analyst makes this fear conscious. He will be reassured because: (1) the interpretation ("You're afraid that I'd be seduced") serves as a promise to not be seduced; and (2) the very act of making the interpretation demonstrates to the patient that the analyst has retained the perspective required to articulate his thoughts and has, thus, not been overstimulated by the patient.

Interpretations may also provide patients with experiences they seek, serving to pass the patients' tests. Because patients invest a great deal of authority in the analyst, they inevitably experience an interpretation as a suggestion. Every interpretation that the analyst makes is assimilated as either supporting or negating patients' pathogenic beliefs. Despite any effort the analyst may make to create a balanced environment, it is impossible to avoid his authority. For example applying this principle to the patient previously mentioned who behaved in a contemptible way, the interpretation, "You're inviting me to put you down" may: (1) Identify a motivation for the patient's current behavior; (2) provide reassurance that the analyst will not put the patient down; and/or (3) enable the analyst to pass a test if the patient experiences the interpretation as evidence that the analyst will not be bothered if the patient behaved in a dignified way that did not invite contempt. The same interpretation can be experienced as a failed test if the patient experiences it as demonstrating that he is in fact behaving in a stupid, irrational manner in his analysis. It is essential to examine how the patient reacts to the interpretation to assess whether it was experienced as a passed or failed test.

The Plan Formulation

How then does the analyst treat the patient from a control-mastery perspective? The first step is to develop a case-specific dynamic formulation, called a plan formulation. For the control-mastery analyst this would consist of: (1) Inferring the patient's goals; (2) identifying obstructions to the goals—pathogenic beliefs; and (3) anticipating the strategies by which the patient may disconfirm his pathogenic beliefs (i.e., identifying testing strategies). The goals for treatment are assumed to be highly individualized yet are also seen as personal versions of common developmental goals. Examples of goals would be: the ability to experience and tolerate one's own affects; the diminution of one's irrational guilt and shame; the ability to rely on and develop close attachments to others; and the ability to maintain one's psychological separateness. Goals that are inferred may be quite different from those consciously articulated by the patient. For example a woman who came to treatment requesting medication for a chronic depression unconsciously sought disconfirmation that she was not entitled to receive any attention and help, or to have anyone devote time to her.

The analyst uses all the information at his disposal in order to infer the patient's plan. Since control-mastery theory emphasizes the patient's reaction to trauma and the role of real experiences in psychopathology, the patient's description of his history and traumas, and his understanding of his problems are all of value in developing a plan formulation. Equally important is the analyst's awareness and identification of his emotional reactions to the patient. Those realizations can be used to hypothesize the patient's goals, obstructions, and tests that will unfold in the therapy. The analyst uses his plan formulation as a set of working hypotheses. As the patient is testing the analyst, the analyst is also testing the patient in order to see how correct his formulation is.

How does the analyst check his plan formulation? This formulation serves two basic functions: (1) It should help the analyst understand as much as possible about the patient's behavior, both in the consulting room as well as in the patient's life outside of the treatment setting; and (2) it should help the analyst pass the patient's tests. If a test or a series of tests are passed, if the patient seeks and receives a series of corrective emotional experiences, the patient will react in one of a number of characteristic ways. He or she may make progress in reaching one or more of their goals. They may express a greater confidence in the analyst, and/or they may show greater flexibility and freedom in their thinking, both in and outside of analysis. These results may be observed in the patient's greater capacity to free associate, retrieve new memories, and/or experience a deeper transference or exhibit a broader range of affects than had been previously experienced. The patient may react to a failed test or series of tests by expressing less confidence in the analyst, becoming more resistant to treatment, having greater difficulty free associating, and/or being more affectively constricted.

If the analyst is passing the patient's tests (as evidenced by the aforementioned patient's specific behaviors), the analyst continues to work in the same manner. However, if the analyst is failing the patient's tests, it is necessary to revise his strategy for working with the patient.

CLINICAL ILLUSTRATION

Jason, a 21-year-old medical student, presented for psychoanalysis because he was having difficulty studying for exams in his first semester of medical school. He was worried about failing and this concern paralyzed him and made him feel suicidal. During the initial hours he mentioned that there was a lot riding on his doing well. Both his girl friend and his mother would be terribly disappointed if he were to fail. He explained that the quality he most appreciated in his mother was the one that he found attractive in his girl friend: Both of them were interested in what he was doing and paid a lot of attention to him. In contrast, Jason's father would tell him that whatever he did was okay, whether he became a doctor or a house-painter. Jason stated that he greatly appreciated his father's "relaxed attitude" and said that he wished he could be more like him.

Jason's family history includes the following: He is the older of two boys. His younger brother adopted a relaxed atti-tude, similar to the father's and had dropped out of college. His parents had divorced when Jason was 10 and he and his brother went to live with their mother. Jason's mother then became quite depressed and focused all of her available energy on him. She would tell him which classes to take, which sports to play, and which strategies he should use to get into a good college. Jason felt that his mother ignored his brother because he wasn't as naturally intelligent or talented as Jason was. In high school Jason complied with his mother's vision of who he should be and relentlessly pursued his mother's goals for him. He studied every night after coming home from sports practice. He played sports for the sole purpose of receiving a scholarship to a college. He reported envying both his father and brother because they knew how to have fun. When choosing a college, Jason selected a state school over the Ivy League schools in order to increase his chances of getting straight A's—his ticket to a prestigious medical school.

Jason maintained his rigid, uncompromising study habits until his third year at college. At that point he became involved with his girl friend, Susan. She encouraged him to relax and spend evenings in music clubs. Jason reported that this experi-ence was transforming, helping him to feel much less anxious. He still managed to get good grades and was accepted into a prestigious medical school. However, in his first semester in medical school he was confused about his identity. He won-dered whether he was a relaxed fun-loving unambitious "Dead-head" or a focused, driven, ambitious student.

Jason began the treatment stating that he was angry at himself for relaxing, that he was intensely fearful that he would fail, and that he was constantly worried. During the first several sessions he made many requests for advice on how to structure his life and become more productive. He was extremely worried and correspondingly generated a lot of worry in his analyst. At the same time, he provided clues suggesting that this worry was unwarranted. He mentioned that he was able to digest large amounts of information in very short periods of time and that in the few practice tests he had been given, he was at the top of his class.

The analyst inferred that Jason had started working within the maternal transference (by imposing his childhood relationship with his mother onto the analyst) in order to test several important pathogenic beliefs. Jason had believed that his mother worried about him because there was something to worry about; that in some way he was defective and incapable of running his own life. He had also inferred that he should emulate her and be a worrier in order to please her. Jason also suffered from separation guilt in that he believed that handling his life in his own way and being psychologically separate from his mother was devastating to her.

The analytic approach utilized in this case involved both an interpretive and a certain premeditated analytic stance that would provide experiences needed to disconfirm his pathogenic beliefs. Specifically, the analyst offered no direct advice on how Jason should structure his life and instead expressed a growing confidence in him. She also interpreted to him that the insecurity he felt about his abilities reflected a compliance with his mother's view of him and that defying his mother's proscriptive to worry by remaining relaxed might be felt by him as an abandonment of his mother.

Jason responded to these interventions in several ways. He recalled experiences of how impotent and constrained he had felt due to his mother's intrusive, controlling style and remembered how angry this made him. Preceding those sessions, Jason had complained of intense anxiety and had even requested medications in order to control his nerves. The analyst refused

to comply with his request (despite her private, unacknowledged fears that he would be too nervous to take his exams).
During the hour following the completion of his finals, Jason
casually remarked that he had "aced his exams." Despite all
the intense worrying and pleas for help, it became apparent
that Jason was actually quite capable and competent. This was
helpful in giving the analyst confidence regarding her stance
and interpretive line with him.

Jason continued to insist that he was incapable of being
psychologically minded or of analyzing his conflicts, and continued to suggest that his analyst had all the answers. Over the
course of the first year of analysis, Jason developed an increased
capacity to freely associate, to analyze his dreams, and to discuss
his conflicts regarding being autonomous, competent, strong,
and powerful. He also came to more deeply feel his sorrow for
his mother and how lonely his independence from her made
him feel. Jason decided to develop a career in academic medicine despite his mother's wish that he pursue a more lucrative
area of medicine.

The second year of analysis marked a shift in Jason's attitude toward treatment. He indicated that he would miss many
sessions due to his increasing responsibilities as a medical student. While there was some merit to this explanation, Jason
would often not show up for sessions he could have attended
and became very indifferent to his treatment. The initial hypothesis was that Jason was working on autonomy struggles and
sought reassurance that his analyst would not be hurt by his
independent behavior. After a period of time in which the
treatment seemed to be stalled—as evidenced by his increasingly resistant behavior and lack of deepening affect-laden material—the analyst began to wonder if Jason had begun to work
in a different way. The analyst's own boredom and withdrawal
led her to suspect that Jason had begun to test her in a different
way. Throughout his life, Jason experienced his father's relaxed
laissez-faire attitude as one of indifference and neglect. This
led the analyst to wonder whether Jason was involved in passive-
into-active testing and behaving in the same indifferent, blasé
manner as his father. This type of testing might serve to challenge the belief that he was worthy of rejection. The analyst

began to more vigorously encourage Jason to come to sessions and was also more active in analyzing his resistance to analysis. She struggled to process and contain her own feelings of rejection and withdrawal. Not only did Jason now find time to come to his sessions, but he began to express a deep sadness and resentment about being deprived of a more engaged father–son relationship. The analyst inferred that Jason experienced her active efforts to engage him in treatment as an acceptance of him and, therefore, felt safe enough to bring forth memories and feelings related to the experience of his father's neglect and emotional detachment.

In the next phase of treatment Jason began to express increasing confidence in his intellectual abilities and he engaged the analyst in discussions related to the philosophy of science, medicine, and a topic that he found especially interesting: moral philosophy. The analyst freely participated in these discussions. Initially, Jason was self-effacing, telling the analyst how inarticulate he was and emphasizing how little he knew or had read. When the analyst challenged these comments and speculated that Jason seemed to be putting himself down and was encouraging her to join him in this way, Jason would change the subject and tell the analyst that he was thinking too much and really just wanted to relax. The analyst persisted in these discussions, telling Jason that he was intellectually quite ambitious, that his interests covered a wide range of disciplines, and that his wish to be analyzed suggested a deep intellectual curiosity. Jason subsequently discussed an aspect of his relationship with his father that was particularly bothersome. Every time he attempted to engage his father in a discussion of science or medicine, his father would tell him to relax. Jason added that his father had finished four years of graduate school in the field of chemistry but had dropped out so that he could have an easier life. Jason experienced his father's dismissive attitude as a reflection of his envy of Jason's intellectual ambition and inferred that his pursuit of intellectual interests would be hurtful to his father.

Jason continued to work in the paternal transference in order to test this pathogenic belief in two other ways. First, he began to slowly develop the capacity to brag. Eventually he implied that he knew more about certain subjects than the analyst (which he did!). Jason experienced the analyst not pulling rank or dismissing him as permission from the analyst to be competitive, proud, and authoritative. He further tested the same pathogenic beliefs in a passive-into-active way by being dismissive of her interpretations. He chided her for being too serious and analytical and felt that she needed to "lighten up and have a little fun." The analyst was not deterred or humiliated by Jason's criticisms and Jason identified with the analyst's capacity to remain undaunted by his rebuffs and to maintain the worthiness of her analytic pursuits. While Jason has since become increasingly ambitious in his pursuit of an academic career in medical ethics, there is a less driven and compulsive quality to his pursuits.

The case of Jason illustrates several aspects of how psychoanalysis and psychotherapy work from a control-mastery perspective. Jason was actively engaged in testing his pathogenic beliefs in relation to his analyst from the beginning to the end of treatment. He began by working on issues of separation guilt and compliance which stemmed from his early relationship with his mother. This was followed by passive-into-active testing and his identifying with his father's blasé and dismissive stance in order for Jason to disconfirm pathogenic beliefs related to his father's rejection. Finally Jason worked on the pathogenic beliefs which had led to his inhibitions regarding his career by expressing confidence and pride and by being competitive with the therapist to see if she would be hurt or envious of his success. In this case the therapist worked by making interpretations as well as by communicating certain attitudes that she thought would be helpful in disconfirming Jason's pathogenic beliefs. Jason's growing sense of confidence in his analyst allowed him to more fully engage in the analytic process.

Control-mastery theory is a comprehensive and coherent theory of the mind that has great theoretical and clinical value. From relatively few basic assumptions regarding how the unconscious mind regulates repressions and how the individual internalizes and reacts to trauma comes an elegant theory of psychopathology and of the psychotherapeutic process. The theory lends itself to a high degree of case specificity. A therapist utilizing control-mastery theory can generate precise ideas concerning the process of therapy as well as remain open to the inevitable spontaneity that has an integral place in all successful therapeutic interactions.

REFERENCES

Bush, M. (1989), The role of unconscious guilt in psychopathology. *Bull. Menninger Clin.*, 53:97–107.

Freedman, M. (1985), Toward a conceptualization of guilt. *Contemp. Psychoanal.*, 21:501–547.

*Gassner, S., Sampson, H., Weiss, J., & Brumer, S. (1982), The emergency of warded off contents. *Psychoanal. & Contemp. Thought*, 5:55–75.

Sampson, H. (1990), The problem of adaptation to reality in psychoanalytic theory. *Contemp. Psychoanal.*, 26:677–691.

*——— (1992), The role of "real" experience in psychopathology and treatment. *Psychoanal. Dial.*, 4:357–361.

——— (1994a), Repeating pathological relationships to disconfirm pathogenic beliefs. *Psychoanal. Dial.*, 4:359.

——— (1994b), *Treatment by Attitudes Process Notes*, 1(1). San Francisco: San Francisco Psychotherapy Research Group.

Stern, D. (1985), *The Interpersonal World of the Infant*. New York: Basic Books.

Weiss, J. (1952), Crying at the happy ending. *Psychoanal. Rev.*, 39:338.

——— (1971), The emergence of new theories: A contribution to the psychoanalytic theory of therapy. *Internat. J. Psycho-Anal.*, 52:459–467.

——— (1990a), The centrality of adaptation. *Contemp. Psychoanal.*, 26:660–676.

*——— (1990b), Unconscious mental functioning. *Sci. Amer.*, March:103–109.

*——— (1993), *How Psychotherapy Works: Process and Technique*. New York: Guilford Press.

*——— Sampson, H., & The Mount Zion Psychotherapy Research Group (1986), *The Psychoanalytic Process: Theory, Clinical Observation and Empirical Research*. New York: Guilford Press.

---

*Recommended reading.

7.

Self Psychology: An Overview

Theo. L. Dorpat, M.D.

INTRODUCTION AND HISTORY OF THE THEORY

Heinz Kohut, the founder of self psychology, was born in Vienna in 1913, and died in the United States in 1981. After his graduation from the Chicago Institute for Psychoanalysis, he joined the faculty at the Institute and began his life-long career as a practitioner of psychoanalysis, including a heavy schedule of teaching, research, and writing on psychoanalysis. Kohut's active participation in the local, national, and international psychoanalytic communities culminated in his election to the presidency of the American Psychoanalytic Association in 1966.

Kohut's (1966) paper, "Forms and Transformation of Narcissism," announced his intense, prolonged involvement with the understanding of the self, its development, anatomy, and psychopathology, as well as the psychoanalytic treatment of disorders of the self.

Self psychology was founded by Kohut in his efforts to expand psychoanalysis to allow for a better understanding and therapeutic approach to a broad range of what he first called *narcissistic personality disorders* and later called *disorders of the self.* His first book, *The Analysis of the Self* (1971), presents a

153

new theory of the self, together with a fresh understanding and approach to the treatment of these disorders.

In his 1977 work, *The Restoration of the Self,* Kohut proposed that the self is the center of the individual's psychological universe and the development and maintenance of the self's cohesiveness is the essential quality of mental health. In his opinion, the problem of "Tragic Man," the individual seeking succor for his or her depleted or fragmented self, has in our time replaced the problem of "Guilty Man," the individual concerned with the problem of avoidance of oedipal guilt, as the current central problem of Western civilization.

BASIC THEORETICAL CONCEPTS

Self psychology is essentially a clinical theory, and its major theoretical constructs were derived directly from the psychoanalytic situation on the basis of sustained empathic–introspective immersion into the subjective worlds of psychoanalytic patients.

The Methods of Psychoanalysis —Empathy and Introspection

In working with patients with disorders of the self, Kohut increasingly suspended his classical approach, as well as any preconceived ideas about the meanings of patients' communications. Instead, he tried to understand the patients' experience in analysis from their point of view. Kohut (1959) described this approach as *empathic immersion* and *vicarious introspection,* and they became for him the defining methods of psychoanalysis. "We designate a phenomenon as mental, psychic or psychological if our mode of observation includes introspection and empathy *as an essential constituent"* (Kohut, 1959, p. 462). Kohut (1984) defined empathy as "vicarious introspection" (p. 82) and also as "the capacity to think and feel oneself into the inner life of another person" (p. 82).

The Selfobject Concept

The structure of psychoanalytic self psychology theory is founded upon the concept of selfobject transferences (the patient's experience of the analyst). Kohut (1978) stated: "The discovery of the selfobject transferences forms the basis of my whole work concerning narcissism and the self" (p. 20).

Wolf (1988) defines selfobject transference as:

> [T]he displacement on to the analyst of the analysand's needs for a responsive selfobject matrix, derived in part from remobilized and regressively altered editions of archaic infantile selfobject needs, in part from current age—and phase—appropriate selfobject needs, and in part from selfobject needs mobilized in response to the analyst and the analytic situation. Selfobject transferences manifest through the expression of direct or of implied demands on the analyst or through defenses against the expression of these demands [p. 186].

As Goldberg (1985) puts it, "Selfobjects are universal, ubiquitous, and enduring. Selfobject transferences, in turn, are the fundamental features of the clinical theory" (p. 76). The first selfobject transferences were described by Kohut (1971) as corresponding to the preoedipal developmental stages of grandiosity and idealization. These constellations were labeled as *mirror transferences* which are derived from the grandiose self, and *idealizing transferences,* which stem from the idealized parental imago. Later Kohut (1977) added a third selfobject transference, the *twinship* or *alter ego transference.*

In the mirror transference, the analysand longs to be validated by the therapist's approval; in the idealizing transference, he looks on the therapist as a powerful and admired helper who will protect him and from whom he can accrue strength; in the twinship (alter ego) transference, the patient seeks the comfort that kinship, "being like" another person, has to offer.

The Affects of Selfobject Experiences

When we take a close look at the content and quality of selfobject experiences we discover that they include as a prominent property a specific emotion as well as nonspecific vitality affects difficult to describe. The specific affects accompanying a posi- tive selfobject experience include feeling comforted, reassured, strengthened, validated, or acknowledged by some interaction with another individual.

The nonspecific quality of the selfobject experience has been studied by Stern (1985) and Lichtenberg (1991). On the basis of his studies of the interactions between infants and their caregivers, Stern (1985) theorized that affective states cannot be adequately appreciated simply by identifying the categorical emotion present (such as enjoyment, anger, fear, guilt, and so on). Their definition must include descriptors that take into account qualities of feeling such as surging, explosive, cre- scendo, bursting, and the like—so-called *vitality* affects (Stern, 1985; Lichtenberg, 1991). Lichtenberg (1991) concludes, "Viewed developmentally, the core feature of the [selfobject] experience lies in the attunement of caregivers to the infant's motivational needs and the vitality of the intimacy this affords" (p. 469).

The Selfobject Dimension of Transferences

Stolorow, Brandchaft, and Atwood (1987, 1994) have chosen to use the term *selfobject transference* to refer to a dimension of all transference rather than to a specific type of transference. In their view, the figure–ground distinction drawn from per- ceptual psychology is helpful in conceptualizing the impor- tance of the selfobject dimension of transference in the analytic situation. This dimension occupies the position of *figure* in the analysis when restoring or maintaining the organization of self- experience is the paramount psychological motive for the pa- tient's specific tie to the analyst.

Even when the selfobject dimension is not figure, however, it is always present in the patient and influencing the analytic relationship and the patient's relationship with the analyst. So long as it is not disrupted, the selfobject dimension operates silently in the background, providing a facilitating medium that enables the patient to confront and work through his frightening and disturbing conflicts.

According to Stolorow and Lachmann (1985), the selfobject dimension of transference is experienced to some degree by the patient as a supporting and holding environment, an archaic facilitating context that reinstates the developmental processes of differentiation and integration that were arrested in the patient's early formative years. The selfobject dimension of transference in and of itself can directly promote a process of psychic development and structure formation.

Kohut's Early and Late Views on Selfobject Transferences

Kohut's concept of selfobject relationships and transferences changed from an early conceptualization that included only archaic (primitive) types of selfobject transferences (Kohut, 1971) to a later, broader concept that included mature forms as well (Kohut, 1984). In the early conceptualization, archaic selfobject transferences were revived in the analytic situation and then through a gradual process of *transmuting internalization* the patient's need for the analyst to provide the selfobject function is done away with. By transmuting internalization, Kohut (1971) referred to a therapeutic process in which a patient unconsciously appropriates specific features of his interactions with the analyst in a way that creates new psychic structures. Thus the archaic selfobject under optimal conditions disappears at the same time as the patient acquires new psychic structures.

For example, a moderately depressed young man with low self-esteem formed a mirror selfobject transference. This bond with the analyst helped him to feel more stable and whole as well as bolstered his self-esteem. As the analysis progressed and he learned new ways to maintain his self-esteem, he no longer had such an urgent need to use the analyst to serve the mirroring selfobject function. Initially the patient's self-esteem was enhanced by the analyst's interventions. Through transmuting internalizations of such constructive interactions with the analyst, the patient gradually learned to maintain a more positive view of himself even during times of stress.

By the time Kohut (1977) wrote his second book, he had modified his thinking about selfobjects and had realized that everyone has selfobject needs. He recognized the existence of mature as well as archaic selfobject transferences and experiences. Also, he no longer believed that a successful analysis required the reduction or even the elimination of selfobject transferences. Instead he indicated that in a successful analysis, the selfobject transferences slowly change from the archaic to the more mature selfobject transferences. The gradual change from archaic (childlike) to more mature selfobject transferences is linked with the following changes: Patients become less demanding of having their needs met instantly, they are not so controlling of the analyst, and they are less apt to become rageful when their selfobject needs are not gratified.

Today there exists a consensus in self psychology for the view that for their well-being throughout their lives, everyone requires others who serve as selfobjects.

Kohut (1977) writes:

> The psychologically healthy adult continues to need the mirroring of the self by self-objects (to be exact by the self-object aspects of his love objects), and he continues to need targets for his idealization. No implication of immaturity or psychopathology must, therefore, be derived from the fact that another person is used as a self-object—a self-object relation occurs on all developmental levels and in psychological health as well as in psychological illness [p. 188].

Self Psychology and Psychopathology

In self psychology all forms of psychopathology are viewed as based on either defects in the structure of the self, distortions of the self, or weaknesses of the self (Kohut and Wolf, 1978). These various pathologies of the self are due to disturbances and traumas in an individual's relationships with selfobjects in childhood.

In contrast to the traditional Freudian theory, self psychology "holds that pathogenic conflicts in the object-instinctual realm—that is, pathogenic conflicts in the realm of object love and object hate and in particular the set of conflicts called the Oedipus complex—are not the primary cause of psychopathology but its results" (Kohut, 1984, p. 53).

In adult life as well as in childhood, the cohesiveness or fragmentation of the self is a result of the success or failure of individuals' relationships with selfobjects. Failures in such self-selfobject relationships often lead to the painful experience of fragmentation. In self psychology, the term *fragmentation* refers to the central pathological experience of the breakdown of the self. According to Wolf (1988), "Fragmentation means regression of the self toward lessened cohesion, more permeable boundaries, diminished energy and vitality, and disturbed and disharmonious balance" (p. 39). In self psychology, fragmentation of the self is the antithesis of cohesiveness of the self. The fragmented self is linked with unpleasurable emotions, whereas positive emotions characterize the more integrated cohesive self.

A Self Psychology Approach to the Oedipus Complex

Kohut (1977, 1984) distinguished between the normal, even joyful, oedipal phase and abnormal oedipal anxieties and conflicts in this way:

> The healthy child of healthy parents enters the oedipal phase joyfully. The joy he experiences is due not only to the fact that he himself responds with pride to a developmental achievement, that is, to a new and expanding capacity for affection and assertiveness, but also to the fact that this achievement elicits a glow of empathic joy and pride from the side of the oedipal-phase selfobjects. Owing to this joy and pride of achievement, the boy's affectionate attitude does not disintegrate into fragmented sexual impulses, his assertiveness is not transformed into destructive hostility, and he is not intensely afraid of his

parents. Only if his parents do not function appropriately as oedipal selfobjects will the child experience high degrees of anxiety [Kohut, 1984, p. 14].

In Kohut's (1977, 1984) opinion, *pathological sexual drivenness* and *destructive hostility* arise secondary to experiences of fragmentation or enfeeblement of the self. The clinical implication of this new view of the Oedipus complex for psychoanalytic technique is clear. Self psychologists do not assume that oedipal anxieties and transferences arising in the analytic situation are the inevitable and universal expression of normal development. Rather, self psychologists investigate and understand these anxieties as arising from present as well as past disturbing interactions with significant others, including the patient's parents as well as individuals in the patient's current environment.

In Kohut's view, narcissism (loosely defined as love of the self) belongs to a line of development that is separate from object love (1977, 1984). In normal development as well as in a successful psychoanalysis, narcissism evolves from archaic to mature forms. Throughout his career, Kohut disputed the traditional views that narcissism, in development as well as in psychoanalytic treatment, is replaced by object love, and that narcissism has only archaic features, whereas object love is a reflection of a mature way of relating (1977, 1984).

Shame and Narcissistic Rage

Beginning with Kohut (1971, 1972), self psychology has made some important contributions toward the understanding of shame and rage responses. For self psychology, shame is an emotion of equal importance to guilt, both phenomenologically and theoretically. Included within the designation of "shame" are a family of related affective phenomena including humiliation, remorse, mortification, embarrassment, and lowered self-esteem. Morrison (1985) writes, "If guilt be the emotion of Freud's conflicted Guilty Man, shame, I would suggest, is the affect central to Kohut's Tragic Man" (p. 71).

Failure in attaining emotionally significant ideals or goals is a major precipitant of shame responses. In Kohut's (1971, 1972) view, shame also arises in adults as well as children when the selfobjects do not respond with an individual's needs for mirroring, approval, and admiration.

Kohut (1977) writes of the guiltless despair and shame of late middle-aged individuals who realize that they have not realized their ambitions or ideals.

> [It is] of utter hopelessness for some, of utter lethargy, of that depression without guilt and self-directed aggression, which overtakes those who feel that they have failed and cannot remedy the failure in time and with the energies still at their disposal. The suicides of this period are not the expression of a punitive superego, but a remedial act—the wish to *wipe out the unbearable sense of mortification and nameless shame* imposed by the ultimate *recognition of a failure of all-encompassing magnitude* [1977, p. 241; emphasis added].

Kohut (1972) views shame and rage as responses to threats or injuries to the self. Self psychology focuses on the developmental, social, and interpersonal contexts within which shame and rage arise. Rage is viewed as a response to frustration such as a loss of control over an archaic selfobject. A common example of this are the toddlers who have temper tantrums when their mothers refuse their demands.

> *Narcissistic rage* is a form of potentially violent aggression that arises to destroy an offending selfobject when the selfobject is experienced as threatening the continued cohesion or existence of the self, particularly when this threat to the self takes the form of imposing helplessness on the self [Wolf, 1988, p. 181].

Shame often serves as a trigger for the activation of rage reactions. But because the shame that triggers rage responses may not be noticed by either the patient or the analyst, frequently inadequate attention is given to the underlying shame experience in the analysis of narcissistic rage responses. For example, a patient tended to become enraged when a therapist made interpretations about her sexual feelings. The therapist was unable to understand her response until he noticed a slight blush on the patient's face immediately prior to her rageful attacks on him. The clinician's hypothesis that her blush was a sign of an underlying shame reaction to his interpretations was soon confirmed by the patient's discussion of her emotional reactions to the analyst's interpretations concerning her sexuality.

BASIC PRINCIPLES OF THERAPEUTIC TECHNIQUE AND CONCEPTS OF HOW THERAPY CURES

The formation, working through, and resolution of selfobject transferences is the core of the self psychology approach to psychoanalytic treatment. According to Kohut (1984), psychoanalysis cures by the laying down of psychological structure and these new structures are constructed (1) via optimal frustration, and (2) by transmuting internalizations of analysand–analyst interactions. The latter "is Kohut's term for a process of structure formation in which aspects of the self-selfobject transaction are internalized under the pressure generated by optimal frustration" (Wolf, 1988, p. 187).

The major kinds of intervention used in analysis conducted according to the principles of self psychology are interpretative. Because sometimes communicating understanding and attunement is more important than explanatory interpretation, the analyst's interventions may be simply statements that reflect back (i.e., mirror) the analyst's empathic understanding of what the patient has said. Confrontations are seldom used in self psychology.

Self psychology views the process of cure as

[A] three-step movement, the first two steps of which may be described as defense analysis and the unfolding of the transferences, while the third step—the essential one because it defines the aim and the result of the cure—is the opening of a path of empathy between self and selfobject, specifically, the establishment of empathic in-tuneness between self and selfobject on

mature adult levels. This new channel of empathy . . . supplants
the bondage that had formerly tied the archaic self to the archaic selfobject [Kohut, 1984, p. 66].

During the first steps of the analytic process as described
by Kohut, the analyst often may interpret defenses against the
establishment of a stable selfobject transference. Though some
patients may quickly after the beginning of treatment establish
a strong selfobject transference bond with the analyst, many
others require weeks or months of the working through of resistances and defenses against the spontaneous emergence of
a selfobject transference before it appears. Mistrust, fears of
intimacy and of being traumatized or exploited by the analyst,
as they have been by significant others in their life, are some of
the more powerful unconscious resistances that many patients
express against the emergence of a stable selfobject transference.

For example, at first a college student was very cautious
and fearful of being rejected by his therapist. The therapist's
accepting attitude together with discussions about the patient's
fear of rejection assisted the patient in trusting the therapist.
The working through of the student's fear of rejection removed the barrier to his establishing a stable selfobject transference.

Along with the development of a stable selfobject transference, patients usually show decidedly definite improvement in
their daily functioning, and experience fewer symptoms. Then
one of the major tasks of the therapist is the interpretation and
mastery of the inevitable disruptions and interruptions of the
selfobject transferences. Some causes of the disruptions, such
as vacations and weekend breaks, are unavoidable. Other
causes of disruptions include the analyst's empathic failures,
mistakes, or any interventions which break the secure bond
between patient and analyst created through the selfobject
transference.

The clinical manifestations of a disruption of the selfobject
transference include a wide range of psychopathological phenomena including anxiety, depression, acting out, hypochon-
driacal trends, and the like. Most commonly these disruptions

lead to the appearance and revival of the same kind of symptoms and painful emotions that brought the patient to
treatment.

The selfobject transference is restored by the interpretation and working through of the transference disruption. The
analyst explains and interprets to the patient the sequence of
events that lead to the disruption and the patient's consequent
emotional disturbance. Such interpretations require tact and
an empathic understanding of how the patient experienced
the disruption, as well as a sense of how the analyst understood
what occurred.

For example, a mirror transference was disrupted after a
patient disagreed with an analyst's interpretation. At the moment the patient disagreed, the analyst made noises by body
movements in his chair. The patient became visibly anxious
and put his hands over the top of his head in a self-protective
way. The patient and analyst then collaborated in investigating
what there was about the noises made by the analyst that triggered the patient's anxiety reaction. During childhood, the
patient's father often hit the patient on the head when the
patient disagreed. For the patient, the noise made by the analyst meant that he was about to hit the patient on the head as
his father had once done—because the patient had disagreed
with him.

The Goals of Self Psychology

One of the goals of self psychology is reached when patients
have learned to seek out and invest mature selfobjects for the
maintenance of their now cohesive states of the self. "The essence of the psychoanalytic cure resides in a patient's newly
acquired ability to identify and seek out appropriate selfobjects—both mirroring and idealizable—as they present themselves in his realistic surroundings and to be sustained by them"
(Kohut, 1984, p. 77).

A psychoanalysis conducted in accordance with self psychology principles aims to repair the developmental defects

brought about by traumatizing or unempathic caregivers and parents. Through the vehicle of "transmuting internalizations" (Kohut, 1971), the patient gradually repairs and corrects these developmental defects. The patient is cured when his or her self is cohesive, and when there has been sufficient new psychic development to allow the individual to love and work successfully.

For example, a young woman came to analysis because she was unable to soothe or comfort herself when she felt overstimulated or otherwise emotionally disturbed. After a few months of analysis, she formed an idealizing transference, and she was able to use the analyst's empathic interventions to soothe herself. Over time she gradually learned to soothe herself through the transmuting internalization of what she experienced as the soothing and calming interventions of the analyst.

A CLINICAL EXAMPLE

Kohut's (1979) paper, "The Two Analyses of Mr. Z," was written to show the differences between the classical theory and approach Kohut used in Mr. Z's first analysis and the self psychology approach he developed later and used in Mr. Z's second analysis. Kohut attributed the marked difference between the poor results of the first analysis and the excellent results of the second analysis to changes he had made in his clinical theory of narcissism and to his discovery of selfobject transferences.

When Mr. Z came to analysis as a single graduate student in his midtwenties, he was socially isolated and his addictive masturbation was accompanied by vivid masochistic fantasies in which he submissively performed menial tasks in the service of dominating women. An important event in the patient's childhood was the patient's separation from his father from the age of 3 until he was 5.

In the first analysis, Kohut, in addition to interpretations, used a combination of educational approaches and critical confrontations to induce the patient to relinquish his narcissistic demands and rages. After the first analysis ended, Kohut belatedly concluded that some of the changes in the first analysis that he thought were therapeutic actually were merely temporary and cosmetic alterations made by the patient in compliance with the pressures placed on him to conform with Kohut's expectations.

In the termination phase of the first analysis, Kohut mistakenly believed that Mr. Z was successfully resolving his core oedipal conflicts and castration fears which he mistakenly believed were illustrated in the following dream:

> In his dream—his associations pointed clearly to the time when the father rejoined the family—*he was in a house, at the inner side of a door which was a crack open. Outside was the father, loaded with giftwrapped packages, wanting to enter. The patient was intensely frightened and attempted to close the door in order to keep the father out* [p. 8].

The Second Analysis of Mr. Z

Four years after ending his first analysis, Mr. Z returned to Kohut for treatment with many of the same symptoms as he had suffered in the first analysis. About eighteen months earlier, Mr Z's mother developed a paranoid psychosis. In the second analysis, the sadomasochistic masturbation fantasies were understood as a desperate attempt to obtain at least some sort of pleasure—"the joyless pleasure of the defeated self"—through self-stimulation.

The patient developed a mirror transference in which he again (as he had in the first analysis) became self-centered, demanding, and inclined to rage whenever he experienced Kohut as out-of-tune with his emotional state. The full unfolding and interpretation of a series of disruptions of the selfobject transference gradually allowed the patient to break his archaic bond with his severely disturbed mother. Most of these disruptions came when the patient felt that Kohut was not sufficiently empathic with his needs for mirroring and approval.

In the second analysis, Kohut no longer evaluated the patient's demands, disagreements, and rages as resistances to be countered by stern confrontations. Instead, he saw the patient "as desperately—and often hopelessly—struggling to disentangle himself from the noxious selfobject [mother], to delimit itself, to grow, to become independent" (p. 12).

The terminal phase of the second and successful analysis was marked by the patient's returning to the analogous activity of the first analysis at the time that he had reported the dream about his father returning home with a load of gift packages. Kohut (1979) writes:

> The new meaning of the dream as elucidated by the patient via his associations, to put his message into my words, was not a portrayal of a child's aggressive impulse against the adult male accompanied by castration fear, but of the mental state of a boy who had been all-too-long without a father . . . [p. 23].

The revised interpretation of this dream was that the return of the father in Mr. Z's childhood was traumatic because of the child's overwhelming need for him. Kohut's report of the second analysis of Mr. Z provides convincing illustrations of the therapeutic benefits obtained through the applications of his theory of selfobject transferences and disorders of the self.

CURRENT AREAS OF RESEARCH, ADVANCES IN THINKING, CONTROVERSIES, AND CONFLICTS

Is Self Psychology an Object Relations Theory?

An important recurring and unsettled controversy among self psychology followers is whether self psychology should be considered a one-person (i.e., wholly or basically an intrapsychic) or a two-person (i.e., object relations) psychology.

One of the more persuasive proponents of the two-person psychology approach is Shapiro (1995). Before he became an adherent of self psychology, his classical orientation led him to believe that patients' transference reactions and transference distortions were wholly determined by their past experiences. Today the two-person psychology approach holds that the "patient's transference reactions, no matter how distorted, are seen as codetermined by both early experiences and the current experiences with the analyst" (Shapiro, 1995, p. 19). In a masterful critique of self psychology, Gill (1994) also takes a stand alongside the increasing number of analysts who maintain that self psychology is an object relations theory.

A Contemporary Relational Perspective on Selfobject Transferences

Bacal (1994) focuses on the relational nature of the selfobject transference in psychoanalytic treatment. The selfobject relationship is not merely some vague, friendly, or supportive connection, but it is instead an experience that is at the very center of the therapeutic process. He claims that the selfobject emotional bond that develops as a result of interactions between the patient and therapist constitutes the central curative determinant of psychoanalysis. For Bacal, the essence of the analyst's contribution to the patient's experience of a selfobject relationship is his or her optimal responsiveness to the selfobject needs of the patient.

There are several major differences between the new relational paradigm and the older Freudian paradigm. The latter was constituted as one-body or single system approach, whereas the former allows for a two-party or multisystem theory. The clinical perspective used in the traditional system was almost always limited to the intrapsychic realm, whereas the concepts used by those who follow the new paradigm include both the intrapsychic as well as the interactional (also called intersubjective or relational) points of view. The conceptual and epistemological underpinnings of the two paradigms also differ. The new paradigm is firmly set in the postmodern camp and the classical theory belongs to the earlier modern period. The objectivist or positivistic epistemological position of traditional psychoanalysis contrasts with the constructivist position of those advancing the new paradigm.

Lichtenberg's Concepts on Selfobject Experiences, Relations, Functions, and Transferences

The child psychoanalyst Lichtenberg (1989, 1991) has recently offered some important modifications and additions to the theories of selfobject functions and the psychoanalytic theory of motivation.

Early on, Kohut defined the selfobject as an individual who supplies a necessary but absent function to another person. According to Lichtenberg (1991), "A contemporary theory of infantile development redefines the term selfobject as referring primarily to a vitalizing affective experience, the selfobject experience" (p. 463). Both Stern (1985) and Lichtenberg (1991) believe that infant research supports Kohut's conception of selfobject as neither self nor separate; both also agree that in infancy as in later life selfobject experiences involve intimacy not merger.

According to Lichtenberg (1991), the core feature of the selfobject experience in infancy lies in the attunement of caregivers to the infant's motivational needs and the vitality of the intimacy that this provides to the infant. In adults as well as in children, "a selfobject experience implies the existence of mental contents comprising an intact or relational, affectively invigorated sense of self, an affirming, and/or like-minded, and/or idealized other; . . . (Lichtenberg, 1991, p. 472). In brief, "selfobject" experience designates an affective state of vitality and invigoration, a sense of vital needs being met and of an intactness of the self. Lichtenberg's (1991) discussion and definition of selfobjects shifts the focus from the individuals who serve a selfobject function to the patient's vitalizing affective experience when selfobject needs are satisfied.

Lichtenberg's Theory of Motivation

Lichtenberg (1989) offers psychology and psychoanalysis a new way to conceptualize motivation that promises to replace the traditional dual drive (sex and aggression) theory while still accounting for all of the relevant clinical phenomena. In his view, "the fundamental level of the unconscious consists, at its core, of schemas for the organization of five motivational systems" (Lichtenberg, 1989, p. 275).

> The five motivational systems are: (1) the need for psychic regulation of physiological requirements, (2) the need for attachment-affiliation, (3) the need for exploration and assertion, (4) the need to react aversively through antagonism or withdrawal, and (5) the need for sensual enjoyment and sexual excitement [p. 1].

Lichtenberg's theory of the attachment–affiliation system of motivation borrows heavily from the work of Bowlby (1969) and others. These writers have provided overwhelming evidence for the existence of innate needs for attachment among humans and other mammals; strivings that are separate from and cannot be reduced to sexual or sensual needs and desires.

Psychic Development from a Contemporary Self Psychology Perspective

Galatzer-Levy and Cohler (1993) provide the first comprehensive study from a self psychological perspective of psychic development throughout the life span. In the past, psychoanalysis emphasized the values of autonomy and independence characteristic of Western cultures and overlooked the life-long importance of other people for maintaining the morale and integrity of the self. These later writers argue convincingly that the old paradigms in psychoanalysis and elsewhere, which emphasized autonomy and independence, not only caused much psychic pain and suffering, but also limited the understanding and study of individuals and their relationships. This cultural idealization of independence and depreciation of even legitimate selfobject and dependency needs causes human suffering because individuals under the influence of these values become ashamed and guilty over their need for affiliation and selfobject relationships. The findings reviewed in their book demonstrate that people seek increasing interdependence, rather than separateness and isolated independence.

These authors made a unique contribution by collating and integrating the contributions from many fields (e.g., sociology, anthropology, developmental psychology, philosophy, psychoanalysis) and explicating the role of significant others for one's development and for the cohesiveness of the self throughout the entire life-span.

CONCLUSION

The influence of self psychology reaches far beyond the borders of psychoanalysis. A wide variety of mental health professionals including psychiatrists, psychologists, social workers, and the like make up the majority of individuals attending the annual self psychology conferences. In addition to its extensive contributions to psychoanalytic theory and practice, self psychology has made significant and enduring contributions to the humanities, psychiatry, our understanding of personality development, and to various other treatment modalities including, among others, individual, group, and conjoint and marital forms of psychotherapy.

REFERENCES

Bacal, H. A. (1994), The selfobject relationship in psychoanalytic treatment. In; *A Decade of Progress: Progress in Self Psychology*, Vol. 10, ed. A. Goldberg. Hillsdale, NJ: Analytic Press, pp. 21–30.

Bowlby, J. (1969), The nature of a child's tie to his mother. *Internat. J. Psycho-Anal.*, 39:350–373.

Galatzer-Levy, R., & Cohler, B. (1993), *The Essential Other*. New York: Basic Books.

Gill, M. M. (1994), Heinz Kohut's self psychology. In: *A Decade of Progress: Progress in Self Psychology*, Vol. 10, ed. A. Goldberg. Hillsdale, NJ: Analytic Press, pp. 197–212.

---

*Recommended reading.

*Goldberg, A. (1985), Psychoanalytic self psychology. In: *Models of the Mind: Their Relationships to Clinical Work,* ed. A. Rothstein. New York: International Universities Press, pp. 69–84.

Kohut, H. (1959), Introspection, empathy and psychoanalysis. *J Amer. Psychoanal. Assn.,* 7:459–483.

———(1966), Forms and transformations of narcissism. *J. Amer. Psychoanal. Assn.,* 14:243–272.

———(1971), *The Analysis of the Self.* New York: International Universities Press.

———(1972), Thoughts on narcissism and narcissistic rage. *The Psychoanalytic Study of the Child,* 27:360–400. New Haven, CT: Yale University Press.

———(1977), *The Restoration of the Self.* New York: International Universities Press.

———(1978), *Search for the Self,* Vols. 1 & 2, ed. P. Ornstein. New York: International Universities Press.

———(1979), The two analyses of Mr. Z. *Internat. J. Psycho-Anal.,* 60:3–27.

———(1984), *How does Psychoanalysis Cure?* ed. A. Goldberg & P. Stepansky. Chicago: University of Chicago Press.

*———Wolf, E. (1978), The disorders of the self and their treatment. *Internat. J. Psycho-Anal.,* 59:413–425.

Lichtenberg, J. D. (1989), *Psychoanalysis and Motivation.* Hillsdale, NJ: Analytic Press.

———(1991), What is a selfobject? *Psychoanal. Dial.,* 1:433–479.

*———Kaplan, S., Eds. (1983), *Reflections on Self Psychology.* Hillsdale, NJ: Analytic Press.

Morrison, A. P. (1985), Shame and the psychology of the self. In: *Kohut's Legacy: Contributions to Self Psychology,* ed. P. E. Stepansky & A. Goldberg. Hillsdale, NJ: Analytic Press.

*Shapiro, S. (1995), *Talking with Patients: A Self Psychological View.* Northvale, NJ: Jason Aronson.

Stern, D. M. (1985), *The Interpersonal World of the Infant.* New York: Basic Books.

Stolorow, R., Brandchaft, B., & Atwood, G. E. (1987), *Psychoanalytic Treatment: An Intersubjective Approach.* Hillsdale, NJ: Analytic Press.

——— ——— ———(1994), *The Intersubjective Perspective.* Northvale, NJ: Jason Aronson.

———Lachmann, F. (1985), Transference: The future of an illusion. *Annual of Psychoanalysis,* 12–13:19–37. New York: International Universities Press.

*Wolf, E. S. (1988), *Treating the Self: Elements of Clinical Self Psychology.* New York: Guilford Press.

8.

Core Conflict Theory

Arnold Winston, M.D., Beverly Winston, Ph.D.

A HISTORY OF THE CORE CONFLICT CONCEPT

The idea of a core conflict dates back to nearly a century ago when Freud (1897) first wrote to Wilhelm Fliess (Letter 71) about the impact that the play *Oedipus Rex* had over its audience. He explained that individuals recognize within themselves the same phenomenon that Oedipus confronted: "I have found, in my own case too, falling in love with the mother and jealousy of the father, and I now regard it as a universal event of early childhood . . . " (p. 265). In general this particular conflict is what is meant when reference is made to the core conflict (Moore and Fine, 1990). Briefly, from ages 3 to 7, the oedipal conflict reigns supreme. The child develops strong positive loving and sexual feelings for the parent of the opposite sex and negative thoughts, competitive strivings, and murderous impulses toward the parent of the same sex.

The next important landmark in the history of the core conflict concept is Freud's development of the concept of transference (1912). Transference can be defined as a repetitive pattern of feeling, thinking, and behaving toward the therapist that is inappropriate and based on patients' relationships with important figures from their early lives such as mother, father, siblings, or caretakers. In his discussion of the transference, Freud suggested that early childhood conflicts are determined, "by the combined operation of inherent disposition and of external influences in childhood. . . . This forms a cliche or stereotype in him, so to speak (or even several), which perpetually repeats and reproduces itself as life goes on . . . " (Freud, 1912, pp. 312–313). Thus Freud set the stage for the centrality of a core conflict in an individual's patterns of interpersonal relationships, including the therapeutic relationship. The term *core conflict* (Freud's cliche or stereotype) implies that there is a basic central underlying conflict that constitutes the driving and motivating force behind an individual's behavior and emotional symptoms.

Ferenczi and Rank in their book, *The Development of Psychoanalysis* (1925), suggested that change comes about through a combination of affect and intellectual understanding that takes place while the patient repeats the original conflict of early childhood within the therapeutic relationship.

Alexander and French (1946) emphasized the importance of searching for a "significant, possibly traumatic, nuclear life experience" (p. 298). They were ahead of their time in advocating the value of finding "a center of conflict" (p. 299) in order to facilitate briefer psychotherapies. They believed that focusing on the core conflict would be more productive than spending time on less important existing conflicts. Balint (1957), French (1958), Malan (1963), and Balint, Ornstein, and Balint (1972), directly or indirectly discussed the concept of focal or nuclear conflicts and the use of focused clinical techniques designed to concentrate on a central explanation of the patient's difficulties or psychopathology.

Wallerstein, Robbins, Sargent, and Luborsky (1956) writing on the Menninger research project, asked the following questions: "what is the core problem as manifest both in the infantile situation and current life situation as recreated in the transference situation . . . what are the reality anchorings of the current suffering and in what way do they recapitulate in fantasy earlier neurotic dilemmas" (p. 244). This group recognized that the core conflict begins early in life, is present in the patient's current life and in the therapeutic relationship.

Beginning in the late 1950s and through the 1960s, contributors to the field of brief psychotherapy utilized a focal approach to treatment based on the concept of a core neurotic conflict. These writers emphasized the concept of a core conflict primarily because of their time-limited approach to treatment. The concept enables a therapist to concentrate on one basic theme.

Malan (1979), who worked at the Tavistock Clinic in London, was a pioneer in the field of brief psychotherapy. He provided a number of well-documented detailed studies on the outcome of psychoanalytically based psychodynamic psychotherapy. He reported that important and lasting changes, both symptomatic and psychodynamic, could be accomplished in patients suffering from severe characterological pathology. As a result of his research Malan developed a set of essential characteristics or principles of psychotherapy to make this form of treatment effective. He emphasized that a central focus or conflict, based on the initial interviews, should be formulated by the therapist. This focus is presented to the patient at the end of the evaluation in the form of an interpretation or explanation and forms the basis for treatment.

In the late 1960s Sifneos (1972) developed a form of psychodynamic psychotherapy, short-term anxiety-provoking psychotherapy, which he applied to patients suffering from anxiety, phobias, obsessions, depression, and a variety of interpersonal problems. In order to be accepted into treatment, patients had to have an oedipal conflict as the basis of their symptomatology. The goal of this treatment was the resolution of this emotional core problem as it was recapitulated in the transference. This was done by pointing out the patient's behavior toward the therapist and linking this behavior with important persons in the patient's life.

Another type of focus was emphasized by Mann (1973), who developed a time-limited psychoanalytic psychotherapy in which separation-individuation is the underlying core conflict. Early in this type of treatment, and generally within the first session, a central issue or conflict is identified. This formulation reflects the therapist's understanding of the patient's present and chronically endured pain which often concerns a negative

self-image. The patient recognizes the pain as a lifelong problem and a "consciously acceptable part of his human condition . . . " (p. 18). The central conflict framed in this way tends
to bypass defensiveness because there is no confrontation of
maladaptive patterns. Instead the therapist and patient join
together and work on the pain endured by the patient over a
lifetime. In this way the therapist provides an empathic environment in which the patient experiences a recapitulation of the
normal maturational stages of life, with termination and separation as the central issue. This is a particularly potent therapy
for individuals for whom separation and loss are their major
sources of conflict.

Davanloo (1980) broadened the idea of a single core conflict as the focus for his treatment modality and therefore was
able to work with a more diverse group of patients suffering
from disorders with a focus on either an oedipal issue or loss,
or both. In this sense he implemented Freud's (1912) concept
that an individual will not have a single "cliche or stereotype,"
but that there may be several paradigms or patterns that repeat
themselves throughout life.

During the past twenty years, a number of clinical researchers (Luborsky, 1977; Strupp and Binder, 1984; Pollack, Flegenheimer, and Winston, 1991) have developed new forms of brief
dynamic psychotherapy using the concept of a core conflict or
pattern as a guiding principle. These approaches have been
developed in conjunction with their research in psychotherapy
process and outcome. Luborsky (1977), developed the idea of
the Core Conflictual Relationship Theme (CCRT) method
which he used to identify central issues within his Supportive-
Expressive Psychotherapy. The components of the CCRT are
the patient's wish or what the patient wants from others, how
others react to the patient's wish or how the patient perceives
others (response of the other), and how the patient responds
to the reaction of others (response of the self). The CCRT is
formulated within an interpersonal framework and focuses on
relationship themes which are the surface manifestations of the
underlying core conflict. The following is a clinical application
of the CCRT.

A 35-year-old woman executive described several conflictual encounters with coworkers which were competitive and antagonistic. She stated that her coworkers were constantly trying to outdo her and seemed always to have the inside track. She felt resentful, frustrated, and defeated. The CCRT formulation is as follows: Her wish or need would be to defeat rivals and receive admiration from supervisors; the response of others is rivalry with the patient; the response of the self is resentment, frustration, competitiveness, and feeling defeated by her rivals.

Several years later, Strupp and Binder (1984) created another short-term modality, Time-Limited Dynamic Psychotherapy, and they proposed their version of the core conflict concept, called the dynamic focus. Ascertaining this core issue relies on the use of interpersonal narratives that describe recurring cyclical maladaptive patterns (CMP) that are the cause of a patient's lifelong difficulties in living (pp. 69–73). According to the authors, the dynamic focus highlights the "self-defeating persistence and inflexibility of a patient's maladaptive and stereotypic interpersonal transactions" (p. 72). The CMP is a central pattern "of interpersonal roles in which patients unconsciously cast themselves; the complementary roles in which they cast others; and the maladaptive interaction sequences, self-defeating expectations, negative self-appraisals and unpleasant affects that result" (p. 140).

Finally, Pollack et al. (1991) developed a form of brief psychotherapy called Brief Adaptive Psychotherapy. In this approach the core conflict is formulated by identifying the patient's major maladaptive pattern. Treatment focuses on the pattern as it is elaborated in the current and past life of the patient and in the therapeutic relationship.

BASIC THEORETICAL CONCEPTS AND PROPOSITIONS

Psychological conflict refers to a struggle within an individual or between that person and the outside world. The conflict usually has its roots in unresolved infantile struggles that have been aroused by an event in the adult's current life. Within the individual, the struggle or conflict is conceptualized as occurring between various parts of the mind or psychic apparatus. Freud's structural theory (1923) of the id, ego, and superego is used to identify the components of the psychic apparatus. The id is postulated to contain the drives, wishes, and needs of a person. Traditionally these have been defined as the sexual and aggressive drives. The ego is conceptualized as embodying the executive functions of the personality. These capacities include engaging in object relations (the quality of relationships with significant others), self concept, defenses, affects, control of the drives, reality testing, and a number of autonomous functions such as thinking, perception, memory, and motility. The superego is viewed as a structure containing two basic functions: the ego ideal and a system of values or morals. The ego ideal contains an individual's aspirations, hopes, and internalized view of the self, while the value system includes conscience and ethical considerations.

The conflict model of the mind relies on the structural theory and the concept of dynamic unconscious processes. People are viewed as attempting to resolve both inner and outer conflicts in order to reduce the unpleasant affects associated with anxiety and depression. The theory holds that individuals use a variety of means to achieve pleasure and avoid painful affects. The patient's psychopathology is seen as originating from the desire to ward off the painful affects of anxiety and depression that are derived from feelings of guilt or grief. According to Moore and Fine (1990), "Psychic conflict or intrapsychic conflict refers to struggle among incompatible forces or structures within the mind, *external conflict* is that between the individual and aspects of the outside world" (p. 44). Although predominantly unconscious, conflicts can be observed through behavior, thoughts, and symptoms. Conflicts arise when instinctual wishes, thoughts, or fantasies "come into conflict with internal or external prohibitions; the ego is threatened and produces signal anxiety; defenses are mobilized and the conflict is resolved via compromise formations in symptoms, character changes, or adaptation. . . . The manifestations of conflict vary according to developmental level, the nature of the psychopathology and cultural factors contributing to the makeup of the superego" (Moore and Fine, 1990, p. 44).

A conflict is composed of three basic components: a wish (or impulse), anxiety, and defense which are defined as follows. An impulse (drive) or wish is a desire which expresses an underlying need. Examples are the wish to be cared for or loved, the need for admiration, the wish to be strong and powerful or independent, and the impulse to lash out or physically hurt someone. Impulses or wishes fall within the two broad categories of sex and aggression.

Anxiety is an affect characterized by an internal sensation of fear often evoking thoughts that something unpleasant is about to happen. Although the danger is often nonspecific a sense of helplessness accompanies this feeling. It is often accompanied by an aroused physiological state consisting of heightened awareness, rapid heartbeat, sweating, muscle tightening, and restlessness. For example, a young woman came to treatment several weeks before her wedding, suffering from paralyzing anxiety. She described the anxiety as the inner sensation of fear along with an inability to take deep breaths, tightening of the muscles in her chest, and a feeling of butterflies in her stomach. When anxiety is more contained, it may act as a signal of impending danger and prevent the painful feelings or emerging wishes from entering consciousness. In this situation the anxiety is so limited that the individual may not be aware of its presence.

The concept of defense is a central one in psychoanalytic theory. Defenses are psychological mechanisms used to mediate between a person's wishes, impulses, thoughts, and feelings, and both internal prohibitions and the external world. They are primarily unconscious, but can also be conscious, operating automatically. They generally involve patterned responses in the sense that individuals tend repetitively to use the same kind of behavior, thoughts, or feelings in response to a variety of perceived dangers. Defense mechanisms come into play regardless of whether conflict is initiated internally or externally. They serve to ward off or push back the unpleasant affects of anxiety or depression associated with the danger situation. Thus, defenses are used adaptively to cope with internal and external stress. They can also be used maladaptively (e.g., pathological denial), which restricts, limits, or inhibits an individual's ability to function optimally and may cause painful symptoms that also limit functioning. To illustrate the concept of defense, the young women described above had previously dated many men, but became anxious, devaluing men (defense), and distancing from them (defense), resulting in an inability to form a relationship.

An example of a conflict that is not unusual in adolescents is the following: A 13-year-old adolescent boy has a wish to be close to a girl in his class. He becomes anxious and withdraws from girls, spending more time in athletic endeavors with male friends. Generally, this is a partially adaptive solution occurring outside the boy's awareness. This conflict involves the wish or impulse to be close to the girl in his class: Anxiety is experienced and the defenses of repression, withdrawal, and turning to another socially acceptable activity follows.

Repetitive fantasies may reflect a core conflict. Arlow (1969) stated that the "traumatic events of the past become part of fantasy thinking and as such exert a never ending dynamic effect . . . " (p. 44). This suggests that fantasies early in life tend to endure with only insignificant changes. Arlow uses a literary analogy, "one could say the plot line of the fantasy remains the same although the characters and the situation may vary" (p. 47). This is another way of saying that people develop core conflicts early in life that are expressed in fantasy as well as behaviorally. The core conflict, fantasies, and behavior retain the same basic theme which is then played out with significant people throughout an individual's life.

THERAPEUTIC TECHNIQUE AND CURE

The concept of the core conflict serves to organize a number of psychodynamically oriented therapies, especially brief or time-limited approaches. The concept organizes the therapeutic situation along several basic lines.

Evaluation

A thorough evaluation of the patient is essential in all psycho-therapeutic approaches. This serves a number of purposes including diagnosis, case formulation, establishing a therapeutic relationship, motivating the patient's interest and commitment to therapy, and determining the technical approach that appears most suitable for a given patient. Case formulation is important because it enables the therapist to understand the patient and, as a result, to be empathic. The formulation generally consists of three areas: dynamic, genetic, and structural.

The dynamic area involves conflicting wishes, thoughts, impulses or fears, and their meanings which may be either conscious or unconscious; and considers how an individual wards off (defends against) their mental contents and the feelings associated with them. These considerations are directly related to a patient's core conflict and especially the contents of the individual's current conflicts.

An example of a dynamic formulation can be drawn from the following data. Mr. T is a middle-aged man whose father has become increasingly debilitated and senile. Mr. T feels anxiety-ridden and is often angry with his wife and friends and later feels guilty about his behavior. The dynamic explanation is that Mr. T had ambivalent feelings toward his father consisting of anger and a wish for his father to die, combined with positive feelings based on rewarding experiences with his father. Mr. T defended against his feelings and wishes toward his father with the defensive behavior of displacing his anger toward his wife and friends. His anxiety serves as a signal of emerging unacceptable impulses which can then be defensively warded off.

The genetic area of case formulation is the understanding of an individual's current situation in light of early development and life events, the genesis of psychodynamic issues. In the previously cited example of Mr. T, his current conflict is based on his father's being highly critical with him when he was a youngster, an attitude that alternated with concern and closeness.

The structural area contains the relatively fixed characteristics of an individual's personality, understood within a functional rather than content-based context. As described earlier,

Freud's (1923) structural theory of the id, ego, and superego is the basis for conceptualizing these functions. The structural area of case formulation assesses an individual's strengths and weaknesses, and his or her overall level of psychopathology which informs the clinician's technical approach to the patient.

The initial evaluation of the patient should be comprehensive and completed in the first hours of treatment so that the therapist understands the patient's core conflict within the context of the case formulation as described above. The evaluation serves as a model for the course of treatment by providing the patient with a therapeutic experience from the beginning so that he or she is motivated for treatment. The therapeutic experience during the evaluation period promotes the alliance between patient and therapist which many clinicians and researchers believe is a major factor in patient improvement.

The evaluation consists of an exploration of the individual's current areas of disturbance followed by a detailed past history. During the course of the evaluation, a trial of therapy is in process (Davanloo, 1980). This treatment modality employs therapeutic techniques such as clarification, confrontation, and interpretation during the initial session, enabling the therapist to determine the patient's suitability and response to core conflict treatment.

Core Conflict Psychotherapy (CCP) is a treatment form that utilizes the triangles of conflict and of person. The triangle of conflict (Freud, 1926; Malan, 1979) (see Figure 8.1) focuses on wishes/impulses/feelings (W/I/F) that are warded off by defense (D) and anxiety (A). In this model, when the therapist is pursuing a patient's feeling or wish she or he is at the W/I/F point of the triangle. Often the patient will respond defensively at this juncture, so as to avoid the conscious experience of a difficult feeling or wish. Defense (D) is the second point of the triangle. When the patient responds in a defensive manner the therapist generally confronts and clarifies the defense until the WIF clearly emerges. The patient also may respond with heightened anxiety because of fear, guilt, shame, or pain related to the conflicted feeling that will be exposed when the defenses are modified. Anxiety (A) represents the third point on the triangle and acts as a signal that unacceptable WIFs are emerging. When this occurs the therapist attempts to explore the patient's experience of anxiety and make it more tolerable, so that difficult feelings or wishes can be expressed.

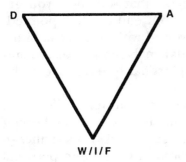

FIGURE 8.1 Triangle of Conflict
W/I/F = Wishes, Impulses, Feelings
D = Defense
A = Anxiety

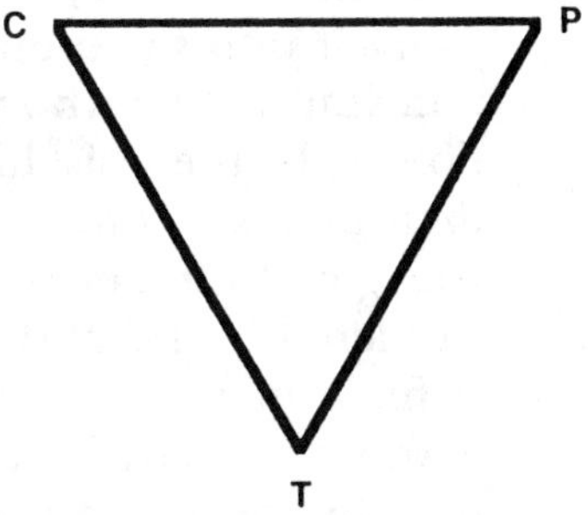

FIGURE 8.2 Triangle of Person
T = Therapist
C = Current Persons
P = Past Persons

Briefly, the triangle of the person (Menninger, 1958; Malan, 1979) has three points, all related to people (see Figure 8.2). These are individuals in the patient's current life (C), past life (P), and the therapist or transference figure (T). This concept of treatment is interpersonal and is always focused on conflict situations involving important people in the patient's life.

The therapist's task is to work within the two triangles, utilizing them to formulate the core conflict. This conflict should be revealed as the therapist examines the patient's relationships in the past and present and, most importantly, in the here-and-now of the therapeutic relationship.

The following vignette is from an initial evaluation session and illustrates the trial therapy approach. The patient is a 31-year-old single man and the session began with his expression of hopelessness about his inability to get his career started. He described a recent incident in which the equipment he was using for a job was not working properly because he hadn't checked to make sure it was in good repair. He was upset and disappointed because he was unable to complete the job. When the therapist asked if this was a fair example of what gets in the way of his success at work, he began a repetitive description

about how difficult it is to get someone to repair faulty
equipment.

T: That may be true, but it seems that somehow you get
yourself into situations where you end up disappointed.
Can you tell me who was involved with you in this situation? [The therapist highlights a maladaptive pattern and
then moves it into the interpersonal sphere, that is, the
triangle of the person.]

P: I called a friend and he never showed up. Then I tried
to fix it again, but decided to use it the way it was, hoping
it would be okay. [The therapist again asks for specifics so
that the conflict can be explored within an interpersonal
context. The patient remains vague and avoids describing
a concrete situation.]

T: You seem to have difficulty talking about who was involved in this work situation and each time we try to look
at this you become vague.

P: [Patient begins to stammer and responds in a hostile
manner.] Why do you need to know these kinds of details? [This led to an exploration of the patient's difficulty with the therapist, who is a woman. He experienced
the therapist as intrusive and attempting to belittle him.]
You keep asking me about it, do you think I'm irrespon-
sible?

T: You seem to be having some feelings about what's happening here between us.

P: You're looking for a chink in my armor, my weaknesses.

T: What does that make you feel toward me?

P: It's annoying.

In this first evaluation session, it became clear that the
patient was defensive with the therapist (vague and hostile)
because he experienced her as devaluing him and looking for
his weaknesses. The therapist pointed out the patient's defensiveness while maintaining an interpersonal focus and the patient perceived this as intrusive and became annoyed. Further
exploration of the patient–therapist relationship revealed that
the patient felt threatened by his female therapist and reacted

defensively with further annoyance. Later in the evaluation session, this behavior in the therapeutic relationship was linked to the patient's relationship with his mother who was an intrusive, critical, and depressed woman.

This vignette illustrates the use of the patient–therapist relationship or transference during the evaluation interview using trial therapy. The patient's expectation that others, especially women, would be critical, provides the therapist with important information with which to formulate the core conflict (see also below).

As therapy proceeds, the core conflict needs to be worked through and resolved in a number of areas. These include relationships with other key people in the patient's current and past life and especially in the therapeutic relationship. The final sessions of a treatment experience constitute the termination phase of therapy. For patients without significant separation and loss problems, this phase entails one or two sessions. Patients who have had traumatic separations and losses will need a longer termination phase. During this phase of therapy, the patient works through the loss of the therapist and the feelings connected to this as well as prior losses.

Core Conflict Psychotherapy (CCP) and other psychodynamic therapies produce change as a result of multiple factors. The most important of these appears to be the therapeutic relationship (Horvath and Symonds, 1991; A. Winston and Muran, 1996). A helping relationship based on a positive therapeutic alliance enables the patient to feel supported and that someone is interested in the patient's well-being. In addition, if the therapist is able to comprehend the prevailing core conflict and assist the patient to develop insight into the origin, development, and workings of the conflict, the alliance will be further enhanced because the patient will feel understood by the therapist. Patient insight should, of course, be experienced both cognitively and affectively if it is to be of value (Laikin, A. Winston, and McCullough, 1991). Finally, affectively experiencing the core conflict in the presence of a benign figure, the therapist, helps to diminish the prevailing conflicts by what has been referred to as the *corrective emotional experience* (Alexander and French, 1946).

CORE CONFLICT PSYCHOTHERAPY: CLINICAL ILLUSTRATION

The patient, Mr. D, is a 31-year-old man who lives alone in a home owned by his family and works sporadically as a video consultant, but would like to be a writer. His initial complaints were that he felt lonely and wanted to develop a significant relationship with a woman, but often found himself becoming angry with them. In addition, he complained that he was too financially dependent on his father and feels hopeless about achieving even modest success in his work. He had flirted with a number of interests, but was uncomfortable about making a firm commitment to any relationship or work-related endeavor. He was a handsome young man, soft spoken and passive, while also subtly hostile and intimidating. (This is the patient who was presented earlier in the illustration of trial therapy.)

Mr. D is the second of three children in a middle-class family. When he was 12 years old his parents divorced and he moved with his mother and two siblings from an urban setting to a suburban area. His father, a withdrawn and remote man is described as preferring to stay outdoors washing his car rather than joining a celebration of his child's birthday party. He was successful financially and was the parent responsible for managing the household, albeit from a distance after the divorce. The patient has had an adversarial relationship with his father largely because he tries to gain economic support from him. His mother is depressed, anxious, intrusive, and critical. Although his mother physically punished his older rebellious brother, the patient rarely was hit since he "acted like a weakling" and kept out of her way. She had one hospitalization for postpartum depression after the birth of the patient's younger brother when the patient was 3 years old.

Mr. D. has a girl friend with whom he has a conflicted relationship. She is described as withholding and critical, yet at times she is caring and shows concern for him. He tends to bend over backwards to take care of her and then becomes resentful and angry. Sexually, he finds her attractive, but feels satisfied only when she allows him to slap her in a "playful" manner and restrain her. He fears humiliation and embarrassment in his relationship with her.

Formulation

A major conflict for the patient involves separation from a difficult mother for whom he has mixed feelings. At times his anger toward his mother is profound. In response, he feels guilty and attempts to pursue women who are needy and dependent, taking care of them in order to repair the damage he imagines he has done to his mother. He does not trust women, devalues them, and at times wants to injure them or restrain them so they will neither hurt nor abandon him. An oedipal configuration also is in evidence in that the patient experiences his father as taking his mother away from him when she was hospitalized. He both fears and loves his father. Mr. D prevents himself from being independent because he fears that his father will withdraw support from him. He behaves as if he's a helpless child and cannot take care of himself. In this sense the patient handicaps himself, presenting and experiencing himself as inadequate, and minimizing and disavowing his achievements. This enables him to avoid feeling belittled by his father, which is a frequent theme in his dreams.

Core Conflict

Mr. D's core conflict involves the wish to be cared for and loved by women and men while dreading and expecting to be criticized, devalued, rejected, and financially cut off by his father. His behavior is to either be passive and helpless in order to obtain both emotional and real supplies or to be hostile and sadistic especially toward women. This behavior distances him from others and thereby protects him, while also preventing him from establishing close relationships.

Technique

In an early session the patient began with complaints about his mother:

P: Each time I visit her she criticizes me. On Tuesday she started in on me again and told me I was dressed like a bum and would never amount to anything. I exploded and really let her have it.

T : [Asks for more specifics] What did you say?

P: I told her she just sits around the house and does nothing. Now I feel rotten about it. [As the therapist explores the patient's interaction with his mother, the patient becomes increasingly passive and unresponsive.]

T: [Confronting the shift in the patient's behavior] As we continue to talk about what happened between you and your mother you are becoming less responsive and more withdrawn with me.

P: [After a brief silence, and with sarcasm, he continued] If you say so.

T: [Therapist confronts the patient's defensive behavior within the patient–therapist relationship] It's hard for you to be direct and straightforward with me, so now you're being sarcastic.

P: I feel like you're pushing and criticizing me.

T: Can you explain how?

P: Well, . . . you said I was withdrawn.

T: You hear disapproval in what I say, but it's important for us to examine the change in your behavior.
[The therapist clarifies the patient's resistance which emerged in the form of passivity and withdrawal, and after some further exploration the therapist comes back to his original narrative about his mother.]

T: Today you began telling me about your mother. As we started examining what happened, you became distant and then sarcastic with me. It sounds like you're reacting to me as you did with your mother when she said you would never amount to anything. Last week you were saying that your mother pounces on you and looks for chinks in your armor.

In this early session, work is done on the patient's defensiveness with the therapist because it reveals part of his core conflictual pattern as evidenced with his mother and the therapist. The pattern is one of passivity and withdrawal or hostility (through sarcasm), based on how he perceives important people in his life and his expectations of them. When this is understood it will be possible to uncover the underlying wish or impulse that serves as the basis for this core conflict. As stated earlier, this patient's core conflict results in behaviors such as withdrawal or hostility based on his perception that others are hurtful, disappointing, and intrusive, and that they do not meet his underlying wish to be appreciated, admired, protected, and loved.

A few sessions later, the underlying wish becomes apparent. On his way to a session the patient observed an interaction between a young child and his mother.

P: A boy was licking an ice cream cone and the ice cream fell out of the cone. The little boy began to cry and his mother kneeled down, wiped his hands off, dried his tears and said: "Don't worry, it's okay, come, we'll get another. Do you want vanilla again or chocolate this time?" I felt a rush of good feelings for the mother.

T: Anything else?

P: I thought how nice it would be if my mother was young again as I remember her before my brother was born, when she was softer.

T: So you yearn for a loving mother who reassures you and is there for you. It's particularly painful when you are wishing for her to be loving and she's critical.

These brief vignettes illustrate how the therapist focused on the core conflict and used the triangles of conflict and person. The therapist asked for details about the patient's interaction with his mother. This kind of information is important in helping to elucidate the core conflict. Global or general information is less useful in delineating this conflict and for providing the patient with experiential understanding. As exploration of the interaction between the patient and his mother proceeded, he became defensive and the therapist confronted his lack of responsiveness and tendency to withdraw from the therapist. This led to work on the therapeutic relationship and his behavior with the therapist is connected to his behavior with his mother. The therapist used the transference to uncover the patient's patterns of behavior that are related to the core conflict, that is, withdrawal and hostility as a reaction to his perceived frustration of an underlying wish to be loved and admired. Finally, a few sessions later the patient related an experience observing a mother and young child that is connected to the wish component of his core conflict, to have a caring and loving mother. As therapy proceeded the core conflict was examined in great detail as it applies to the important relationships in this man's life.

CURRENT AREAS OF RESEARCH

There are two distinct approaches to research on the core conflict concept. The first involves studies that examine the efficacy of a given psychotherapy that makes use of core conflict formulations. The second approach entails studies that specifically examine patients' core conflicts, how they are used by the therapist, and their effects on outcome.

The first approach is in the area of clinical trials research, that is designed to determine the usefulness of a given mode of psychotherapy as compared to a control group and/or another therapy. Malan (1963) was one of the first therapists to systematically investigate a form of brief dynamic therapy that used a focal approach. He conducted clinical studies that demonstrated relatively good outcomes to these treatment efforts. In addition, he reported that the more focused the therapy, the better the outcome. However, the focused approach may not involve the identification of a core conflict, so it remains uncertain whether these studies have a bearing on core conflict forms of treatment.

In a study of short-term dynamic psychotherapy, A. Winston, Laikin, Pollack, Samstag, McCullough, and Muran (1994) demonstrated good results for Brief Adaptive Psychotherapy, which, as mentioned earlier, defines a patient's major maladaptive pattern, that is derived from his or her core conflict. In this study, patients with personality disorders were randomly assigned to Brief Adaptive Psychotherapy (BAP), Short-Term Dynamic Psychotherapy (STDP) based on Davanloo's model (1980), or a waiting list. In the two therapy conditions, patients improved significantly as compared to the waiting list control group, doing so on symptom and social adjustment measures as well as the patient's major complaints upon entering treatment. This indicates that therapies based on working through a core conflict can be successful.

Binder and Strupp (1991) also have reported good results with Time-Limited Dynamic Psychotherapy (TLDP), which uses a concept related to the core conflict idea. As described earlier, their formulation is termed the cyclical maladaptive pattern (CMP). Their research also supports the efficacy of a core conflict approach.

More specific studies on the nature of core conflict were conducted by Luborsky and his co-workers (Luborsky and Crits-Christoph, 1990). They studied the Core Conflictual Relationship Theme (CCRT), and demonstrated that the CCRT changes from the beginning to the end of treatment. They found that a patient's habitual way of interacting with others shifted so that the CCRT showed a decrease in negative responses of self and other and an increase in positive responses from the other. The "response of the other" is the manner in which others react to the patient's wish, or how the patient perceives their reaction. The "response of the self" is how the patient responds to the reaction of others. In addition they found that patient wishes or needs did not change. Thus, while the wish component of the core conflict remains the same, the person's perception of others, as well as his or her behavior, do change as a result of psychotherapy. This implies that individuals can learn to deal more effectively with their needs and wishes by altering their behavior and sense of others.

In another study Crits-Christoph, Cooper, and Luborsky (1988) reported a relationship between the accuracy of therapists' interpretations based on the CCRT and its relationship to therapy outcome. Accurately interpreting components of the core conflict appeared to effect outcome positively. Interestingly, interpreting the response of the self was not related to outcome, whereas interpreting wishes of the patient and responses of the other were related to positive outcome. Luborsky's "response of self" includes both defense and affect.

Other studies (Salerno, Farber, McCullough, A. Winston, and Trujillo, 1992; Orlinsky and Howard, 1986) have shown that interpreting or confronting affect is counterproductive or of little value. However, clarifying and confronting defensive behavior appears to be beneficial. B. Winston, A. Winston, Samstag, and Muran, reported (1994) that the more a therapist addressed a patient's defensive behavior, the better the outcome in two psychotherapies (BAP and STDP).

A contrasting view on the fate of the defenses in psychotherapy is presented by Brenner (1982). In a theoretical discussion regarding change in defense, he stressed that "particular modes of defense neither disappear, nor do they change in any regular, uniform, or predictable way as a result of analysis. What happens as analysis proceeds is not that defenses change in a progressive way, but that the patient's compromise formations change in a progressive way" (p. 82). Although not specifically stated, Brenner implies that in psychotherapy, the wish or impulse component changes in a more systematic way, but the defense component does not change in that manner. This is the theoretical converse of Luborsky's findings and thus in need of further exploration.

Freud (1924) took both points of view regarding the resolution of the core conflict. He talked of the ideal outcome as a "destruction and abrogation" of the conflict. Later, in "Analysis Terminable and Interminable" (1937), he talked only of the "taming of the instinct," stating that the demand does not disappear "so that nothing more is ever heard from it again" (pp. 224–225).

Based on the findings that are available to us, we tend to agree with Freud's later observation that pathological impulses (instincts) or wishes do not disappear. In follow-up interviews of patients who were successfully treated in brief dynamic psychotherapies, we have found that old conflicts assume less importance, but are still discernible. Therefore, from both a clinical and research perspective, it appears that wishes and impulses endure after treatment and the core conflict is not totally resolved. What seems to occur is that the conflicted wishes and impulses become less demanding or decrease in intensity, possibly as a result of both a shift in defensive behavior leading to more adaptive coping skills, and a decrease in the patient's expectations of others.

CONCLUSION

This chapter has defined the core conflict concept, recounted its history, and highlighted its use in case formulation and ongoing psychotherapy, particularly brief dynamic psychotherapy. As demands increase for short-term psychotherapy approaches, the use of organizing concepts such as the core conflict idea becomes increasingly important. Early identification of a patient's core conflict enables the therapist to proceed in an organized, goal-oriented manner. Whether these basic conflicts are resolved or become muted may not be crucial from a clinical point of view, provided that the patient functions better, has improved relationships, and feels relatively comfortable.

REFERENCES

*Alexander, F., & French, T. M. (1946), *Psychoanalytic Therapy*. New York: Ronald Press.

Arlow, J. (1969), Fantasy, memory, and reality testing. *Psychoanal. Quart.*, 38:28–51.

Balint, M. (1957), *The Doctor, His Patient and the Illness*. New York: International Universities Press.

---

*Recommended reading.

————Ornstein, P. H., & Balint, E. (1972), *Focal Psychotherapy.* Philadelphia: Lippincott.

Binder, J. L., & Strupp, H. H. (1991), The Vanderbilt approach to time-limited dynamic psychotherapy. In: *Handbook of Short-Term Dynamic Psychotherapy,* ed. P. Chrits-Christoph & J. Barber. New York: Basic Books.

Brenner, C. (1982), *The Mind in Conflict.* New York: International Universities Press.

Crits-Christoph, P., Cooper, A., & Luborsky, L. (1988), The accuracy of therapist's interpretations and the outcome of dynamic psychotherapy. *J. Consult. & Clin. Psychol.,* 56:490–495.

*Davanloo, H. (1980), *Short-Term Dynamic Psychotherapy.* New York: Jason Aronson.

Ferenczi, S., & Rank, O. (1925), *The Development of Psychoanalysis.* New York: Nervous and Mental Disease.

French, T. M. (1958), *The Integration of Behavior,* Vol. 3. Chicago: University of Chicago Press.

Freud, S. (1897), Extracts from the Fleiss papers. *Standard Edition,* 1:173–280. London: Hogarth Press, 1966.

————(1912), The dynamics of transference. *Standard Edition,* 12:97–108. London: Hogarth Press, 1958.

————(1923), The Ego and the Id. *Standard Edition,* 19:1–59. London: Hogarth Press, 1916.

————(1924), The dissolution of the Oedipus complex. *Standard Edition,* 19:171–179. London: Hogarth Press, 1961.

————(1926), Inhibitions, Symptoms and Anxiety. *Standard Edition,* 20:75–172. London: Hogarth Press, 1964.

————(1937), Analysis terminable and interminable. *Standard Edition,* 23:209–253. London: Hogarth Press, 1964.

Horvath, A. O., & Symonds, B. D. (1991), Relation between working alliance and outcome in psychotherapy: A meta-analysis. *J. Counsel. Psychol.,* 38:139–149.

*Laikin, M., Winston, A., & McCullough, L. (1991), Intensive short-term dynamic psychotherapy. In: *Handbook of Short-Term Dynamic Psychotherapy,* ed. P. Crits-Christoph & J. Barber. New York: Basic Books.

Luborsky, L. (1977), Measuring a pervasive psychic structure in psychotherapy: The core conflictual relationship theme. In: *Communicative Structures and Psychic Structure,* ed. N. Friedman & S. Grand. New York: Plenum Press.

*————Crits-Christoph, P. (1990), *Understanding Transference. The CCRT Method.* New York: Basic Books.

Malan, D. H. (1963), *A Study of Brief Psychotherapy*. New York: Plenum Press.

*———(1979), *Individual Psychotherapy and the Science of Psychodynamics*. London: Butterworth.

Mann, J. (1973), *Time-Limited Psychotherapy*. Cambridge, MA: Harvard University Press.

Menninger, K. (1958), *Theory of Psychoanalytic Technique*. New York: Basic Books.

Moore, B. E., & Fine, B. D. (1990), *Psychoanalytic Terms and Concepts*. New Haven and London: The American Psychoanalytic Association & Yale University Press.

Orlinsky, D., & Howard, K. (1986), Process and outcome in psychotherapy. In: *Handbook of Psychotherapy and Behavior Change*, ed. S. Garfield & A. Bergin. New York: Wiley.

Pollack, J., Flegenheimer, W., & Winston, A. (1991), Brief adaptive psychotherapy. In: *Handbook of Short-Term Dynamic Psychotherapy*, ed. P. Crits-Christoph & J. Barber. New York: Basic Books.

Salerno, M., Farber B. A., McCullough, L., Winston, A., & Trujillo, M. (1992), The effects of confrontation and clarification on patient affective and defensive responding. *Psychother. Res.* 2:181–192.

Sifneos, P. E. (1972), *Short-Term Psychotherapy and Emotional Crisis*. Cambridge, MA: Harvard University Press.

*Strupp, H. H., & Binder, J. L. (1984), *Psychotherapy in a New Key*. New York: Basic Books.

Wallerstein, R. S., Robbins, L. L., Sargent, H. D., & Luborsky, L. (1956), The psychotherapy research project of the Menninger Foundation: Rationale, method, and sample use. *Bull. Menninger Clinic*, 20:221–278.

Winston, A., Laikin, M., Pollack, J., Samstag, L. W., McCullough, L., & Muran, J. C. (1994), Short-term dynamic psychotherapy of personality disorders. *Amer. J. Psychiatry*, 151:190–194.

*———Muran, J. C. (1996), Common factors in time-limited psychotherapy. In: *American Psychiatric Press Review of Psychiatry*, Vol. 15, ed. R. McKenzie, L. J. Dickstein, J. M., Oldham & J. B. Riba. Washington, DC: American Psychiatric Press.

Winston, B., Winston, A., Samstag, L. W., & Muran, J. C. (1994), Patient defense/therapist interventions. *Psychotherapy*, 31:478–491.

9.

The Work of Melanie Klein

O. Weininger, C. Whyte-Earnshaw

KLEIN'S PLACE IN THE CANON

Originality combined with a thorough understanding of both the pathological and normal processes of human functioning embody the work of Melanie Klein. Her contribution to psychoanalytic theory both acknowledges and challenges the ideas of Sigmund Freud. Ultimately, within the larger discipline of psychoanalytic practice, the writings of Melanie Klein have come to be associated with object relations theory.

In object relations, as in all psychoanalytic theory, psychodynamics play an important role in formulating a description of mental phenomena. The psychodynamic aspect of object relations is concerned with the interplay of complementing and opposing motivational forces that make up the mental contents (e.g., thoughts, feelings, representations) of individuals. Motivational forces refer to such things as felt needs, ideals, conscience, attempts to avoid becoming overwhelmed or disorganized in the face of life's demands (e.g., delaying gratification), and the action to contain, modify, and redirect emotions and impulses. In addition, psychodynamics are concerned with

We want to thank Daniel Blais for his help in the preparation of this chapter.

the dynamics of the unconscious mind in the process of its active engagement with the other, including the mind of the other; the interaction between the internal (intrapsychic) and the external (intersubjective) world.

Object relations theory furthers the understanding of the unconscious realm and of general psychological functioning through the incorporation of an implicit premise of intersubjectivity, a theory which sees human beings as primarily object seeking (Fairbairn, 1952). *Object* in this usage refers to a person, part of a person (e.g., the lactating breast), and/or a symbolic representation (e.g., shoes to one who has a fetish for footwear). By contrast, Freud's original (i.e., classical) theory of psychoanalysis holds that humans are primarily pleasure seeking (Brenner, 1973; Greenberg and Mitchell, 1983; Marx and Cronan-Hillix, 1987). In Kleinian thinking an individual's primary, yet not exclusive, motivation is to seek out relationships with others (i.e., whole or part objects) (Weininger, 1993).

Klein saw her work as continuous with classical theory (Lindon, 1966; Weininger, 1992). She conceived of her efforts as representing the truest development of that model and saw them as consistent with its most fundamental principles. Therefore, distinctions made between her own work and ongoing developments in classical theory were meant to delineate her position vis-à-vis innovations represented by, for example, the work of Anna Freud (1969). Both these women sought to extend Freud's seminal ideas despite differences in their respective theoretical viewpoints.

Kleinian theory is an entirely psychological theory. Unlike classical theory, Klein's theory attempts to account for the contents and processes of mental dynamics outside any apparent reliance on biology as an explanatory framework. Object relations theory departs from classical theory mainly by eclipsing *instinct theory*, the cornerstone of the classical model, and replacing it with an individual's innate orientation to objects. In the Freudian model, theory conceptually precedes clinical accounting. Kleinian practice places clinical experience first, thus making it a compelling feature of the theory. Ultimately, object relations theory posits an alternative psychoanalytic model of human functioning. The Kleinian model of object relations is arguably the most dynamic and complex of theoretical offerings in the area of developmental psychology (Weininger, 1984).

Klein's elaboration of the death instinct has proven instrumental in clinical interventions with psychotic patients, a population that had previously been thought beyond the reach of psychoanalysis. In Kleinian theory the death instinct exists as a threatening sense of destruction from within, emanating from the aggressive impulses the individual projects to the caregiver who then becomes feared as a potential aggressor. This dynamic operates at the level of the unconscious yet can manifest itself at a behavioral level; for example, the infant who experiences feelings of discomfort, muscle tension, and generalized anxiety, or the young child whose wreckless behavior places him or her in constant physical peril. The internal conflict is over damaging or destroying the caregiver and gives rise to a sense of feared annihilation connected to a sense of dislike for the self which is felt to be bad. Additionally, the self may feel as if it is under constant threat of being destroyed due to the badness that is being expressed just by having personal needs and feelings. The death instinct exists as a potential from birth onward. It strives to annihilate the needs, the perception of needs, or even the ego which perceives such needs as experienced by the individual (see Hinshelwood, 1991; Weininger, 1996).

Klein's most important contributions relate to her development of the theoretical and technical implications of human aggression. Inextricably linked with this dimension and equally significant is the development of a model of child analysis which incorporates the basic insights and principles of psychoanalytic understanding and practice. In addition, Klein filled in the previously sketchy picture of the maternal figure in psychoanalytic theory and balanced the emphasis on the role of the father in neurosis. She located the infant's relation to the breast and the maternal figure at the very center of the story of human development—the same center which in Freudian theory is occupied by the phallus (Freud, 1916–1917). Klein also developed the concept of internal reality (Hinshelwood, 1994; Hughes, 1989). In delineating the content and processes of mental life which comprise the internal world, she stressed the reciprocal influence this inner world and external reality have on one another. In conjunction with these achievements in clinical practice, Klein's elaboration of the developmental and clinical implications of the death instinct created the theoretical and technical foundation for the treatment of psychotic patients. Overall, Klein has presented a compelling, clinically based theory of the relationship between early mental life and subsequent development in both the normal and the pathological case.

THE BASIS OF KLEINIAN THEORY

Klein asserts that the ego[1] is in existence in a rudimentary form at birth and furthermore that its earliest experience of the world is shaped by the intrauterine environment. There exists therefore a correspondence between the ego and the loving mother's sense of the distinctive "self" of the newborn child she has carried. Klein sees the ego as being able to develop, perceive, and make decisions of a sort from the first day of life in the outside world. The infant approaches its environment through a complex process of bodily sensation and unconscious phantasy. The external world brings meaning to the internal world of the infant's mind as it is formed through unconscious phantasy. Conversely, unconscious phantasy gives meaning to "actual events" in the external world. Simply put, unconscious phantasy accompanies all experience of reality (Hinshelwood, 1991).[2]

---

[1]A figurative term to identify a literal belief there exists, at birth, a constellation of functions. These functions (or defenses) informed by affect, perception, and experience in the world, and defined by mental activity, influence an individual's capacity to adapt to the demands of life. Such a constellation of functions takes shape acquiring a self/boundary (e.g., me vs. not-me) and having the capacity to identify objects. The ego evolves in the form of conscious (e.g., insight, judgment) and unconscious mental representations (phantasies) as it grapples with anxieties that arise in its relations with objects (see Hinshelwood, 1991).

[2]The word *fantasy* has to do with the act of imagining as a process of conscious thought. *Phantasy* has to do with the expression of instinctual impulses as *unconscious* mental activity. The particular content of such impulses, urges or feelings (e.g., wishes, fears, anxieties, love, sorrow, etc.) can together or singularly dominate the mind at any

After birth the infant ego makes a monumental effort to assimilate and cope with its new environment. The infant uses phantasies to help define an external reality which is in turn introjected to reshape the original internal phantasy and thus the child's perception of reality. For example, the young toddler who experiences that something bad (i.e., the gnawing sensation of hunger) is in his or her tummy can in turn experience the feeding by mother as a good object going in and replacing the something bad and thus saving the child. The experience of having good objects safely located inside leads to an internal sense of goodness, self-confidence, and mental stability. So we see that introjection operates as the experiencing of the external world (e.g., the situations the child lives through) taken into the self to become part of the child's inner life. In effect, introjection facilitates construction of the child's internal world.

Projection is also active from the beginning of postnatal life. Projection and introjection can operate simultaneously with the former referring to a capacity on the part of the child to attribute to objects (e.g., human or nonhuman) around his or her feelings, predominantly those of love and hate. Consider the previous example of the hungry toddler but under different circumstances where the wait for nourishment is too long to bear. Such a child would then project those feelings of persecution and attribute them to the external object (i.e., mother) associated with the experience of being deprived of food. Through a process of interaction with the mother, which is continuous, reciprocal, and dynamic, the child gradually moves through a series of positions of ego development which remain active throughout emotional and intellectual maturation.

THE TWO POSITIONS

By the term *position* Klein meant a mental configuration that was characterized by a specific aspect of object relations (e.g.,

---

given moment (see Isaacs, 1948). As the mental representative of an instinctual drive, phantasy can be shaped by basic experiences of either a satisfying/pleasing nature and/

the paranoid–schizoid position and the depressive position). The object stands as the internalized version of an external, but constructed object (e.g., whole or part; animate or inanimate) to whom the ego has accommodated. The object relation would then represent the main type of anxiety, the predominating phantasies, and the preferred defenses.[3] The ego in the infant operates first in the paranoid–schizoid position primarily because the immature ego is as yet unable because it is not developed (strong) enough to do otherwise. That the ego is functioning within this paranoid–schizoid position has more to do with the individual's phenomenological experience of internal and external reality than its age.

Babies during their earliest experiences develop differentiation between themselves and the object as the inner world becomes built up. The infant has experiences such as satisfaction, pleasure, frustration, disappointment, and reacts to these experiences in relation to the state of the ego. The position then refers to the anxieties and the defenses toward the object (e.g., mother) which is or is not providing such things as nurturance, safety, or stimulation. The change to another position would then mean that the ego has achieved the capacity to tolerate earlier anxieties, having now greater confidence in the internal good object. Such a change would mark as a developmental success, albeit never an absolute one. With the developmental accomplishment of overcoming the paranoid–schizoid anxieties and the working through of the depressive position phantasies, the infant is able to go on to develop symbol formation, cognitive, and socialization skills.

The paranoid–schizoid position and the depressive position refer to early object relationships with their own configurations of anxieties, defenses, and phantasies. The infant is

---

or a frustrating/painful nature beginning even before the child leaves mother's womb (Weininger, 1984). Phantasy is the psychological phenomenon that best approximates the biological nature of humans (Hinshelwood, 1994). As the mental corollary of instinct, phantasy is born of every instinctual urge and every impulse experienced by the infant.

[3]The term *defenses* refers to a protective mental state as a function of the ego operating at the level of the unconscious and associated with levels of development ranging in form from primitive through neurotic to mature. An individual holds no conscious awareness of the defenses used to ward off danger (e.g., loss of the object's love) yet as a result may be left with feelings of anxiety, shame, guilt, envy or depression. Reality may come to be distorted or deleted by the severity, rigidity, type, and extent to which the ego avails itself of a given psychological configuration as defense.

involved from the moment of birth in a complex process of action and reaction. The infant ego assumes a responsible position and in a very practical way directs the total creation of the baby's world. This development is due to the complex association of the infant's unconscious phantasies with the parents, in particular the mother. The initial bias in infant behavior may or may not be expressed or may be distorted in its expression, depending on the facilitating effect of the environment. The varieties of positive or negative outcomes of the complex internal drama of the earliest stages of ego development must depend to a great degree on the mother's reactions to the baby's emerging self. The infant is an active, dynamic human being from the first moments of birth; by the same token, he or she is very much in need of sensitive responses and understanding from caretakers.

Framed within the to and fro of development, Klein delineates the psychodynamics of the evolving personality in the form of the paranoid–schizoid and depressive positions. In using the term *position* rather than the Freudian *stage,* Klein's analysis of infant development emphasizes its gradual and flexible movement. She sees the baby's progress through the positions as an economical in-and-out process rather than a series of complete steps to a level from which there is no backtracking. At the same time, Klein recognizes that there can be serious regressions that occur as a result of a transient or chronic situation caused by some trauma. When a parent dies, when a comfortable home setting becomes a stressful one, when the parent cannot provide the necessary food on some fairly adaptable schedule, or when the mother experiences a serious psychological difficulty that robs her of the emotional energy to care for her baby, then the infant is apt to experience a regression. Klein, however, sees the normal progression as one in which the baby progresses to a certain point only to regress a bit and then move on again, gradually accumulating the necessary experiences for further ego development.

The earliest stage of development, the paranoid–schizoid position, is characterized by the split—separation of good and bad—of both the ego and the object with a prevalence of projective processes and of persecutory anxiety and omnipotent phantasy (that one is in control of the world). Persecutory anxiety experienced by the infant is met by processes (defenses) which threaten and have the potential to disrupt and fragment the mind. Splitting as one such process can lead to *projective identification* resulting in a depletion of the ego (e.g., sense of feeling lost; empty) and the ego's subsequent difficulty introjecting good experiences.

PROJECTIVE IDENTIFICATION

Projective identification is a rudimentary example of an aggressive object relationship. It is the forcing of parts of the ego into the object in order to take over the object or what the object contains. It is the phantasy of certain aspects of one's ego being located elsewhere. In projective identification there is a primitive relationship with the object—first the breast and then the whole mother. Klein sees projective identification as a defense where parts of the ego and the internal objects are split off and projected onto the external object, which is then possessed and controlled by the child who identifies with the projected part. Essentially, the child is now saying, "I am giving all these things which I have perceived and associated with me out to you, the object in reality (e.g. mother)," and the object now comes to embody the ego. This process can involve the projection of both good and bad. On the one hand, the child may see the object as allowing him to express aggression, "All my bad parts are now with you; the object can be attacked to get rid of the bad as well as the object." On the other, through identification of the mother (object) with the good, projected in order to keep it safe, the child gains the sense of security from anxiety: "You are the guardian of all my good and I have to stay with you forever (thereby avoiding separation)." Essentially, projective identification is an attempt to gain control over anxiety and hostility.

But if the infant is able to tolerate the discrepancies between phantasy and reality, the split gradually diminishes. The good and bad objects and the good and bad parts come closer together. The infant or child becomes more aware of his or her ambivalent feelings about a mother who is both good and bad (i.e., I hate/I love). Thus the paranoid–schizoid position represents the earliest state of mind beginning in the initial few months of life wherein exists anxieties, defenses, and object relationships.

Klein theorized a further constellation of characteristic anxieties, defenses, and object relationships developing in or around the fourth through to the sixth month of life. The infant reaches a physical and emotional maturity that enables it to begin to integrate its fragmented perceptions of mother. The child is now able to unite the good and bad versions of mother that she or he had previously perceived (the *depressive position*). Klein theorized that the depressive position continues throughout life and is never totally worked through. The integration of part objects to form the whole object leads to the painful recognition by the individual that his or her feelings of love and hate (ambivalence) are directed to the same whole object (e.g., mother). Concern for the object is the central theme in this developmental position. The mix of hate and love for the object results in a sadness Klein termed *depressive anxiety*. In the bringing together of part objects to form the whole there is a concomitant feeling that the latter may be damaged (i.e., as a result of mixing the bad with the good). The emotional turmoil over the phantasied damage is experienced as guilt, loss, and concern leading to feelings of remorse. It is the sense of having done something wrong and the subsequent self-imposed imperative to put things right, to repair the damage. Nevertheless, the hallmark of this position remains the infant's recognition of the object's separateness and independence. The development of symbolic thought and creativity evolve through the achievement of this position with generosity and altruistic intent devoted to the well-being of the object (see Weininger, 1992).

Klein pointed out that fundamentally, for the child, environment or reality means the *object*, that is, the representations of persons within the unconscious mind, in whole or in part (e.g., the nursing breast), including the experience of the functions they perform. The mother (as object) who performs the functions of nurturance is the person on whom the infant depends physically and emotionally. As a result the mother and child share what is the most intense of psychological relationships.

The infant attributes qualitatively different motivations to objects based upon subjective experience at the sensorimotor, perceptual, psychic, and emotional levels. Understandably, the unconscious registration of the experiences of objects and their associated motivations will tend to bias subsequent felt expectancies in relation to the object. As a consequence, the physical approach taken by the infant with regard to objects will also be affected. And so in the infant's mind unconscious and conscious contents can be close and immediately related. Thus attempts to distinguish between phantasy and direct experience of the world will lead us to misunderstand and misconstrue from misconstruing the psychological life of the infant by failing to recognize that the phantasy of the object *is* for the infant the infant's object. For example, consider the very hungry baby who is subject to the unpleasant, even hurtful physical sensations associated with this condition. The baby may be observed turning away from the very nipple which objectively could bring it relief from its suffering. From such behavior we may infer that subjectively for this baby the nipple represents something bad and to be avoided. This phantasy affects not only the infant's behavior, as we have seen, but in turn the feelings, thoughts, and behavior of the maternal figure. For some mothers such behavior by their babies contributes to feelings of inadequacy, anxiety, or anger. Other mothers will respond by redoubling their feelings of sympathy and concern for their babies, and will resort to behaviors that reflect tenderness and sustained patience.

Thus, the intentionally attributed to the object need not reflect reality in an objective sense, but merely reflect the infant's subjective experience. These experiences, it may be stressed, are necessarily conceptualized in relational terms. The infant constructs an internal reality which has a relative degree of correspondence to external reality, including the actual intentions of caretaking figures. It is therefore also important to give appropriate attention to the nature or quality of the caretaker. This is because it is through a continuity of good experiences at the breast that the infant begins to construct a sense of self, other, and the world as essentially benign or good. Thus, Klein recognized that there are two sources of input that shape the infant's experience—the actual nature of external reality and the infant's ability to experience what is offered by reality (e.g., the breast as present and providing vs. absent and withholding).

The premature infant kept in a hospital for a period of time provides a further example of how external reality and the infant's interpretation of that reality may differ. Here the physical problems related to respiration and intake may insure that the most tender ministrations of a parent are experienced as painful (i.e., the environment is experienced as attacking). This baby's world is a very different one from the healthy full term infant with similarly caring parents. Of course the experience of a healthy, full-term infant in need of normal care will again be different where the caregiver is excessively incompetent, overburdened, or directly abusive. It should not be forgotten that normal care refers to the emotional and social as well as the physical realm. Normal needs include, for example, help in the management of those inevitable periods of seemingly inexplicable and extreme distress which all infants are subject to either occasionally or regularly—their fussy, clingy, or crying times. Klein's point is that in addition to physical variables, there are psychological ones that have a bearing upon the infant's ability to make positive use of what is good in the environment. These psychological variables can be expected to vary across infants, the measure of aggressivity being a case in point.

THE ROLE OF AGGRESSION, ANXIETY, AND ENVY

If the first rule of Kleinian theory is the primacy of object relations, the second is the centrality of aggressivity in psychological development and functioning. Aggression is a constitutional feature of human psychological functioning and object relations. Aggression mixes with dependency in shaping the infant and the infant's relation to the world. Aggression is necessary for survival. In its many manifestations both necessary and destructive it may contribute both to the development and/or the disorder of the mind. The fact that aggression exists is beyond qualifications (i.e., whether beneficial or harmful). It is an instinctual force that must be reckoned with in each individual.

Klein believes aggression is stirred up by the trauma of birth, the moment in which the nascent ego recognizes that it trembles between annihilation and becoming. The initial splitting and projection of the bad, by which the vulnerable ego defends itself, leaves behind a residue of hostility which is incorporated into the libido, the basic drive toward becoming and experiencing itself. Without aggression, no doubt, we would perish: Klein speaks of children dying of marasmus (i.e., caloric starvation) as children who are unable to express the aggressive need to reach out, and are then unable to become. Similarly, anxiety, as the result of the perception of internal loss, is part of the human condition. Klein views anxiety as originating from the hostility which must emerge in the initial defensive splitting of good and bad elements by the ego.

In the infant, anxiety is freed from conscious perception of loss and hostility and is experienced as discomfort, an inability to maintain an inner or outer calmness. The unsatisfied baby whose sense of persecution overpowers the internal stability conferred by the good breast is an anxious baby. To try to cope with just the symptoms of anxiety and deny the underlying hostility will not be effective. When the baby can reexperience some of the hostility in doses that have been made manageable by the mediation of the good enough mother, his or her anxiety will lessen.

Anxiety evoked in the baby as a result of his or her own hostility affects the infant in at least two ways: (1) the baby becomes afraid of being annihilated by his or her own feelings, that is, afraid of being destroyed by the aggression, if it is liberated; or (2) the baby's fears are focused on external objects and their sadistic feelings are turned toward these external objects, and therefore these objects become a focal source of danger. For example, since the mother is the first object to give satisfaction, she is also the first object to withhold it, and all of the baby's feelings of intolerable fear of danger and extermination are projected onto the mother. The internal danger has been exchanged for an external one. However, in doing so, the baby must now seek ways to protect him- or herself and their immature ego from this object. Thus the basic defense system evolves: introject the good and project the bad.

The war between love and hate starts at birth, accompanied by the experience of pain, fear, and rage. If the infant is to survive, it must split the good and bad. The good becomes the ideal and helps the infant to deal with the bad, the persecutor, who must be sent away. In this process the mother participates, unconsciously forming an alliance with her infant that helps the baby maintain the goodness. Because she does this, the mother–baby relationship becomes idealized for both. In Klein's view, this ideal provides the prototype of love, trust, gratitude, and hope; there cannot be an effective development of these basic feelings without the idealized relationship. This is the foundation for hope—mother is always there as an ally.

Klein also developed the first psychological theory of envy, which remains one of the least understood and most controversial elements of the theory. In Klein's view the illusion of oneness, that is, the felt experience of being the receptacle and wellspring of all pleasing and satisfying experiences, meets up with the beginning awareness that the source of satisfaction-goodness resides outside the self. When such a challenge to the illusion of oneness occurs the infant becomes subject to two potential phantasies and affective responses. The first is gratitude toward the object which has come to be recognized as the source of relief and pleasure. The second is envy of the object which contains all good things.

Evolving from the more basic feelings of bad and good, envy enters into clear view as a distinct emotion experienced in terms of real relationships. However, early on it is the most primitive and fundamental emotional reaction (i.e., primary envy is the envy of the breast and occurs within the paranoid–schizoid position). Envy forces the person to be as good and capable as the object but, on finding that this is impossible, attempts to spoil the object's goodness in order to remove whatever is envied. Anger resulting from the feelings that someone else, namely the mother, possesses and enjoys things that are desirable, forces the infant to turn the good into the bad, and by projection to render it no longer desirable. The infant is then unwilling to introject the object, because it is not only useless but would be internally destructive. While the ego was within the paranoid–schizoid position, the phantasy was to take in the loved object, the breast, and to establish it entirely within the ego. But external reality aspects, such as hunger, fatigue, and ill-health, create feelings of frustration and deprivation, and complete gratification is never achieved, and as a consequence envy of all the goodness of the object is experienced. Because of envy, the necessary good introjections cannot be achieved; envy is destructive. It is "the angry feeling because another person possesses and enjoys something desirable—the envious impulse being to take it away or to spoil it" (Klein, 1957, p. 181).

Envy appears to be expressed as attacks upon the mother's body (e.g., biting of the nipple; scratching of the breast) in an attempt to take the desired object, to have it all to oneself. This original envy is the ego's relation to a single object, the phantasy of a singular possessive relationship to and desire for the breast-mother. Envy includes the desire to put badness into the desirable object in order to render it less desirable. When defenses against envy are not successful these envious feelings become too powerful to be contained within the mother–child relationship. As a result, persecutory anxiety arises in the infant and is experienced as a continual impulse to destructively attack. For example, a baby for whom a sense of internal gratification cannot be maintained will become angry and more demanding of the breast leaving mother feeling she is an inadequate nurturer. The baby driven by greed and the anxiety of a phantasied retaliation will not respond to the affection and attention given by the mother. In fact, mother's affection seems to accentuate the baby's greed. Greed does not permit the goodness of the object to be assimilated into the ego. In such a pathological state the capacity to regain an effective balance is lost.

When the ego phantasizes excessive envy, the splitting process or primary defense of the paranoid–schizoid position is
hindered. The ideal breast only intensifies envy and is therefore
continually damaged or destroyed. Introjection of an ideal
breast, with a subsequent sense of identification and satisfaction, is thwarted. In this way the infant will undermine their
own capacity to experience the good object, thus jeopardizing
the development of a sense of other, self, and the world as
good. No object can provide the sense of love or care. Rather,
a feeling of despair is experienced, along with a sense of continual persecution coming from the damaged objects. Since there
are no good introjections, the ego remains at an immature
level with the persistent phantasy that "Others have everything," and the need to try to destroy because of envy.

With effective care in a trusting relationship, the infant
works through the paranoid–schizoid position, with its ruling
persecutory phantasy; as babies enter the depressive position
their ego experiences the ambivalence of hate and love toward
the loved object, the phantasy of harming the object by making
excessive demands upon it, and of losing the love of the object.
Within the depressive position the ego experiences guilt for
demands and aggression toward the loved object, along with
the desire to repair any damages that might have been done
to it. These phantasies are the defenses and anxieties of the
depressive position. The phantasy of loss and actual loss
through weaning, for example, created the groundwork for
these depressive anxieties, as if the ego phantasized that it had
taken too much or had damaged the breast. However, since
reparation did not provide complete satisfaction, envy of the
desired object arose.

The baby has created the phantasy of what the breast
should be: an inexhaustible object, with an unlimited flow of
love and milk. When there are deprivations and frustrations,
the baby sees the breast as the cause of these and sees it as bad:
It keeps milk, it keeps love, it keeps tenderness to itself. So he
or she hates and envies what is felt to be a mean and ungiving,
grudging breast. Any kind of emotional or social deprivation
will increase the enormous feeling of primary envy, and in our

work we see this in parentally deprived children who continually express the feeling of never having had enough, always demanding more. Sometimes these children seem to want an unusual amount of food. They do not seem to be able to eat when their plate is neatly or sparsely filled. Only when they have taken more onto their plate do they eat. It is almost as if they were destroying, robbing, or trying to exhaust the source of food. Some of these children will frequently vomit after eating—perhaps because they ate too fast, or perhaps because the desired food, in association with their envy, created the phantasy of ingesting something bad and poisonous. Envy will occur even when the breast is satisfactory; that is, the mother is "good enough" and feeds her baby well. When there is an easy flow of milk from the breast (or bottle), part of the phantasy becomes: "I can't get it all at once, it's still coming and I can't take in any more." The breast, as phantasized by the infant, should be both within the baby and fill it continuously, and since he or she must stop to breathe and the milk is still available, ironically, envy of this satisfactory breast can be experienced.

With envy the capacity for enjoyment is spoiled. By the same token, feelings of enjoyment and the gratitude that is then occasioned counter the feelings produced by envy. The child's relationship with the mother's breast becomes the foundation for the stability and strength of the ego. With good internal objects the infant will not be damaged by a temporary state of envy. A well-loved, well-mothered child does experience hate, envy, and greed but the ego will have the capacity to regard reality accurately and adjust the destructive phantasy to be more in accord with reality. Every child will have some of these feelings, but within the loving, stable relationship he or she will be able to maintain an effective balance. The strength and stability of the ego are based on the regaining of the good object not only once but time and time again. The repetition is the important aspect, for then the ego can experience the transient state of losing the good object without harm to the child's basic feelings of goodness about him- or herself. As the child is able to internalize the good object again and again, it increases in value. The ego's stability and ability to perceive reality are enhanced and envy is held at bay.

THE PLAY TECHNIQUE

In developing a technique appropriate for work with children Melanie Klein recognized that children's play could perform the same function as did verbal free association with adult patients. Both give access to the unconscious of the individual and thus to the nature of the conflicts, anxieties, desires, and phantasies that comprise the inner world. Kleinian technique is perhaps most sharply distinguished from other forms of psychoanalytic practice in the work with children. There is an explicit prohibition against making judgments, giving instruction, or attempting to alter the behavior of the child either to suit the demands of others or one's own sense of propriety. Play is the way children try to understand and to control outside situations and events. However, play at home or in the classroom is very different from play in the therapeutic treatment room where it becomes the medium of communication between the child's ego and the therapist. Klein argued theoretically and preserved in practical terms a set of defining technical features of analytic practice within her play technique.

In play psychotherapy, the therapist is trying to help children carry on with their growth and to help them get rid of some of the mechanisms that prevent growth. The psychoanalytic framework provides an understanding of these mechanisms, but it is play which is itself a therapy. The therapist comes in when the play is blocked or becomes so frightening for the child that it stops. The therapist learns from the play what has frightened the child and offers an interpretation. Thus, for example, a frightening dream may be played out, but the anxiety originally provoked by the dream may be so frightening that the child stops playing. The therapist needs to understand the dream and its frightening aspects by observing the play, the child's manipulation of particular materials and toys, and the feelings with which the child endows them.

Materials

Toys and the setting are important in the play technique. The toys used are little dolls: mothers, fathers, a variety of children, small and large cars, trains, airplanes, domestic and wild animals, bricks, balls, a small house, fences, paper, Plasticine™, string, pencils, paints, and crayons. The toys are usually very simple so that the child can use them "in many different situations, actual or phantasized, according to the material coming up in his play. The fact that the child can thus simultaneously present a variety of experiences and situations also makes it possible for us to arrive at a more coherent picture of the workings of the mind" (Klein, 1964, p. 119). Each child's toys are kept in a box assigned for his or her exclusive use and is brought to each session by the therapist. No one else uses these toys and this means that each child's objects are safe from intrusion by others. To the child this means that no one else can damage his or her objects, no one else will see what he or she does to them, and that the therapist considers them sufficiently important to keep them safe. Essentially, the box becomes the container for the child, the repository of his or her feelings which will be guarded by and known only to the child and the therapist.

Children are often interested in other children's boxes (i.e., the possibility that their therapist may be seeing other children). While no child's box is shown to another, discussion about why they are interested may ensue. Usually they begin to understand their curiosity about events and things that are happening around them, events that were previously too frightening for them to talk or even to think about. Their curiosity is not stifled; the therapist encourages children to explore within the safety of the relationship between the two of them and within the special room (Weininger, 1982). The room itself is simple, and the child always returns to the same room for sessions. The same room, at the same time of day, for the same length of time, has particular meaning for children. They do not just become "attached" to the room, but rather it acquires the meaning of being the place where this intimate relationship between child and therapist occurs. Klein points out that the "transference relationship can only be established and maintained if the patient can feel that the consulting room, or the playroom, indeed the whole analysis, is something separate from his ordinary life" (Klein, 1964, p. 279). Nothing in the room should be easily breakable: The floor should be made of material that is easy to clean, the room should have a water supply, a table and at least two chairs, a small couch, and walls that are sturdy enough to withstand some aggressive activity without being damaged.

Toys represent important objects, and the child transfers feelings and thoughts to them. The toys themselves are then used in the same way as the child might want to use the original object (i.e., the toy is equal to the object). Sometimes a child will tell you "This piece of chalk is my mother, this piece is my father, and this is me," and then play out some family drama which he or she could not talk about in relation to actual people, but can do so by using the chalk pieces as if they were actual people. It is important to find out what and/or who the toys represent and, as Klein points out, "who these [toy figures] people [are] meant to be, what their relation to each other is, and what they are supposed to be doing" (Klein, 1964, p. 280). The child talks about these toys as people when he or she "comes to realize that the toys stand in his mind for people and therefore the feelings he expresses toward the toys relate to people. . . . He is gaining insight into the fact that one part of his mind is unknown to him, in other words, that the unconscious exists" (Klein, 1964, p. 280). Children who suggest that the toy figures are mommy, daddy, and siblings offer the opportunity to explore their unconscious world of phantasy through dramatic play (Weininger, 1979, 1982). Therapists should give an interpretation in language appropriate for the child and in words that are understandable. An interpretation implies that the play item or event is a disguise for the expression of an object relationship. It is important therefore to know what the toys symbolize to the child, and what words the child uses to talk about the item or event. We have found that verbal clarification of the symbols enhances the interpretation and seems to strengthen the transference relationship.

The Transference

The transference relationship is a relationship between the child and the therapist. It *is* the object relationship. The transference goes on as long as the therapist remains "neutral." By "neutral" I mean the therapist does not reveal secrets to the parents and is able to provide effective containment by not becoming encumbered by parental wishes and anxieties for the child. This transference relationship contains within it love, fear, anger, anxiety, guilt, pain, and all the maneuvers the child will go through to try to undo, or destroy, or deny the unconscious object relationships. Through the transference process the child projects his or her internal object world with its interwoven mix of inner and outer reality brought about by early experience. The therapist then becomes the good or bad parent—"a new edition of an old object relationship" (Winnicott, 1986, p. 75). Through the therapist's interpretive comments the child begins to understand his or her feelings toward their parents and gradually is able to integrate the projections as their own.

Transference is a very powerful relationship. It has its basis in the earliest phantasy object relationship and makes use of projection and introjection. It is as if the transference provides the opportunity for the "reverie" (Bion, 1962) process where the parent takes in the anxious, difficult feelings of the baby, thinks about them, and gives them back to the baby when the baby is strong enough to handle these powerful feelings. The *containing* aspect of transference is the therapist's capacity to hold, to clarify, and to help identify strong feelings and poorly defined thoughts and actions, to reduce the general feelings of anxiety and distress so that the child can move on to become aware of these states, and then gradually "take them back." This is done primarily through interpretation within the transference process. Klein held that the child's "intellectual capacities are often underrated and that, in fact, he understands more than he is credited with" (1964, p. 284).

The child begins to realize his or her painful phantasies do not damage the therapist, and that the therapist lives on in spite of the hostility, envy, and persecutory feelings projected by the child. The child slowly constructs her or his own effective and resilient container and gives herself or himself the time to think about problems and feelings rather than impulsively projecting them and then worrying about consequences. The therapist does not try to deny or to get rid of these feelings, but rather provides the container and the reverie so that the child gradually takes these feelings back.

The unconscious phantasy, revealed in the child's play, comes about and is interpreted within the transference relationship. The therapist becomes the repository for the child's earliest phantasies. How the child will respond becomes a function of the therapist's ability to accept and contain, and to interpret when appropriate, the anxiety and defense mechanisms (e.g., projection, splitting, projective identification) attached to the phantasy. Children project their early phantasies onto the therapist by the means of play materials. The therapist interprets the play as the symbolic equivalent of early object relationships along with the feelings of anger, pain, dependency, and fear attached to these early objects and the relationships the child phantasizes them to be. These interpretations allow less painful, less threatening, or even less powerful objects to be introjected, but basically help children to explore further through playing and to talk through the characteristics of their early object relationships.

The Role of the Therapist

Within the therapy room the therapist is a special adult, for not only is he or she with the child for the full session, but is also interested in whatever the child is doing. However, the therapist must also be in control of the setting and not allow the child to harm him- or herself or the therapist and must be able to stop any activity that is dangerous to the child, the furniture, or contents of the special room. Children need to be contained, not simply because they might hurt themselves or others, but also because by damaging materials, destroying furniture, walls or windows, they are symbolically destroying objects that are important to them. By causing damage, the child will anticipate retaliation, and will behave accordingly. Either the child will become more aggressive or withdraw from a fearful reality. In either case, nothing is gained other than that the child once again believes that the world which was dangerous before entering into therapy, is still dangerous. If a child attempts to destroy the room, the therapist not only prevents this but also interprets it (Weininger, 1989).

When Johnny, a 3-year-old, said he would kick the wall and knock it down, he was told that I thought he was very angry with his therapist. Johnny wanted me to bring in more toys and it was explained to him that this would not occur because if it did he would think that the toys we now had were not good enough. Johnny was trying to avoid the therapeutic relationship by getting so many toys in the playroom that he would be able to flit from toy to toy and never become involved with anything; that is, never become involved in the therapeutic relationship. Johnny's response was to look sullen, get pouty, and lie down on the floor. When he was offered the interpretation that he wanted to be a little baby again and get all the good things, he got up and began to kick the wall. Johnny needed a lot of good objects, but he could not introject them because he was afraid that the badness inside him would make good objects bad as well. Johnny saw himself as a very bad boy, and if not given new toys he could get angry and blaming. By my interpreting his need to keep things good, he was able to talk about how bad he was, how he wanted to take everything away from his little brother, even eat him up because "he got everything from mommy all the time." The therapist makes interpretations to help the child "revise these early relations at their root and thus effectively diminish his anxieties" (Klein, 1964, p. 285). These interpretations are directed to the level at which the therapist considers the anxiety to be dominant and at which the child is primarily behaving and are made always within the transference, that is, within the object relationship.

Sometimes therapists have the reward of clear confirmations of their interpretations even outside the therapeutic setting. For example, when Kevin, a 3-year-old patient, said that he was "sad." It was possible to interpret to him his concern about helping to repair and restore his mother who had recently undergone an appendectomy. Kevin made a round object out of clay on which he made some deep impressions with his fingers. He went on to paint each indentation with a different color and when this was completed he said that this was a gift for his mother. His mother said that Kevin had wrapped the gift in tinfoil and presented it to her while she was still in bed. Kevin said that he made it "special" for her, that he made sure it was clean by wrapping it in tinfoil, and she did not have to worry about him because he would always be a good boy. Kevin's mother told him that he was a good boy, that she loved him, and that his gift made her feel much better.

She confirmed Kevin's attempts at reparations by accepting the gift and telling him that it helped her feel better. Thus, a conscious act on the part of Kevin is responded to by a conscious act on the part of his mother. His mother's response confirmed for Kevin his phantasy of being responsible in some way for her operation. Mother accepting Kevin's gift became proof that she was damaged and in need of reparation. By mother accepting the gift the result was a diminishing of Kevin's sense of anxiety. Kevin sorted out his phantasy (i.e., that he hurt mommy and she needed an operation to get out the bad thing in her tummy) from her real physical problem. He gradually accepted the thought that he was not responsible, but still felt sad because his mommy had to have an operation, but happy because he could make her feel nice because as he said "I gave her a nice thing." The sadness at her pain became reality based and not phantasy directed. Kevin could feel sad and yet not think he caused his mother's problem. However this sort of confirmation is not always readily available.

Another kind of confirmation is often provided by the child's immediate reaction to an interpretation. A change in posture or facial expression, or words, or play activity may indicate the effectiveness of a particular interpretation. After hearing an interpretation about his rivalry with his sibling, 4-year-old Charles said, "I don't want to talk about that anymore." When told that he was really angry with his brother and his mother, Charles replied, "Don't talk funny, I won't listen to you," and he went to play in the sand box. Within 10 minutes he returned to where his therapist was sitting and said that he had bad dreams about dogs, about a big dog biting a puppy. Talk about the dream and I think the interpretation created the possibility for him to describe his dream even though he seemed to reject the interpretation itself.

Whether the interpretation can be tolerated-accepted by the child, is at times, secondary to the emotion it evokes in the child. If words of understanding are offered to the child within the confines of the therapeutic setting this will allow the child to hear things in a more uncompromising manner. In such an environment the child is allowed to think and feel and say whatever he or she wishes. This freedom is, of course, conveyed at the beginning in the gradual development of rapport and trust in the safety of the therapeutic setting. Given these conditions, any words spoken by the therapist by way of offered interpretations can more directly be responded to emotionally. Once the emotion is felt the child can then sense whether he or she feels frightened by or safe with such emotion. The latter feeling will emerge if the beginning work of the therapy has been successfully achieved. The degree of safety the child feels will determine to what extent he or she is then able to engage the therapist.

Children become anxious and upset but do not know why, and to ask them why generally just increases their anxiety because they cannot "do" or "give" what is expected of them. Such questions strengthen the sadistic characteristics of children' superegos and add to their pain. The young child then has the phantasy of destructive, punishing internal objects (phantasy of parents) which constitute "a particularly savage superego with which the child's ego cannot cope" (Segal, 1979, p. 38). Anxiety, pain, and symptoms become split-off bad parts with which the child cannot cope and which are transferred to the therapist in play psychotherapy. Interpretation is used to help reduce children's anxiety so that they can begin to talk about and play out the things that have created the problems for them. This approach entails understanding the play communication, not to try to get the child to "warm up" to the

therapist, but to rely "on the fact that this interpretation re-
lieves unconscious anxiety to maintain the child's interest and
cooperation" (Segal, 1972, p. 405).

Play, drawings, constructions, and verbalizations help the
therapist to understand the internal conflicts, phantasies, and
problems and provide an avenue to the child's unconscious.
But, as we have seen from the child's point of view, drawings
act also as a form of reparation (re: Kevin). The act of creation
and giving gifts to a real mother diminishes the dread of the
phantasized terrifying mother. The child can imagine her re-
paired by his or her gift or art and existing in the "full possession of her strength and beauty" (Klein, 1929, p. 443).

How do you play with the child, how much do you do with
the child? A child may, for example, want the therapist to fly
around the room or eat the Plasticine, or to crawl on the floor
as if he or she were a worm. I do not think the therapist doing
these things, if possible, would strengthen the transference relationship. The therapist should be part of the play, participate
but not limit the phantasy expression of the child. One does
not know how the child wants the therapist to crawl, or how to
fly, and if attempted would prevent the expression that the
child gives to his or her phantasies. However, the therapist will
engage in many degrees of pretense from the possible (pretend
to eat) to the impossible (pretend to fly) and help a child to
fill in all the descriptions about the pretending. To participate
in a more direct way is to become involved in a form of peda-
gogy rather than therapy. It is true a therapist's involvement is
not limited by the pragmatics of the physical world or his or
her adult conceptions of reality. It is, however, limited by the
therapist's understanding of and desire to respect, by never
broaching the boundaries that define, the impossible possibilities of a child's phantasy.

In other words, by unsolicited actions and movement, the
therapist risks defining (i.e., interpreting in a nonverbal way)
that part of the play in which they are involved by virtue of
their own thought and feeling. This would, in essence, confuse
the interpretation with the play. Responding to the child's request, regardless of how much direction given will inevitably
bring a personal and subjective interpretation to the play. The

therapist's personality then becomes a part of the play and counterproductive to the process, because it is precisely the therapist's role to give interpretation *of* the play and not *to* the play (the latter, of course, contaminates the opportunity to aid the child in gaining insight into what exactly is his or her unique reality). This is not play in the recreational sense, but play at the service of a mental and emotional reworking for the child of their experiences in the world. Therefore, the play must remain completely the child's, seen and felt by the child as being completely their own. It is the child's world we wish to understand; therefore, anything we can do to promote the child's exploration of his or her thought and feeling in a safe place is most beneficial to the therapeutic effort. It is incumbent upon the therapist to avoid becoming confused about the function of the play. Of course, there are times when the therapist may join the child in play but then it is the joining and the child's willingness to share in the event that demands understanding (i.e., the ways and issues around which the child wishes to relate).

Termination

The termination process is part of the ongoing therapy. The therapist continues to interpret the anxieties with the play and the child's verbalizations. Transference interpretations also continue to be made, but now for the child the therapist becomes a real person and the separation from, and loss of, this person have to be worked through. The loss does occasion the pain of grief; the experiences of successful work completed with the help of an accepting and kind person provide the basis for the impending grief at termination. Separation, loss, and mourning must be dealt with and this occupies the period of the termination process (Klein, 1950b). This process is "bound to stir up painful feelings and revive early anxieties; it amounts to a state of mourning" (Klein, 1950a, p. 80). Even after the therapy has ended the child still has to carry out by him- or herself part of the work of mourning. For example, a child functioning within the depressive position will usually feel abandoned and must be helped to recognize his or her internal strength. However, the child may react to terminating by symptom development, unhappiness, anxiety or dissatisfaction. With the awareness of an impending termination depressive anxieties are evoked once again and the child believes he or she has done something wrong or has been bad. Interpretation relating to the desire to prolong treatment helps the child to understand that he or she is not bad and has not taken too much from the therapist, and that the therapist is not tired and fed up with the child, sick, bored, or busy with someone else. Gradually, children can carry the therapist in their thoughts, and at the same time gain more good internal objects which makes them feel that they have "rights to their objects" (Balint, 1950, p. 197).

CONCLUSION

The life and work of Melanie Klein cannot be overlooked by the serious psychoanalytic practitioner. Equally, the student of child development has much to profit from understanding the essence of Klein's work. It is true that there has been much contention about and criticism of her ideas. Klein's work has often been neglected, her ideas have been used but there has been some reluctance to cite her as a reference, and the spirit of her creative and intuitive mind has often been ignored. In fact, it remains almost as it was over thirty years ago when Zetzel (1961), in a tribute to Klein, wrote "Many contemporary psychoanalysts are relatively unfamiliar with her work . . . in this country [America] in particular, failure to acknowledge her contribution is so prevalent that papers on infantile development and early responses to separation and loss typically omit detailed reference to her concept of the depressive position, to her recognition of the positive functions of early anxiety . . . to her formulations concerning the role of symbol formation in the learning process" (p. 442). This, I feel, is to the mutual detriment of all psychoanalytic schools (Weininger, 1996).

REFERENCES

Aron, L., & Harris, A., Eds. (1993), *The Legacy of Sándor Ferenczi.* London: Analytic Press.

Balint, M. (1950), On the termination of analysis. *Internat. J. Psycho-Anal.,* 31:196–199.

Bion, W. R. (1962), *Learning from Experience.* New York: Basic Books.

Brenner, C. (1973), *An Elementary Textbook of Psychoanalysis,* rev. ed. Garden City, NY: Anchor Books.

Fairbairn, W. R. D. (1952), *Psychoanalytic Studies of the Personality.* London: Routledge.

Freud, A. (1969), *Indications for Child Analyses and Other Papers 1945–1956.* London: Hogarth Press.

Freud, S. (1918), From the history of an infantile neurosis. *Standard Edition,* 17:1–122. London: Hogarth Press, 1955.

———(1916–1917), Introductory Lectures on Psycho-Analysis. *Standard Edition,* 15, 16. London: Hogarth Press, 1966.

Greenberg, J. R., & Mitchell, S. A. (1983), *Object Relations in Psychoanalytic Theory.* Cambridge, MA: Harvard University Press.

Grosskurth, P. (1986), *Melanie Klein: Her World and Her Work.* New York: Knopf.

Grotstein, J. (1992), Foreword. In: O. Weininger, *Melanie Klein: From Theory to Reality.* London: Karnac, pp. ix–xvii.

Hinshelwood, R. D. (1991), *A Dictionary of Kleinian Thought.* London: Free Association Books.

*———(1994), *Clinical Klein: From Theory to Practice.* New York: Basic Books.

Hughes, J. M. (1989), *Reshaping the Psychoanalytic Domain: The Work of Melanie Klein, W. R. D. Fairbairn, and D. Winnicott.* Berkeley, CA: University of California Press.

Isaacs, S. (1948), The nature and function of phantasy. *Internat. J. Psycho-Anal.,* 29:73–79.

Klein, M. (1921), Eine Kinderentwicklung [The development of a child]. *Imago,* 7:251–309.

———(1929), Personification in the play of children. *Internat. J. Psycho-Anal.,* 10:193–204.

———(1950a), *Contributions to Psycho-Analysis.* London: Hogarth Press.

———(1950b), On the criteria for the termination of an analysis. *Internat. J. Psycho-Anal.,* 31:204.

* Recommended reading.

————(1957), *Envy and Gratitude*. London: Tavistock.

————(1959), Our adult world and its root in infancy. *Hum. Rel.*, 12:291–303.

————(1964), The psychoanalytic play technique. In: *Child Psychotherapy, Practice and Theory*, ed. M. R. Haworth. New York: Basic Books, pp. 119–121; 277–286.

Lindon, J. A. (1966), Melanie Klein: Her view of the unconscious. In: *Psychoanalytic Pioneers*, ed. F. Alexander, S. Eisenstein, & M. Grotjahn. New York: Basic Books, pp. 360–372.

Marx, M. H., & Cronan-Hillix, W. A. (1987), *Systems and Theories in Psychology*, 4th ed. New York: McGraw-Hill.

Piaget, J. (1983), Piaget's theory. In: *Handbook of Child Psychology, Vol. 1, History, Theory, and Methods*, ed. P. H. Mussen. New York: Wiley.

Segal, H. (1972), Melanie Klein's technique of child analysis. In: *Handbook of Child Psycho-Analysis*, ed. B. B. Wolman. Toronto: Van Nostrand.

————(1979), *Klein*. Sussex, U.K.: Harvester.

Spillius, E. B., Ed. (1988), *Melanie Klein Today: Developments in Theory and Practice*, Vol. 1. London: Routledge.

Weininger, O. (1979), *Play and Education: The Basic Tool for Early Childhood Learning*. Springfield, IL: Charles C Thomas.

————(1982), *Out of the Minds of Babes: The Strength of Children's Feelings*. Springfield, IL: Charles C Thomas.

————(1984), *The Clinical Psychology of Melanie Klein*. Springfield, IL: Charles C Thomas.

*————(1989), *Children's Phantasies: The Shaping of Relationships*. London: Karnac.

*————(1992), *Melanie Klein: From Theory to Reality*. London: Karnac.

*————(1993), *View from the Cradle: Children's Emotions in Everyday Life*. London: Karnac.

*————(1996), *Being and Not Being: Clinical Applications of the Death Instinct*. London: Karnac.

Winnicott, D. W. (1986), *Home Is Where We Start From: Essays by a Psychoanalyst*. New York: W. W. Norton.

Zetzel, E. R. (1961), Melanie Klein: 1882–1960. *Psychoanal. Quart.*, 30:420–425.

10.

Dreams and Other Aspects of Jungian Psychology

Aryeh Maidenbaum, Ph.D.

WHAT IS JUNGIAN PSYCHOLOGY ABOUT?

There is a well-known story in Jungian circles, told about Jung himself. A psychiatrist from another city in Switzerland came to consult with Jung about a particular patient. After hearing the case history in question, Jung presented his view of the situation, including diagnosis and prognosis. The psychiatrist, taken aback, mentioned to Jung that he had already spoken to someone at the Jungian Institute and had been given a different assessment of the patient's problems and recommended treatment plan. After hesitating for a moment, Jung's response was: "Thank God I'm Jung and not Jungian."

This brief, anecdotal, story reveals much about Jung's approach to psychotherapy. For unlike Freud, and founders of other schools of thought who followed him, Jung did not attempt to systematically set up an approach that was "Jungian" per se. Indeed, his feelings on the subject were that the world of psychology is diverse and there is not one theory to explain everything and/or help everybody. In fact, Jung's exact words on the subject were "When I am not sure about a patient I give him books by Freud and Adler and say, 'make your choice.' "

(Jung, 1936, p. 143). Indeed, training with an analyst taught (and analyzed) by Jung, by anyone's standards a Jungian, I was taken to task for using the word *Jungian*. Meanwhile, as irony and fate would have it, twenty years after this initial reprimand, literally hundreds of books have been written on the "Jungian" approach to psychotherapy. Moreover, as if to emphasize the distance between the earlier and later generation of Jungians, courses in "Jungian" psychology are taught at universities throughout the world with the term freely used at numerous international, and interdisciplinary, conferences.

Nevertheless, in Jung's well-known Tavistock Lectures, his groundbreaking work on "psychological types," and indeed throughout his life, he made it quite clear that neither he nor any particular school of psychology held a monopoly on the correct way to approach the psyche. He wrote: "I know that what Freud says agrees with many people, and I assume that these people have exactly the kind of psychology that he describes. Adler, who has entirely different views, also has a large following, and I am convinced that many people have an Adlerian psychology. I too have a following . . . and it consists presumably of people who have my psychology" (Jung, 1936, p. 140).

Jung basically validates a viewpoint that in order to be an effective psychotherapist, one must be familiar with different psychological approaches and techniques—whether the classical Freudian or that of object relations, self psychology, or communicative psychoanalysis, to name but a few. "I have patients with whom I have to make a Freudian analysis and go into all the details which Freud has correctly described. I have other cases which force me to an Adlerian point of view, because they have a power complex," Jung stated over a half-century ago (Jung, 1936, p. 140).

It is clear that Jungian psychology does in fact exist as a separate, unique approach that can be utilized by clinicians in the healing process. It is an integrated theory. It is something that Jung himself practiced and would sanction today. Nevertheless, interestingly enough, while Jung in effect was exhorting his students to familiarize themselves with different approaches to the psyche, few academic or psychoanalytic training institutions have offered courses or instruction in the Jungian approach to therapy. Inclusion of Jung's psychology and ideas within this volume is commendable and representing at long last a more open attitude toward the "Jungian" message, if not toward Jung the messenger.

Perhaps a helpful way to begin delineating a "Jungian" approach to the psyche is to point out some of the contributions Jung brought to the field of depth psychology and understand how and why his approach helps heal, and is of practical use in the consulting room. We should remember that until his break with Freud, Jung was considered by Freud as his "crown prince, the heir apparent" to the Freudian leadership worldwide. In effect, at that point in time, Jung was considered the leading Freudian in the world after Freud. In fact, one of the basic tenets of all psychoanalytic training originated with Jung's suggestion to Freud that analysts should themselves undergo a "training analysis." In short, Freud looked to Jung as not only his successor but as the one who would lead the psychoanalytic movement into the future and ultimately validate Freud's own work. In a letter written by Freud to Jung, dated January 19, 1909, he declares that "We are certainly getting ahead; if I am Moses, then you are Joshua and will take possession of the promised land of psychiatry, which I shall only be able to glimpse from afar" (Freud to Jung, 1/19/1909 in McGuire, 1974, p. 197).

Through the encouragement of his mentor Eugene Bleuler, Jung read Freud's ground-breaking book, *The Interpretation of Dreams* published at the turn of the century (Freud, 1900). Shortly thereafter, Jung began a correspondence with Freud which lasted until their break which occurred in 1912. The correspondence, punctuated by several powerful meetings between the two, and including a joint trip to the United States in 1909, led to a strong bond between Freud and Jung for the next decade or so. One must remember, however, that Jung's first exposure to the field of depth psychology came through his own work in the realm of psychiatry (i.e., dealing with psychoses and institutionalized patients). Additionally, Bleuler, father figure, mentor, and supervisor to Jung, is known for his pioneering work in the area of schizophrenia. Indeed, the term *schizophrenia,* and its basic diagnosis, was first coined by Bleuler during Jung's period at Burgholzli (in Zurich), one of the leading psychiatric hospitals in Europe at the time.

Meanwhile, Sigmund Freud, because he was Jewish, was snubbed by the University of Vienna and denied the professorship he both desired and deserved. Additionally, Freud was ostracized by the city's medical and social establishments for threatening the accepted mores of the time with his emphasis on sex as part and parcel of the neurotic symptoms he was describing in his work. Understandably, Freud welcomed an alliance with Jung who was both connected with established and respected psychiatric circles and, equally important, a member of the Christian world. In Freud's eyes, Jung had much to offer in terms of having Freud's pioneering work accepted as more than just a "Jewish psychology." However, and this is crucial to understanding some of the ensuing differences between the two men, Jung's psychology and ideas about the structure and dynamics of the psyche came from Jung's extensive experience and understanding of the psychoses and the psychotic process, while Freud's innovations came wholly through his work with neuroses.

ARCHETYPES AND THE COLLECTIVE UNCONSCIOUS

Jung's fascination with what he termed the *collective unconscious* was a direct result of his early career as an alienist (psychiatrist) at the Burgholzli Hospital. The manner in which Jung first became aware of what he eventually termed *archetypes* is described in several places. The most revealing summation of how he first formulated his idea on the nature of the collective unconscious was made by Jung in his discussion of the ramblings of a psychotic patient he treated for schizophrenia. According to Jung, his discovery of the collective unconscious, an impersonal nature underlying the psyche, occurred during his period at the renowned Burgholzli Psychiatric Hospital in Zurich when a patient took him aside and over to a window one day and said: " 'Stand here and look at the sun. What do you see?' " The doctor, understandably, saw only the sun, whereupon the patient said: 'But don't you see the tail on the sun?' The doctor answered 'I am not so sure.' 'Well,' said the patient, 'look carefully and move your head as you look; you will see the tail move. The moving tail is the source of the wind' " (Meier, 1959, p. 18).

The incident took place at the time Jung was Bleuler's assistant at Burgholzli. Coincidentally, or synchronistically as Jungians would put it, at the time Jung happened to be reading a recently published, ancient Greek papyrus. As C. A. Meier, Jung's one time assistant and himself the first President of the Jung Institute of Zurich, relates it, Jung took notice of the fact that at a certain stage initiates into the Greek mysteries were asked to look at the sun where they were told to look for a tube hanging down, "swinging first to the right producing the East Wind, and then to the left producing the West Wind." The patient at Burgholzli had not only been hospitalized for many years, but was also uneducated and knew no Greek. There was no possibility that the patient could have seen the recently published Greek papyrus that Jung was then reading and, had he even seen it, he could not have read it (Meier, 1959, p. 19).

To many, this incident might have been dismissed as sheer coincidence but Jung remembered it years later. During the course of his researches Jung found many similarities between the fantasies of mentally disturbed people and the motifs of mythology texts and folk literature. Ultimately, he was able to discern many of these myths in the dreams of his patients and of children who could not possibly have had any intellectual knowledge of them. Subsequent research has borne out the fact that myths of different peoples, with no possibility of cultural contact, bear striking resemblances between them.

The Jungian use of the term *Archetype* (from the Greek word *Arche,* meaning origin or beginning and *Type,* standing for imprint or pattern, together signifying inherited patterns or forms) is describing the psyche's predisposition to produce over and over again the same mythological ideas, at times (collectively) in the form of myths and at other times (individually) through the appearance of symbols in a given person's dreams and creative work. Jung took the term *archetype* from the ancient Greeks and defined archetypes as "factors and motifs that arrange the psychic elements into certain images." He saw these archetypes as human, psychological instincts whose "origin can only be explained by assuming them to be deposits of the constantly repeated experiences of humanity" (Jung, 1917, p. 69).

Jung is saying that archetypes are present in every individual, in addition to his or her personal memories. For Jungian clinicians, there is a need (within a therapeutic situation) for understanding both the personal unconscious, one's individual past from childhood onwards that needs to be dealt with therapeutically, as well as a collective, or impersonal, unconscious which serves as the source for the formation of symbols and myths within our own psyches. Thus, while for some patients, dealing with personal material might suffice in the therapeutic situation, for others, confronting not only their personal histories and backgrounds, but connecting their patterns of experience to ancient myths and/or fairy tales where the hero or heroine is identified with similar psychological issues is a necessary ingredient in the patient's healing process. As Jung saw it, it is essential for the therapist to be familiar with the worlds of myth and symbols, as well as their patients' personal unconscious, so that when archetypal images or psychological instincts (for example: hero; father, mother, child) appear in a patient's psyche through dreams, or other unconscious material, the therapist should take note of parallels between the individual's behavior or attitude and similar motifs that appear in the great myths of mankind and are thus natural and "impersonal."

Understanding precisely what Jung meant by the term *archetype* is probably the most difficult aspect of Jungian psychology. To begin with, even Jung found it almost impossible to give an exact definition, noting that "the best we can hope for is to begin to understand by talking around it." In describing what he meant by archetypes, Jung wrote that they are "by definition, factors and motifs that arrange psychic elements into certain images . . . in such a way that they can be recognized only from the effects they produce. They exist preconsciously . . . " (Jung, 1936, p. 149). What Jung describes is the ability to communicate unconsciously through the formation of archetypes. In short, the term *archetype* is not referring to an inherited idea or myth per se but rather to an inherited pattern of psychological thought, a psychological instinct that will spontaneously form a symbol or connection to a myth to help in the healing process. The individual accesses these archetypes within through a wide variety of experiences, through dreams, fantasies or any creative aspect such as writing or drawing.

An example of how the psyche produces an archetypal image can be seen in the example of a patient whom I treated years ago. M, a 35-year-old, married, Israeli male, was in prison in a foreign country and awaiting trial for theft. I was called in for a consultation to ascertain whether a reported suicide attempt of his was in fact "real," or staged to aid in his release and/or transfer to a hospital setting. During the course of the initial interview, with much trepidation as to the potential consequences if I was incorrect in my appraisal of the situation, I came to the conclusion that the attempt fell within the realm of a plea for help and need for therapy rather than a genuine attempt to kill himself. Fortunately, I'd guessed right and was able to convince prison authorities to authorize a weekly therapy session. These sessions took place in the prison, and continued for almost a year and a half.

For most of the first year we worked together, my help consisted of little more than simply being someone to relate to because he was held in solitary confinement for most of that time. I brought him newspapers and journals for which he was grateful, but when trying to reach him personally by discussing his life and past, I came up against a blank wall. Here was a man with no more than an elementary school level of education, who could not relate to psychotherapy let alone a Jungian approach. His ability for self-reflection was minimal to nonexistent. Denial was not only merely a defense, but a way of life. It was clear that he suffered from depression, yet aside from blaming his imprisonment, he claimed to have no other issues that were troubling him. Thus, for example, when discussing his family of origin, or his relationship with his wife, he spoke only in terms of love and devotion despite the fact that his wife seldom wrote to him, and had never visited him in prison. In this case, not only was there an absence of unconscious material in our therapy sessions, there was almost no conscious material brought by M to therapy. In short, for close to a year, it was almost impossible to get through to him and effect any change whatsoever.

After almost a year of weekly therapy sessions, he had the following dream: "I dreamt that I was Samson and was strong enough to pull the bars of my cell apart and walk out of prison." Rather than see any archetypal material here, one might easily dismiss this dream as little more than wish fulfill-ment. After all, his reality was imprisonment; with such super-human strength he could indeed be freed from what was clearly a difficult, depressing situation. Still, why Samson? Why not a figure that would be closer to his own socioeducational level like Superman, Batman, or Tarzan? All sorts of heroic figures abound in the popular culture. Furthermore, he himself had not read the Bible and his only association to the story of Sam-son was that he had heard the tale told by his fourth grade teacher. When I asked him what he remembered from that story, he recalled only that Samson was the all powerful hero.

Yet, in examining the dream from a Jungian point of view, one cannot help but be struck by its archetypal nature, by the psyche's production of an archetypal image as an ingredient for breaking through beyond the conscious, interpersonal level of therapy. Indeed, as it turned out, this dream marked an important turning point in our work together. The archetypal image produced was related to the story of Samson, but not on the conscious level of sheer strength. Rather, as I pointed out to my patient, a key element in the story is Delilah, the woman responsible for Samson's predicament. By simply pos-ing the possibility of existing parallels, and explaining to him in simple language the importance of dreams in our ongoing mental health, I was able to reach him. The denial and resis-tance that had previously characterized the therapy was re-placed by trust and an attempt at self-understanding. As soon became evident in our discussions, the relationship M had with his wife, combined with memories of his father's petty thefts so as to buy his wife, M's mother, expensive gifts, had played a role in M turning to theft as a means of enabling him to purchase jewelry, furs, and fancy cars for his wife as well. In turn, upon M's imprisonment, his wife neither forwarded money to him to hire an attorney, nor came to visit him once during the period of his initial incarceration.

THE ARCHETYPES OF ANIMA AND ANIMUS

The concept of the femme fatale, as referred to in nonclinical language, is in reality a connection to what Jung terms the Anima, an archetypal, unconscious, contrasexual aspect of a man's personality. As Jung sees it, men and women each have within them both masculine and feminine aspects. The contrasexual component is embedded within the unconscious and is known as the anima in men and the animus in women. Ultimately, the goal for both men and women is to raise to consciousness and then integrate within the totality of the personality these unconscious, archetypal, contrasexual dimensions present within each of us. An important aspect to bear in mind is that, throughout Jung's work, the terms *masculine* and *feminine* are used advisedly and in no way meant to convey an impression that there are stereotypical men's and/or women's roles in life. On the contrary, both men and women have masculine and feminine traits which, if developed constructively, serve as a kind of inner balance to prevent a one-sided approach to life. As Jung used the terms, masculine represents logos (thinking or logic), differentiation, objective reality, aggression, power, and the conscious realm among other attributes of the personality. Alternatively, feminine would stand for traits more closely identified with eros, relatedness, feeling, and intuition.

The worlds of literature, film, and theater are filled with examples of how men and women fail to deal with inner aspects of themselves and project these qualities onto members of the opposite sex. Intuitively, the great authors and creative artists have understood what psychologists and others in the field have come to postulate intellectually. For, while a woman may serve as the carrier of a man's anima projections or, alternatively, a man hold the quality of the animus for a particular woman, the real task of each individual is to understand the nature of these projections, remove them by seeing the other individual as he or she really is, and integrate these qualities into his or her own being.

An example of how an anima projection manifests itself can be seen in the classic film *The Blue Angel*. One of the primary characters is a professor who falls in love with a cabaret girl (played by Marlene Dietrich) and leaves his former life to blindly serve her. What emerges is the professor's loss of identity and place in the world. Caught up in this archetypal anima projection, the professor, out of touch with his long repressed feelings, sexuality, and inner needs, soon disintegrates as an adult, mature man. Another example, one that shows the projection of a woman's animus onto a man, can be see in the novel *Anna Karenina* where the result of Anna's concretizing and living out the projection by running away with her lover who is an officer in the Russian Army. Rather than understanding the inner need for developing her own masculine identity, she concretizes the experience by acting out and leaving her child and family behind, an action that ends in disaster. In short, the danger for an individual man or woman comes not from the projection but from identifying with the projected archetype (anima/animus) through the person of another individual. At that point, when one is wholly caught up in the archetype, there emerges an unrealistic, ungrounded dimension to the individual's real life with potentially dire consequences.

Because making these connections to one's own unconscious is not an easy task (Jung is reported to have once stated that the trouble with the unconscious is that it is *un*conscious), like many other personal psychological revelations, it is generally first experienced through the phenomenon of projection. For example, we react negatively to another individual's personality traits while all along it is a trait that lies within us and is being denied, a part of ourselves we dislike and deny. In this manner, powerful feelings are activated and the task of understanding more about our own, inner psyche can begin.

In a positive vein a classic example given by Jung is that of "love at first sight" whereby one projects all sorts of qualities onto another while knowing very little about that person. The qualities one "loves" are in reality inner aspects of one's own personality, the anima or animus in Jungian terms.

While Jung's concept of the anima and animus might well need, and indeed has been undergoing, debate and redefinition in light of changing attitudes toward homosexual and lesbian relationships, his basic concept of these contrasexual archetypes provides a useful vantage point in understanding how heterosexual relationships often work. In this light, within gay and lesbian relationships as well there exists the need for each of the couple to define his or her own masculine as well as feminine sides.

Returning to M's dream, and our subsequent exploration of it within the context of his therapy, we might say that by seeing his own issue in the context of the archetypal field, he was better able to understand his problem as more than merely one in which he, as an individual, was caught up in an unhealthy relationship. By realizing his own overidentification with, and literalizing of, the archetype, that is through having his wife carry his inner projections of what he thought the feminine was about, he was better equipped to reach the next stage of personal development, i.e., contact with his own anima. By removing his projections and understanding his own negative connection to the feminine, he would ultimately be able to form healthier relationships with women in the future.

THE IMPORTANCE OF DREAMS

One does not always come across clear and precise archetypal images of the anima or animus within a given dream. Nor does such a clear, distinct, heroic or historic figure as Samson generally appear as he did in M's dream. More often than not, as dramatic as working with dreams generally is, the situation requires the analyst approach from the stance of good, basic analytical training and skills. This would include first rate detective work, a wealth of knowledge about symbols, myths, and fairy tales, and well developed intuition. A metaphor for how this works can be seen in the Jungian position that in approaching a dream one must be careful not to separate the dream from the dreamer. To properly understand the significance of a given dream, a therapist must be familiar with the age, sex, occupation, education, religion, and specific associations of the dreamer. In short, the biography of the dreamer plays an important role in framing the context of the dream.

On a practical, concrete plane, Jung offers specific categories in helping understand a dream. His approach comprises what he terms the *object level* and the *subject level* of a dream. On an object level, a Jungian approach would not differ dramatically from that of any other clinician. It represents that aspect of the dream which relates to one's personal unconscious or individual history. In other words, this type of dream usually revolves around people or issues currently active in the dreamer's life and it needs to be examined on that level (i.e., what the dream is telling us about the dreamer's current situation). On a deeper, subject, level, the content connects the dreamer to either his or her "complexes" or, through the appearance of universal symbols or myths, to the realm of the archetypal. To use the Samson dream as an illustration, the dreamer was both forced to face both his own personal situation (having surrendered his ego to his wife) as well as able to understand the archetype of the femme fatale (e.g., Delilah) that he shared in common with others.

Without minimizing the essential need for good clinical skills, one might say that for Jung working with dreams is the alpha and omega of understanding the unconscious messages an individual's psyche is sending. Jung saw a natural balance between the conscious and unconscious parts of one's psyche. The dream serves to bring light to that which is not being seen or said by the individual's conscious personality. Thus, after first obtaining all the relevant biographical data of an individual's life story and patterns, his or her dreams reveal the portions of the personality left out or ignored in the conscious attitude. In short, Jung sees the psyche as a self-regulating system with the dream serving as a compensatory function for the conscious personality. In fact, Jung would in all likelihood caution one to bear in mind that in approaching a dream, the first questions that must be asked are: "What is this dream trying to tell me? What am I not seeing in my conscious life?" In other words, "what conscious attitude is the dream trying to compensate for?"

Jung sees the dream as a message, a bridge between the conscious and the unconscious. However, he emphasizes that dreams are not to be seen as moral statements, telling one to "behave better," or as carrying ethical judgments per se. Rather, he describes the dream as providing a balance to the lopsided nature of one's conscious mind. When one is asleep, with ego defenses reduced, it is through the mechanisms of the dream that one might bridge the gap that exists between the outer personality, and the inner "Self," what Jung defines as the true "objective psyche," that part of us which controls the entirety of the personality: conscious and unconscious. Within these various aspects of the self lie a number of subtexts—a connection with such archetypal images as anima, animus, hero, caretaker, or even what Jung calls the "Shadow," an unexpressed dimension of our personal unconscious which is often in direct conflict with the persona—the outer image of ourselves which we present to the world or consciously identify with. Through the answer to the riddles inherent in each dream, and by learning how to connect to these various dimensions within the structure and dynamics of our psyches, healing and individuation (self-realization) can begin to take shape.

WORKING WITH DREAMS

How does one work with dreams within a Jungian analytic setting? What secrets must be gleaned and which skills honed before one dares to feel comfortable and proficient in that world? Perhaps the best place to begin is by understanding that the analyst must not adopt a preset, dogmatic theoretical position. Rather, it is important to keep in mind a broad, all-encompassing attitude that does not preclude any particular approach. It is crucial to be conscious of the fact that there are many areas within the patient's life which he or she may be too sensitive to discuss early on in the analysis. In such situations the individual must be approached with tact, nuance, discretion and, above all else, timing. Defenses such as avoiding certain subjects (sexual identity issues, family secrets, etc.) are there for a reason and must be respected. The need for caution, however, needs to be balanced with the fact that recall of the dream itself is usually an indication that the conflict, or issue being raised in the dream, is one that the patient is ready to bring to consciousness. Nevertheless, in ascertaining whether or not to probe deeply and explore the dream's hidden content, it is crucial to ascertain if sufficient ego strength exists to deal with this unconscious material. To this end, the following factors need to be taken into consideration:

1. *Biography of the dreamer:* age, sex, family history, religious affiliation (if any), medical profile (if applicable), marital status, occupation, etc. In short, the dream must be placed within the context of the individual's life. Some dreams, as we have seen, are to be looked at from a "subject" level while others need to be taken more interpersonally ("object level"). It is helpful to know as much as possible about the dreamer's present reality and past background before plunging into interpretive waters. For example, if the dreamer is dealing with current health problems or struggling financially, dreams presenting issues of sickness and/or money issues would be dealt with on an object level rather than examined symbolically. Similarly, for an individual of an Orthodox Jewish background a dream of the symbol of a cross would mean something entirely different from its meaning for someone who was raised as a strict Catholic.

2. *Associations:* Once the biographical data are collected, the next important step is to obtain the dreamer's personal associations to the dream. For, above all, it is the dreamer's associations to the dream that mark the first step of the journey toward understanding a specific dream. In this regard, both Jung and Freud begin with those associations. They entail the first active step toward beginning to decode the language of

the dream, a message from the unconscious in a foreign language (i.e., the vocabulary of the dream comes in symbols and images that need to be deciphered). The associations provide an entry point, the first words of this language, so to speak, which can help the dreamer approach the unconscious.

Jung, however, differs from Freud at this point in that his method of looking for associations is more directed than Freud's and not a mere starting point for general psychological work. In other words, the Jungian approach is to look for "direct associations" to the specific images and symbols that appear in a given dream. The aim, as Jung would put it, is to hit upon the "complexes" (feeling toned affects) that lurk behind the particular image, symbol, or person that appears in the dream. Thus, while Freud saw dreams as the "royal road to an understanding of the unconscious," Jung saw the complex as that very same royal road. The complex, in effect, is the architect of the dream edifice.

3. *The Complexes:* Jung's work on the "complex," the key element of all dreams, grew out of his research known as the "Association Experiment," an area of study Jung began before his encounter with Freud. This experiment was designed in the hopes of using it as an aid in the diagnosis of schizophrenia. While Jung's association experiment failed to provide a useful tool in the diagnosis of psychosis, it turned out to prove a useful aid in identifying the core of an individual's complexes.

Jung saw the complex as a split-off part of the personality, an alter-ego or splinter psyche with a strong feeling toned affect behind it (Jung, 1934, p. 97). As Jung saw it, complexes are the main actors in our dreams with each figure in the dream representing a particular complex, a part of one's personality, either positive or negative in nature. Alternatively, another complex indicator in the dream might be situational, for example an adult dreaming of being back in an elementary school classroom. By first identifying the complexes raised in a particular dream, one can then proceed to trying to understand the meaning behind it. In this context, Jung would suggest first asking the patient "why is this particular dream coming now?" For instance, when a patient is asked for an association to a person or place in the dream, what the therapist should be looking for is a direct association to a specific person, place, or thing that is tied to a specific complex. For example, if a patient reports dreaming of a desk, it is important to ascertain what kind of desk? If in a classroom, which desk, in which particular classroom? Thus, it could be a grade school desk that was in his or her fifth grade classroom, which might then lead to a particular complex, originating at that age and in that school experience.

Unlike approaching dreams from the vantage point of Freudian "free associations," Jungian technique emphasizes focused, direct associations. For from Jung's point of view, while it is true that free associating around a dream's images might lead to a complex as well, so too would reading the *New York Times* and free associating to some words in a particular article. One doesn't need a dream to get at complexes in general. As Jung sees it, the dream is coming at a specific point in a patient's life, in order to deal with a specific problem, an identifiable complex that is giving him or her difficulty and is in need of attention. The link to understanding the origin of this particular complex in time is being revealed in the dream. That is not to say that complexes are all bad, destructive, and to be eliminated. On the contrary, from a psychological point of view, complexes are an indispensable element of psychic life. An individual without any complexes would be creatively and affectively debilitated. For example, any creative force within us is fueled by a complex which drives the creative process as in a drive for approval, power, or perfection. As Jung put it, the question is not whether or not we have complexes, but whether the complex has us.

4. *Amplification:* When there are no associations to a dream, or after they have been given and exhausted, a Jungian approach would then encourage the analyst to insert elements that might help shed light on the dream. These elements would be developed in the context of some historic, mythological place. The purpose of bringing to bear these myths, fairy tales, and symbols (i.e., archetypal images) is to place the contents of a dream that lacks personal associations into a context of the general human condition. This connection, through the world of archetypes, is one that helps the dreamer understand

the individual situation on a deeper, richer level. This effort, called "amplification," must be handled with reserve and prudence, and only after the personal unconscious material (or lack of it) has been worked through in terms of what is going on in the patient's life that calls for attention. Often, however, it is only through connecting to the archetypal level that a therapist can take the potency out of what might otherwise be experienced as a place of deep shame and despair. For example, incestuous feelings toward a parent carry a great deal of shame in our society, but when the story of Oedipus is understood on a symbolic level, the message that comes across that the archetype behind it is universal if the feeling is acted out rather than understood on a human level. Or, by using fairy tales such as Cinderella, the Ugly Duckling, or Rapunzel as models one can often help a woman understand the universality of her particular feelings of worthlessness, unattractiveness, and shame in inspiring parental abandonment and disapproval. Through a link to the archetype that is at work for this particular complex, the patient might come to realize that he or she is not alone in having this type of problem. It is, in essence, a universal problem and thus easier to talk about, and ultimately deal with openly. In short, this specifically Jungian method of amplification should only be utilized when the personal, associative material is exhausted. At that point, it can serve as a springboard to a breakthrough on a deeper level. Initially, however, the dreamer's personal level problems and more immediate issues, must be dealt with by the analyst in order to help heal the patient's inner wounds.

5. *Subject vs. Object Level:* This is, as noted, an important aspect of Jung's approach to the dream. If someone close to the dreamer (i.e., spouse, child, good friend, family member, or indeed anyone he or she interacts with often and is present in their everyday life) appears in the dream Jung would say that the dream should be interpreted on what he calls an "object level," that is, interpersonally. This level should be fully explored before one approaches a deeper, possibly archetypal, "subject" level. Thus, a dream that has a character in it who is distant from the patient's current life (e.g., an unidentified fireman, hospital attendant, stranger, or even person not seen

in many years by the dreamer), he or she is not taken on the object level but rather on the subject level. That is, such a dream would have something to do with an internal issue and not concern a specific person or issue in their lives. Both levels are important, one being a foundation for the other. We first need to exhaust the object level and then move to the subject level. As a rule of thumb, at the beginning of an "analysis" the object level dominates, especially with younger people but also with adults. In other words, neglected, pressing life issues must always be dealt with first. Only later, when one's outer, everyday life is truly balanced, can a person progress to a deeper, inner level of issues.

6. *Compensation, Interpretation, and Repetitive Dreams:* Jung saw a natural balance, a self-regulating system within each of us, between the conscious and unconscious levels of the psyche. For Jung, one of the most important elements of the dream is its compensatory aspect, the unconscious bringing to light of something that the dreamer was not aware of before it happened in the dream. Moreover, the dream, which is a message from the unconscious, is portraying something which the dreamer might find at odds with his or her conscious, or ego attitude toward the world. In fact, a question the therapist must always ask when approaching a dream is, "For what conscious attitude is this dream coming to compensate?" Simply put, "What is this dream trying to tell me?"; "What am I not seeing in my conscious life?" In brief, we might say that the dream message functions in such a way as to fill in the "blind spots" of one's conscious personality (Whitmont and Perera, 1989, p. 57).

Another way to understand the compensatory aspect of dreams is to start from the premise that dreams are not dreamt to repeat previously understood information. An example of this is seen in the case of repetitive dreams which can be taken to indicate that the dreamer has not grasped the psychological significance of the issue being dealt with in the dream. In order to break through and reach the dreamer's consciousness, the dream keeps recurring; the message has to be driven home over and over again until its importance and meaning is extracted.

Nevertheless, notwithstanding the fact that Jungians have written hundreds of books on the subject of dream interpretation, there have been cases reported which describe the healing aspect of dreaming taking place even without any interpretation of the dream itself. C. A. Meier, in fact, indicated that it is not always necessary to interpret a dream. In a series of introductory lectures he gave on analytical psychology, Meier reports the case of a 57-year-old American attorney who had been suffering for several years with severe depression to the point of hospitalization in a mental institution. When first seen by Meier, his condition was rather grim; he was completely detached from life and not interested in his surroundings or in those around him. At first, he couldn't even speak during his sessions. He was seen for a period of six weeks, for a total of fourteen sessions. During this time, the patient remained mute while Meier was likewise silent. The patient was, however, able to dictate his dreams to his wife at first and, later, a secretary. Altogether twenty dreams were recorded and brought to the therapy sessions. Notwithstanding the fact that none of the dreams were interpreted, Meier reports that the depression lifted enough so that the patient could begin talking about his issues within the therapeutic setting, an example of what Jung calls the functioning of the "objective psyche," in this case the healing power of the dream with or without analytic interpretation.

Nevertheless, this is not to imply that the Jungian approach to the use of dreams is amorphous or advocates noninterpretation. As we have seen, understanding and interpreting dreams encompasses detailed, multifaceted work on the part of the analyst. This work includes not only an in-depth knowledge of the dreamer's life and personal unconscious, but an extensive knowledge of the worlds of symbol, myth, cultural anthropology, and the natural sciences to name but a few. Furthermore, Jung himself saw the world of dreams as an area that deserved much attention and which should be grounded within the context of the therapy.

TECHNIQUE IN INTERPRETING DREAMS

In addressing the practical issue of how to interpret dreams, one possible method Jung suggested was to approach a dream from the perspective of an inner theater. Jung saw dreams as inner dramas that cast each and every dreamer in the role of not only author and chief protagonist, but also that of producer, actor, and director. Thus, in anticipation of the current spate of self-help and how-to books, Jung offered an interesting approach for analyzing a dream. This particular technique called for utilizing the classical literary method of dissecting a Greek drama as follows:

Write out the dream and then subdivide it into the following categories:

(1) *Exposition:* characters, time, place, and setting of the dream.

(2) *Plot:* What is the story? In short what is happening in the dream itself?

(3) *Crisis:* Describe and isolate the conflict or crisis raised in the dream.

(4) *Solution:* The solution usually, but not always, is left to the dreamer when he awakens (i.e., it is a function of bringing consciousness to bear on the psychological confrontation evident in the dream).

As an example of the way one can break down a dream into these above mentioned components (as well as obtain some insight into countertransference) I will cite the following dream I had concerning M, the above mentioned patient.

> My patient, his wife, and I were in Israel, driving along a lovely highway by the sea. His wife was behind the wheel of the car, and he was beside her. The scene was a romantic one, as if out of some beautiful opera, yet we seemed to be heading nowhere. There was operatic music playing on the radio, the day was sunny and clear, and the sea was to our right. However, no matter how fast or far we were driving, we always seemed to be in the same place.

1. *Exposition* (time, place, and characters): myself, the patient, and his wife. The locale: Israel! In analyzing the dream,

a discrepancy between the reality of the dreamer's conscious world, and the image produced by his or her unconscious, can prove to be an important detail. Thus, the first thing I needed to note was the reality of the therapy itself taking place in Switzerland. I needed to be alert to the fact that the dream might be commenting on the fact that the therapeutic work was not grounded in time or place.

2. *Plot:* (the story) We were taking a ride; or, one might say, I was being taken for a ride. The wife of my patient, whom in actuality I'd never even met, was driving. I was a passive observer of what seemed to be a scene that reminded me of a romantic opera.

3. *Conflict:* (crisis) We were getting nowhere. One begins from the premise that if the therapist is dreaming of the patient it is a commentary on the therapeutic situation, a countertransference reaction to what is transpiring in the therapy, a corrective that must be taken seriously.

4. *Solution:* None in the dream! Some, rare, dreams actually contain a solution; for example a voice heard in which the dreamer is actually given a solution. Jung refers to this as a voice from the self, but in general he observes that the solution of the dream is generally left to consciousness. My own solution was to tell the dream to my patient—a highly unusual step, but given the unique circumstances of working with someone within a prison setting I felt it was worth the risk.

In this particular case, I realized immediately that the dream contained within it a message regarding my own countertransference reaction to the therapeutic work that was taking place. I was fascinated with this patient both because he was from Israel, a place I felt closely connected to, as well as wanting to believe his story of a happy, romantic marriage. However, there was a problem; nothing was happening in the therapy. Parallel to what was taking place in the dream, the focus of the therapy was being "driven" by the absent wife. The therapy was going nowhere. I had been listening to my patient's descriptions of his love for his wife and bought into it. No matter how hard I had tried to get through his defenses (in this case, denial of his awful marriage), we had apparently made no headway, as the dream clearly pointed out. My dream raised an important question for me: Can a Jungian approach work for someone with little or no education and no previous therapy. After all, much of what Jung had written was not only directed toward second half of life issues, but seemed to imply that the person in analysis required a degree of knowledge ranging from anthropology and the Bible on the one hand, to Greek mythology, psychology, and even theology on the other. At this point, I was reminded of what Jung had said of his own work, namely that if his approach to psychology could not be understood by the farmer in the field it was not worth anything. With this in mind, it became clear to me that it was important to take the risk of revealing my dream.

By relating the dream, in effect serving as a role model for respecting the unconscious, I was able to break through the patient's defenses and reach a deeper level of work with him within the therapeutic framework. He, in turn, following the relating of my dream, shared his Samson dream with me and we were able to connect at a level that had not existed in our work to that point. Subsequently, as a result of this particular encounter with the unconscious, I came to understand that what was required in any analytical work was the ability of the therapist to put Jung's multilayered, often complex ideas into plain language. What is called for is a genuine dialogue between patient and therapist; between, as Jung put it, analyst and analysand. On the one hand, the therapist must maintain an analytical, neutral stance and must realize that the situation is an asymmetrical one. Yet, on the other hand, the analyst must approach the patient as an analysand, as an equal partner in the process. Jung saw the role of therapist as akin to that of a midwife. The therapist must always remember that he or she is there to help the patient give birth to a new aspect of the self that until then had been hidden within the psyche. There is no reason why language, terminology, or even education should be a barrier to communicating the basic concepts of Jung's ideas to most individuals.

What became evident to me as a result of working with M within a prison setting, was that while the psyche is a complex, often difficult to understand aspect of ourselves, there is no right or wrong way to reach an individual and there is more than one possible way to deal with a dream. Often, like a work of art, one can understand much from several different perspectives. Thus, for the therapist, it is important to be able to maintain a fluidity in moving from the conscious to the unconscious and back again. From a Jungian approach, the dream can provide the starting point for the vehicle needed for this movement—a multipronged, internal and external dialogue between the conscious and unconscious of the patient and that of the therapist.

A BRIDGE TO THE UNCONSCIOUS

The leading role dreams can play in the individuation (self-realization) process cannot be underestimated. Dreams bring about psychological confrontation. They are messages from the unconscious, a bridge between our conscious and unconscious lives. The dream, according to Jung, often undermines the conscious aims of the ego, of the individual's conscious desires and intentions. In other words, dreams are what Jung views as spontaneous representations of the unconscious, much like an X-ray of what is going on internally for the individual. For a Jungian, the dream world is as rich and diversified as the conscious world—at times even more so. What is crucial to keep in mind is that the dream provides an interior balance to the external, conscious life of the patient. This being the case, the dream can serve, within the therapeutic work at least, as a compensatory function for what is not being dealt with on a conscious plane.

Nevertheless, while keeping in mind the importance of dreams, it is crucial to understand that they represent only one bridge to the unconscious, one possible pathway within the therapeutic process. The primary goal of every Jungian therapist must still be to help in the healing process, to provide the necessary support, insight and feedback. This takes place by placing the patient's offered material first—not by forcing the therapy into a theoretical framework that calls for the patient to bring in dreams as a requirement of the therapy. Often, one can work for years with an individual and not deal with a single dream. Indeed, it is helpful for therapists to remember the etymology of the very term *psychotherapy*, from the Greek word psyche, soul. Jung believed that each individual, each soul, has its own particular need and mode of expression and what is taking place in the consulting room was exactly that, therapy for the soul. At times, working with dreams might be the key to unlocking hidden material; at other times, what is called for may be working with and interpreting drawings the patient may bring into therapy, treating daydreams or fantasies as unconscious material to be analyzed, or even simply just talking to the therapist about everyday problems. The primary goal must always be to help nurture the process of individuation. Dreams are but one aspect, one tool, one bridge to help that along.

PSYCHOLOGICAL TYPE

There are many areas in which Jung delineated his psychology and ideas and which, when understood and utilized within a Jungian analysis, can further the therapeutic work. To this point, I have covered a number, but by no means all, of Jung's basic concepts. A tool to help a patient understand more about his or her personality (conscious and unconscious), and a concept that is being actively applied today on a practical, everyday level can be found in Jung's theory of psychological type. For Jung, psychological type meant delineating the primary attitude (extravert or introvert) and function (thinking, feeling, intuition, sensate) with which each person consciously approaches the world. It defines the way we problem solve, how we relate to friends, colleagues, and loved ones, and our general outlook on life.

Often loosely referred to among Jungians as "Typology," Jung's theory of psychological type marks a starting point for understanding how his psychology differs from that of Freud and Adler. As Jung broke away from Freud, but acknowledged some points of agreement with Adler, he tried to understand how all three analysts could have useful theories of the workings of the psyche. The outcome of Jung's personal struggle with this question was his development of the ideas found in his book *Psychological Types*. In it, Jung describes how his own, as well as Freud and Adler's, personal psychological type is mirrored in their own particular, unique, approach to psychoanalysis (Jung, 1921). With his theory of psychological types, Jung provides a model that is useful in helping to understand how each of us approaches the world. Additionally, it is especially useful in working with couples to help them understand and appreciate their differences and at times opposite approaches to the conscious world. Or, another valuable area of application is its use by career counselors where this concept of Jung's resulted in development of the Myers Briggs Type Inventory (MBTI), a personality test based on Jung's theory of psychological type that today is one of the most widely used career counseling tools in the United States.

Briefly, Jung describes two different "attitudes" or stances that individuals have in approaching the world: extraverted and introverted. The extravert's attitude is directed toward the outer object while the introvert directs his or her attention primarily toward the inner world, the subject. To be more precise, the introvert is mainly concerned with what Jung calls the "subjective factor," while the extravert derives energy from the outer object, other individuals and/or events.

These two attitudes, introversion and extraversion, are modified by what Jung called the four functions: thinking, feeling, intuition, and sensate. In this view, he described thinking and feeling as rational and judgmental functions while intuition and sensate were seen as nonrational in nature. Intuition and sensate functions are what we use to gather information, while thinking and feeling serve to process that information (i.e., help us in the decision making process based on the information gathered). Jung, throughout his writings, describes both the attitudes and the functions as constituting pairs of opposites; thinking is the exact opposite of feeling; intuition and sensation represent polar opposites. Similarly, extraversion and introversion are the reverse of each other. For example, when one has a strong feeling function, thinking would be the weakest of his or her functions with the same constellation true of the others (introversion/extraversion and intuition/sensate approaches to the world). In other words, each pair of opposites, according to Jung, is mutually exclusive of one another (e.g., when using the thinking function, one tends to exclude its counterpart or opposite, feeling). To offer some examples of the way these functions manifest themselves, it is helpful to follow the descriptions provided by Meier in his *Introductory Lectures to Analytical Psychology*:

"Sensation" tells one that there is an object. It has certain qualities which the senses perceive, such as color, shape, and size. "Thinking," however, enables one to logically deduce what it is. Thus, for instance, it is a glass of such and such color, shape, or size. In this model, "intuition" would be described by Jung as analogous to "seeing around corners," getting information in a way that is neither conscious nor explainable. Thus, in the above cited examples, one could intuit that this glass, filled with wine, contains within it the wine that I gave to a friend three years ago for his fiftieth birthday. The opposite of thinking, the feeling function, carries within it judgments. For example, "I like or don't like the wine being served at such an occasion." In other words, it is a judging function that values or devalues as the case may be.

Jung's concept of psychological types, like much of his theory of the structure and dynamics of the psyche, revolves around a series of opposites. Jung believed that these pairs of opposites within each individual provide much of the impetus for personal development, "individuation." Some of these opposites that Jungian psychology is built around are, for example; masculine/feminine; shadow/persona; self/ego; conscious/unconscious; power/relatedness, all of which help to shape who we are. These, and the various components of functions and attitudes within the psychological type framework, are a few of the psychological issues most individuals must deal with as part and parcel of what Jung has termed the "individuation process."

CONCLUSION

The individuation process, getting in touch with one's own self, or "self-realization," as Jung described it, is "the key concept

in Jung's contribution to the theories of personality development'' (Samuels, 1986, p. 76). The movement toward individuation is a life-long process. Similarly, the primary goal of any
Jungian, long-term analytic treatment is to provide a containing
frame for helping to facilitate the psyche's push toward self-
realization. How this is accomplished within the therapeutic
situation is a mystery to the conscious aims of the ego. It cannot
be simply willed by the patient; nor can it be controlled, guided,
or even jump-started by the analyst. In general, Jung did not
write extensively about so-called techniques and methodology.
His assumption was that the unconscious will provide both the
material and the timing to dictate the pace of the individuation
process for each individual.

More recent generations of Jungians have continued to
mine the fields of analytical psychology and in many instances
charted waters not dealt with in depth by Jung himself. For
example, where Jung once remarked that the healing occurs
despite the transference, today several of the most reputable
Jungian Institutes adopt the position that transference issues
in therapy are a focal point of the analytic work. And, finally,
where Jung and the first generation of his students avoided
using the couch as part of the analytical treatment, some current day Jungians espouse its use as part of their treatment of
patients with certain, specific issues.

In conclusion, since Jung first began his pioneering work
in the field of what is today known as analytical psychology,
changes and evolution in both theory and practice have taken
place. To Jung's credit, however, this is in keeping with the
spirit of his work. For despite his dislike of the very term *Jungian*, Jungians have carried on in his tradition of not being
locked into dogma. Jungian psychology, since Jung's death in
1961, has moved forward and kept pace with developments in
the fields of psychiatry, psychology, and the helping professions
in general. To paraphrase a well-known quote of Jung that ''I
would change all my theories to help a single patient,'' one
might say that a good, contemporary Jungian clinician is open
to learning all there is from all schools of thought and is prepared to integrate that which has proven sound into the framework of Jungian psychology. In short, Jung's own theoretical

eclecticism, unappreciated, indeed unknown to many Jungians and non-Jungians alike, is very much in the post-Jung, Jungian tradition.

REFERENCES

Freud, S. (1900), *The Interpretation of Dreams*. New York: Avon Books, 1965.

Jung, C. G. (1917), The personal and the collective unconscious. In: *Two Essays on Analytical Psychology*. Princeton, NJ: Princeton University Press, 1972.

———(1921), Psychological types. In: *Psychological Types: Collected Works, Volume 6*. Princeton, NJ: Princeton University Press, 1974.

———(1934), A review of the complex theory. In: *The Structure and Dynamics of the Psyche, Collected Works, Volume 8*. Princeton, NJ: Princeton University Press, 1969.

———(1936), Analytical psychology: Its theory and practice. In: *The Tavistock Lectures*. London and New York: Routledge & Kegan Paul, 1968.

McGuire, W., Ed. (1974), *The Freud-Jung Letters*. Princeton, NJ: Bollingen edition, Princeton University Press.

Meier, C. A. (1959), *Jung and Analytical Psychology*. Newton, MA: Department of Psychology Publication, Andover Newton Theological Seminary.

Samuels, A. (1986), *A Critical Dictionary of Jungian Psychology*. London and New York: Routledge & Kegan Paul.

Whitmont, E. & Perera, S. (1989), *Dreams: A Portal to the Source*. London and New York: Routledge & Kegan Paul.

11.

An Evolutionary Biological Perspective on Psychoanalysis

Malcolm Owen Slavin, Ph.D., Daniel Kriegman, Ph.D.

In a book, *The Adaptive Design of the Human Psyche: Psychoanalysis, Evolutionary Biology and the Therapeutic Process* (Slavin and Kriegman, 1992) and a series of papers, we have tried to demonstrate how thinking in "evolutionary-adaptive" terms provides a way of fitting various psychoanalytic models—classical, relational, and self psychological—into a larger picture that more fully embraces the many facets of human nature. We have addressed some of the important debates and complexity of the contemporary Darwinian perspective at greater length in these works (cf., Gould, 1980; Kitcher, 1985, 1987). This chapter presents a brief summary of certain aspects of our extended work and its application to clinical practice. We hope to give the reader a taste of what we believe are the novel possibilities for theory and therapy of using this new perspective.

WHAT EVOLUTIONARY BIOLOGY IS NOT

The very term *evolutionary biology* brings a flood of connotations with it, many of them highly misleading. So we feel we must say something about what evolutionary biology does *not* mean. It does *not* mean neurobiology, physiology, psychopharmacology, or any of the other current physical or biochemical approaches that are commonly equated with what is "biological." These aspects of biology deal with physical and chemical mechanisms that may correlate with, and are presumed to underlie, experience. We draw, instead, from a branch of contemporary biology that is quite different. Whereas the neurobiologist may look at psychological structures and ways of organizing experience and ask the question, *"How* are they physically built into *the brain?"* the evolutionary biologist asks a markedly different question, "Why have they become a fundamental feature of human *psychological experience?"*

As Ernst Mayr (1982, 1988), one of the foremost scholars of biology, has noted, it is not simply that there are complex interactions between two realms of human existence—one *psychological,* the other *biological.* There is a biological patterning within the psychological realm itself—within our very way of construing and ordering experience. This patterning has been shaped by a huge amount of evolutionary history. Our minds are not biological entities *because* they are connected to brains made up of neurons and biochemical processes. As a set of *psychological* phenomena, the operation of the human mind—the structure and process of feelings, perceptions, cognitions—itself defines an active biological organ, designed for living as a human being within a very complex human environment.

FEAR OF ESSENTIALISM AND BIOLOGICAL UNIVERSALS

It is more than interesting and productive to consider what evolutionary biology can say about the human condition. In a sense, it is inescapable. All of us do it—explicitly or implicitly—all the time. All psychoanalytic—indeed, all psychological—models are, at some level, biological models. That is, they are all founded on a set of basic assumptions about what is "primary" in human nature (Greenberg and Mitchell, 1983).

These assumptions include positions on issues such as what is and isn't innate, essential, and universal in ourselves and the world into which we are born. In this broad sense, even the most "antibiological" of psychoanalytic models are only nonbiological in the narrow sense of their rejection of a particular kind of physicalistic speculation found in Freud's classical drive theory. The models that every "nonbiological" theorist constructs are rife with their own sets of implicit biological assumptions about human nature (Slavin and Kriegman, 1992).

Indeed, as Diana Fuss, the feminist literary critic, has argued "any radical constructionism can only be built on the foundations of a hidden essentialism" (1989, p. 12). In other words, you simply can't make a theory of human experience and subjectivity without making assumptions, however limited, about what is basic and universal about the mind as well as what is universally "average and expectable" about the relational world in which the mind develops. In a sense our approach is actually dedicated to making this "hidden essentialism" more open and explicit. We believe it is possible, indeed crucial, to move beyond the simplistic dichotomies of social constructionism versus essentialism, postmodernism versus scientific objectivism. In regard to theory and therapy, we also hope to show that listening with the "evolutionist's ear" can better attune us to the inevitable biases in our own subjectivity as well as to some of the deepest, most vital, adaptive, individual meanings within the communications of others.

EVOLVED PSYCHODYNAMIC DEEP STRUCTURE

Let us briefly consider a way of talking about biological design that can serve as a clearer, more concrete bridge between evolutionary concepts and psychoanalytic constructs. Chomsky (1972) has shown that a complex, "hard-wired," universal, biological program is required for the immense amount of cognitive processing needed to master languages, even though each language is, patently, a culturally constructed product. It was only possible, however, to recognize the need for such underlying, innate linguistic structures when, after extensive study, the magnitude of the adaptive problem facing the child and the fluent adult language user was appreciated. Chomsky's contribution lay in good part in his recognition that simple models of learning grounded in a tabula rasa notion of the mind simply could not begin to explain the stunning success with which each new generation solved an adaptive challenge that would be insurmountable for a mind that was not prepared to meet the challenge with a built-in, evolved design. This evolutionary conception echoes the philosopher Emmanuel Kant's insight into the paradoxical need for "knowlege" that precedes experience. "The world is itself, complex in ways that are not . . . analyzable or deductible without an enormous amount of *a priori* knowledge. In order to solve a task you must already know a great deal about the nature of the circumstances in which the task is embedded" (Tooby and Cosmides, 1990, p. 12).

Extending Chomsky's notion that there must be universal, preexisting psychological structures underlying the mastery and use of language, we have shown that many aspects of our psychodynamics can be usefully understood as also having preexisting, underlying, "deep structural" organization (Slavin and Kriegman, 1992). Subjective constellations of thought and feeling such as those that, in different psychoanalytic traditions, we call the "self," "introjects," "transferences," "empathy," "drives," "ego," etc., may exist precisely because we have evolved flexible, responsive innate programs for generating such "structures of subjectivity." Remember, this is not to reify these psychological terms, to reduce them to some kind of *physical* entities. Nor does it diminish the role of *experience* in shaping the individual psyche. Rather it is to say that these subjective, psychological entities will only arise because our minds have come equipped with an evolved program that will enable us to use our experience to generate these kinds of inner, dynamic forms and processes. Moreover, as we shall see, the deep structural, adaptive design of the human psyche may serve as a way of solving the staggeringly complex adaptive dilemmas universally faced by the human child and the socially interacting adult.

PARENT–OFFSPRING CONFLICT THEORY: LOVE AND INTERSUBJECTIVE CONFLICT IN EARLY DEVELOPMENT

The Meaning of "Adaptation" and the Broader Concept of "Inclusive Fitness"

The essential principle in evolution is that all life forms represent structures that enhance the survival and replication of copies of their underlying genetic codes. Those that succeed become more common, eventually characterizing the species as a whole. Those that fail disappear. All life forms and structures (physical as well as mental, as well as behavioral inclinations) can be understood in terms of the benefits they provide to the genetic material underlying them (Mayr, 1983; Kriegman and Slavin, 1989).

The term *adaptation* has a long, complicated history both within and outside of psychoanalysis. Let us be clear about its evolutionary biological meaning. As we noted, whenever anything (a structure or behavior) about an organism is called "adaptive" in contemporary evolutionary theory, we mean that it is organized so as to maximize the pursuit of ends that are advantageous to its individual genotype (Mayr, 1983, 1988; Trivers, 1985). Although most of us are familiar with this idea in terms of the Darwinian metaphor of "survival of the fittest" there is an important extension of this idea in contemporary evolutionary thought.

Since our genotype is always shared, to some degree, with kin, motivations that are actually most advantageous to it will necessarily include the welfare of these other individuals—albeit always in somewhat "discounted" form relative to one's own interests. This has led to a reconceptualization of "fitness" as *"inclusive* fitness" (Hamilton, 1964). Inclusive fitness is based upon the recognition that the survival of copies of an organism's genes in other individuals, and eventually in the future gene pool of the species, is the only real measure of evolutionary success or fitness. What is "adaptive" is what ultimately maximizes inclusive fitness, not simple personal fitness (Hamilton, 1964; Trivers, 1985). Let us now look more closely at the implications of this whole view of adaptation as it applies to the interactive dynamics that occur in the course of the prolonged period of human child development.

The Genetics of "Self" and "Other" and the Inevitability of Intersubjective Conflict

Because of the very close genetic relationship between parents and offspring in all species, there is a large degree of overlap between the individual self-interests of parent and child. They inherently share many of the same aims; in many respects, what is advantageous to one is advantageous to the other. This is particularly obvious from the parents' point of view. We need little biological sophistication to appreciate that the parents' own reproductive success, their "inclusive fitness," is intimately tied to the future reproductive success—the inclusive fitness—of their offspring.

This is also true, to some extent, in terms of the child's tie to the parent. Not only is the child tied to the parent for more obviously selfish, or individual, reasons, but also because the child derives distinct benefits to its inclusive fitness from the parents' successful pursuit of the parents' own fitness. Remember, the average parental genome includes half of the child's own genetic material. In this sense, the separateness of parent and child within the dyadic relationship is, in part, a *phenotypic illusion*. Parts of the child's genetic "self" are, literally, included within the parental "self" (and vice versa).

Though this may sound like a psychotic version of reality (a fusion or primitive merger of identities), it is, at root, nothing other than the actual biological reality that underlies Winnicott's (1965) telling aphorism, "there is no such thing as an infant, only a nursing couple." In this important biological sense, the notion of the child's individuality is, in some respects, an illusion based on our conscious overestimation of the phenotypic (overt, observable) physical separateness of the two organisms. At some level, this fundamental biological truth can be seen to underlie the basic metaphors, or visions of human nature, that characterize the relational tradition in psychoanalysis. It is implicit in the notion of the "selfobject" in

Kohut's (1984) work. While there is clear evidence from recent infant studies (Stern, 1985; Beebe and Lachmann, 1988; Lichtenberg, 1989) of an extremely early ability to differentiate the *skin bounded self* from others, we must also note that the interests of parents and children do overlap as emphasized by Ornstein (1989) and Stolorow, Brandchaft, and Atwood (1987). Yet simultaneously, each skin-bounded individual is unique. This uniqueness also has enormous significance.

For example, if we view family dynamics from the subjective perspective of the child's self, that is, from the perspective of the child's genetic interests, we would expect the child to value itself twice as much as it values its full sib with whom the child shares 50 percent of its genes. In contrast, the parent has a subjective view in which, on average, each child is valued relatively equally (half as much as the parent's self). So in interactions between siblings, parents—who are equally related to all of their offspring—want altruism between their offspring whenever the benefit to the recipient is greater than the cost to the altruist; and children only want to act altruistically whenever the benefit to a sib is greater than twice the cost to themselves. Likewise, in interactions between siblings, parents want their children to forego selfishness whenever the cost exceeds the benefit, and children ought to only be willing to readily forego selfishness when the cost to a sibling exceeds twice the benefit to themselves.

We therefore must emphasize another biological fact: Despite the overlap in their interests, parents and offspring are genetically distinct, unique, separate individuals. Thus, to some degree, from the moment of conception onward (Haig, 1993), their interests necessarily diverge as well as potentially compete and conflict. So, the biological support for Winnicott's view of the "nursing couple" notwithstanding, we must also affirm that, in an equally fundamental, psychologically relevant sense, there definitely *is* such a (separate) thing as a baby; and a (separate) nursing mother. There is a baby with a genetically distinct, unique self from the very beginning of life; and there is a mother (an average, "good-enough," devoted mother) with interests, aims, and views that are intrinsically different from her baby's aims and interests.

The universality of this basic, biological matrix has the following major implications: On virtually every crucial psychological issue in the course of development (indeed of the full life cycle), the parent—as a functioning biological organism—is likely to have been psychologically "designed" to operate with a subjective interpretation of reality that is consistent with its own inclusive fitness—derived in a self-interested fashion from its own subjective experience—biased toward those individuals (usually kin) to whom it is most closely tied. We shall call this the parents' inclusive self-interest. We can also borrow Erikson's (1956) apt term and call this the parental "psychosocial identity."

Thus, because the inclusive fitness of parent and child are only in part the same, there is a basic biological reason to assume, as Robert Trivers (1974), the leading theorist in contemporary social biology, put it, that "conflict is . . . an expected feature of [parent-offspring] relations . . . in particular, over how long the period of parental investment should last, over the amount of parental investment . . . and over the altruistic and egoistic tendencies of the offspring" (p. 249). Put more broadly, at the level of the psychological phenotype, we expect problematic, normative (as opposed to simply pathological) conflict to occur in the complex developmental process by which the child's identity is formed. Problematic conflict should also be a regular, ongoing feature of the interaction between the identities of parent and child. Our hypothesis is that, over vast evolutionary time, the realities of this "universal relational matrix" represent a chief selection pressure that shaped important aspects of the psychodynamic "deep structure" of our minds.

THE ADAPTIVE DILEMMA OF THE HUMAN CHILD

A Few Facts Concerning Human Adaptation

Let us keep in mind a few facts concerning human adaptation:

1. The prolonged childhood of the human species entails a period of extreme dependency and immaturity in which an

enormous amount of innate, hard-wired responsiveness has been "sacrificed" in the course of human evolution in order to create the flexibility in the child's capacity to construct an identity through social interactions. This plasticity in the psychosocial representation of its own inclusive self-interest can thus permit an exquisite attunement to the complex, changing realities of the sociocultural world into which it is born (LaBarre, 1954; Mayr, 1983).

2. The long developmental period of parent-child interaction (as well as the interactions between the child and the wider social environment) is one in which most interpersonal transactions—arguably the most important ones—take place through language and other forms of symbolic communication. Language and other forms of symbolism enable the child to construct a map of the world that far exceeds (and differs in quality from) anything that could be created from direct experience (Konner, 1982).

3. Yet, as numerous theorists have noted (Mitchell, 1985; Trivers, 1985), deception is a pervasive, universal intrinsic feature of all animal communication. In the pursuit of their own inclusive fitness, organisms do not simply communicate in order to convey a truth about reality to others, but rather to convey a "presentation of self": to hide certain features and selectively accentuate others that they need or desire others to perceive. The unique feature of human symbolic communication—its displacement from direct observation—greatly amplifies this power both to convey realities accurately and to hide them. Subjectivities—including an individual's sense of what reality is—inevitably clash (Slavin and Kriegman, in press; Kriegman, 1996a,b, 1997).

Psychological Implications of Human Prolonged Childhood, Language, and the Role of Deception in Human Communication

With its prolonged childhood, learning, and language in mind, let us try to formulate the central adaptive dilemma of the human child; that is, the essence of what it must accomplish psychologically in order to know and enhance its own inclusive fitness. Biologically, we know the child must strive to maximize the amount of investment (time, interest, love, guidance) given by parents. Psychologically, we know that the child must also incorporate from its parents whatever is in the child's own interest to learn accurately (about itself and the world) as this is transmitted through the parents' vision of reality. These aspects of the problem are well known and are essentially the sole focus of theories of "attachment" (e.g., Bowlby, 1969) that have accurately stressed the motivational significance of innate relational ties. But attachment theories have viewed these important functions in isolation, that is, outside the context of the inherently competing interests that also characterize the kin environment.

The adaptive problem of the human child is far more complex than has ever been dealt with by attachment theories. The child is almost totally dependent on direct investment from an environment which only partially shares its self-interest. More problematically still, the only chance for it to develop an internalized map of reality—a well-structured inner guide to the relational world—is to have a way of dealing adequately with the inherent, often covert, biases in the parental environment (by correcting or compensating for them) so that it can use its parents' interpretations of reality to define and build crucial aspects of its own self. In short, the human child is dependent upon self-interested parental figures, not only to survive, learn, and grow, but also, as objects to internalize in the very process of forming a self and a defined sense of its own self-interest. How, then, is it able to maintain and promote a clear enough sense of its own self-interest throughout the developmental process?

The evolutionist asks, How did the human child evolve the basic structural–dynamic capacity to accomplish this task? In functional turns, how would one want to "design" a child to be capable of developing a viable, internalized self derived through interactive relationships while, simultaneously, successfully looking out for its own specific interests under such conditions? We would like to suggest that the concept of repression provides a basic clue as to how this took place.

REPRESSION AS THE CORNERSTONE OF AN EVOLUTIONARY-ADAPTIVE SOLUTION

A Functional Redefinition of Repression

Repression is a psychological process in which attention or conscious awareness is structurally diverted away from certain wishes, aims, affects, or images of self and others. Into the more conscious realm, go those wishes and aims that are overtly more acceptable to, and internally more congruent with, the close kin environment of the family (including parental identities and views of reality). At the same time, however, the dynamic conception of repression describes a process that insures that many of the child's aims and views (that are less acceptable to or less congruent with parental views) will not be permanently lost as potential representations of, or guidelines for, the pursuit of the child's individual interests. Unlike a simple model in which behavioral responses are learned and unlearned, the process of repression insures that repressed aims can be put away, out of consciousness, but held in reserve, to return or be retrieved when it may be in the child's interests to do so (Slavin, 1974, 1985).

From an evolutionary perspective, what may be the most critical function of repression is not its more obvious diversion of conscious subjective experience, but, rather, its use of such a diversion to preserve future access to temporarily unacceptable, but potentially vital, aims and needs. Indeed, the evolutionary biology of parent–offspring conflict theory (Trivers, 1974) predicts precisely that such potentially conflictual, individually self-interested aims will surface when (1) conditions of direct parental investment decrease or threaten to decrease, and/or (2) the parents' control over and view of reality is less closely aligned with the child's interests than it was when the repression took place.

Repression thus can be seen as a very central psychological process that makes possible a certain "innate skepticism"—a normative resistance to "oversocialization" into the family culture (Slavin, 1985, 1990). This dynamically accessible storage then actually permits the child to risk being far more open to and influenced by the culture of that environment.

> From the evolutionary–adaptive perspective, what may be the most critical aspect of the classical concept of repression is that it signifies or alerts us to the fact that at the very center of psychic organization lies an organized inner system that enables us to use a diversion of awareness, an alteration of consciousness—in effect an act of "intentional" or strategic self-deception—while simultaneously preserving the possibility of access to temporarily unacceptable but potentially vital versions of the self [Slavin and Kriegman, 1992, pp. 158–159].

Trivers (1976) notes that:

> [If] deceit is fundamental to animal communication, then there must be strong selection to spot deception and this ought, in turn, to select for a degree of self-deception, rendering some facts and motives unconscious so as not to betray—by the subtle signs of self-knowledge—the deception being practiced. Thus the conventional view that natural selection favors nervous systems which produce ever more accurate images of the world must be a very naive view of mental evolution [p. vi].

The question of the importance of such situations remains: Are there enough human interactions that require deception to render this a central feature of the human psyche? In fact, there appear to be more than enough.

Development as an (Intrapsychically Regulated) Negotiation Process

We are suggesting that it may be useful to view the human child as centrally involved in the negotiation of a kind of provisional identity in the course of its development. This provisional psychic structure represents a kind of working compromise between the child's interests and the interests of the kin environment. It allows the child to keep alternative impulses, affects, and narcissistic and creative elements in reserve, out of awareness, perhaps, but not out of the realm of future "renegotiated" possibility (Slavin and Slavin, 1976).

What are the future events that may require renegotiation? There are expectable but unpredictable changes in parental and kin investment (e.g., the birth of siblings, the health and emotional state of parents, as well as the myriad ways in which family fortunes and dynamics can drastically change over time). We know that there are usually substantial shifts in the quality and attunement of most interpersonal environments under such changing conditions (Erikson, 1964b).

More significantly, however, there is a major predictable change built into every child's life cycle—adolescence. A prolonged childhood in the context of primarily very close kin relations is, to be sure, an excellent environment in which to develop. Although we have emphasized intrafamilial conflicts of interests, biases, and normal deceptions, it should be clear that "kin altruism"—the motivation to identify with the interests of kin, based on highly overlapping self-interests—is real and adaptively indispensable. No one but parents and close kin could conceivably be counted upon, in any regular, predictable way, to make the degree of investment that is necessary to insure a human child's present and future development (Kriegman, 1988, 1990).

There is, however, a radical shift at adolescence. The biological change that takes place at adolescence is not only the well-known physiological maturation of the body, the brain, and the capacity for reproduction. It is also an equally fundamental, equally "biological," shift from an environment composed primarily of interactions between close kin to an environment of more distant kin and unrelated individuals bound together primarily by ties of reciprocity and exchange.

Although there are, of course, vast differences (between social classes, cultures, and historical eras) in the degree to which adolescents are expected to move away from the family in the process of establishing an adult life, there is, nevertheless, always a relative movement away from primary relationships with close kin toward more distant and unrelated individuals (for mating and exchange relationships) in virtually every human society. Biologically, there are vast differences in the meanings of relationships with different degrees of relatedness (Trivers, 1985). Psychologically, the complicated process of forming a provisional identity within the family invariably entails significant (often costly) compromises in terms of the repression-dissociation of potentially vital aspects of the self. We would therefore expect that a major developmental dynamic would have to exist by which those elements of individual identity developed in the context of kin investment and kin altruism can be reevaluated and renegotiated in the context of the drastically different conditions of reciprocal exchange outside the nuclear family.

The ubiquity of regression in adolescence that has long fascinated psychoanalytic theorists (see A. Freud, 1958; Erikson, 1964a; Blos, 1979) may be understood within the evolutionary framework as an adaptive process that has been "prepared for" by the operation of repression in childhood. In this view, adolescent regression represents the process by which selectively repressed aims and identity elements that did not fit the family environment are retrieved at a later point in development when they may provide a uniquely valuable means with which to renegotiate what is essentially a "new compromise" between individual interests and the new parameters and possibilities of an altered environment. Inclusive self-interest—provisionally internalized in a childhood identity—is thus reopened, and, in the course of interaction with new objects, redefined into its adult form (Slavin and Slavin, 1976).

The Function of Endogenous Drives (and the Drive–Defense System) in This "Negotiation/Renegotiation" Process

If the dynamics of repression do represent a strategy for hiding, preserving, and retrieving those aspects of our aims and experience that cannot fit within the formative environment—especially the more self-interested aims—we still need to account for those affect states or emotional signals that press us to act in intensely self-interested ways in the first place. From our evolutionary perspective, we ask how a socially or relationally constructed self—a self that, to a significant degree, is built out of biased familial–cultural meanings—can still be counted upon to generate the pursuit of a whole range of passionately individual aims? What allowed the human child to take the historically unprecedented "risk" of "sacrificing" a huge amount of innate, hard-wired adaptedness? Especially, what enabled us to rely upon a program that is dependent upon symbolic, deception-prone interactions with powerful, needed objects whose own interests inevitably lead them to try to shape our identity toward what is beneficial to them?

With these questions in mind, reconsider the notion of endogenous (or instinctual) drives. First note that all innate (naturally selected) motivations are "endogenous." What distinguishes the classical drives from relational needs or motivations is the asocial nature of the classical drives. We are suggesting that while it is necessary to correct the extreme classical overemphasis on asocial, selfish drives (Mitchell, 1988; Kriegman, 1988, 1990; Kriegman and Knight, 1988), there is an important aspect of such "selfish drivenness" that must not be discarded. It is in the asocial aspect of the drives that we have a mechanism that guarantees access to some types of motivation that arise from nonrelational sources and are, in a sense, totally dedicated toward the promotion of our individual interests (Slavin, 1986). The unique functional feature of such drives—conceived as a type of motivation rooted in our bodily nature—is the way in which they serve as a guarantee against having one's genetic self-interest usurped by the social influence of important others, notably those serving as models for introjection and identification. As Wrong (1963) pointed out, theories that do not adequately address the question of how individuals are equipped with motives that are not entirely social in nature, will always present us with an "oversocialized image of man," an incomplete and absurdly unrealistic picture of human motivation.

This conception of the "balancing" function of the drives echoes Rappaport's (1960) notion of the way in which the drives guarantee a certain "autonomy from the superego"; or,

as Eagle (1984) put it, the instincts serve to resist the individual's "enslavement by society." It is critical to note, however,
that the evolutionary argument for the adaptive function of
the drives differs radically from its ego psychological predeces-
sors (e.g., Rappaport). Beyond any of the modifications introduced by ego psychology, the evolutionary paradigm revises
the assumptions of classical theory in several ways: (1) It puts
the drives and their role into a clearly subsidiary position in
relation to other, superordinate principles of motivation; (2)
it acknowledges the existence of fundamental, primary, irreducible social motivations (Kriegman, 1988, 1990); and (3) it
emphasizes the existence of pervasive biases in the motives and
aims of normal adults within the thoroughly "good-enough"
environment—the essentially nonpathological, yet profoundly
self-interested environmental influences that the child must be
equipped to both internalize and resist in the course of normal
development.

Thus, evolutionary theory suggests the need for a type of
motivation which, in this function, resembles the instinctual
drives of the classical model. The drives provide a unique
source of adaptively relevant information (Peterfreund, 1972)
operating within the larger functional organization of the aims
of the individual (Lloyd, 1984). Yet, simply because such endogenous motives are highly dependent on input from the body
(and relatively resistant to social modification) there is no reason to equate them with what is "animal" or "biological" in
our nature; nor, certainly, do they exist in basic opposition
to something that is, in any basic sense, "nonbiological" or
"cultural" in our nature. From an evolutionary perspective this
is a completely false, misleading dichotomy (Mayr, 1974, 1982).

IMPLICATIONS FOR DEVELOPMENTAL STABILITY AND CHANGE

The Compulsion to Repeat versus the Capacity for Creative Repetition

From a clinical vantage point, we rarely, if ever, see repression
operate in a direct way. Instead, we see repetition. That is to

say, the operation of repression is inferred from repeated patterns of behavior that often appear to contradict conscious aims and intentions. In these, at times painful repetitions, we assume that repressed aspects of the self are either excluded from expression or are being expressed in restricted, indirect ways—usually in the form of certain actions or symptoms. Thus the clinical meaning that is given to patterns of repetition will derive in good part from our underlying assumptions about why and how repression operates.

From the classical perspective, problems in adaptation arise because the exclusion of repressed needs from awareness cannot be maintained (A. Freud, 1936; Fenichel, 1945; Brenner, 1976). The frustration, fixation, or traumatic overstimulation of infantile aims creates an imperative, continuous need to seek new arenas for their expression—albeit in distorted, disguised form. Caught in a web of continuing conflict (essentially over the selfishly sensual and aggressive character of these primary needs), individuals are driven to enact painful repetitions of their original failures to find acceptable ways of fulfilling their aims. This is related to Freud's (1920) metapsychological speculations about the existence of a fundamental "repetition compulsion" and is the essence of the clinical notion of the so-called compulsion to repeat (Bibring, 1943; Fenichel, 1945; Glover, 1955). The compulsion to repeat is a motivational concept that goes hand in hand with the classical view of repression and invariably plays an absolutely central role in the classical and ego psychological definition and basic understanding of psychological disorder (Kriegman and Slavin, 1989).

In this view, patterns of symptomatic experience, transference repetitions, and the persistence of subjectively painful (otherwise inexplicable) actions are ultimately described as extended ways of reliving the past without consciously experiencing or knowing it. Most clinically observed repetitions are thus regarded not as persistent efforts at accomplishing something new, but rather as deceptive strategies for maintaining or restoring something old, some prior state of equilibrium, or status quo ante (Bibring, 1943). The emphasis is thus on repetition as signaling self-deception—as a way of keeping the connection alive but out of awareness. In effect, it becomes a way of not remembering, of not changing, of distorting meanings, of not knowing.

As we have seen, the evolutionary perspective clearly suggests that the process of repression is indeed based, in part, on a kind of functional self-deception that serves to divert awareness from certain highly conflictual aims in a fashion that will insure the possibility of their later return as part of on ongoing, relational negotiation process. Thus we would expect that a whole range of earlier developmental experiences, affects, and motives will be readily revived and repeated at other points in development; it is assumed that the need to conceal and distort some of their more conflictual meanings will certainly continue to operate during the whole repetitive process of retrieving, reliving, and renegotiating both the internal and the interpersonal dimensions of one's identity or inclusive self-interest.

Thus the elements of overlap with the classical model are apparent: There is assumed to be a certain built-in tendency to return to and "relive" aspects of the past, as well as a persistent need to alter the subjective experience of reality in ways that would conceal certain selfish and aggressive aims that are likely to diverge and compete with those of needed others. However, the differences between the evolutionary paradigm and the classical model are also significant, perhaps, ultimately, farther reaching. From the evolutionary perspective, the most important dynamic aspect of clinically observed repetitions—and the whole range of phenomena that are readily referred to as manifestations of "the repetition compulsion"—is the fact that they cannot be understood apart from the larger adaptive context in which they occur (Kriegman and Slavin, 1989).

Specifically, this means that the universal salience of early experiences and the persistence of infantile attachments are not primarily understood as a function of the inherent conservatism of the instincts or the persistence of the child's immature distortions of adult reality. Rather, these phenomena are seen as elements in a far broader adaptive system that is designed to preserve repressed early experiences because—given the assumed biases in the familial version of reality—"the repressed" represents a version of reality that contains substantial subjective truth. It is a version of reality that is particularly crucial for the process of redefining self-interest in changed environments and thus adaptively reorganizing the self.

The repetitive enactment of repressed meanings is thus, ultimately, less accurately understood as an effort at self-deception and distortion of reality—though it inevitably includes this—than as a striving to make use of certain highly subjective meanings for the adaptively relevant information they contain, and to use them as renewed developmental guidelines. There is always an effort to communicate them in some form to others and—to the extent that the new environment is reliably different from the old one—to renegotiate their place in the structure of the self. Repression confers, in effect, a capacity for future repetition—a capacity that may well appear to be (or even be experienced as) a compulsion.

Unlike the repetition compulsion, repetitive enactments of repressed meanings often do not simply operate in the service of restoring and maintaining an inner "equilibrium," in the sense of a status quo, but rather as part of a complicated process of experimentally promoting developmental repair and change while simultaneously holding onto the old solution until a new, more effective one has begun to develop. In this way, the evolutionary perspective profoundly validates the view of Winnicott and Kohut that developmental strivings toward the resumption of thwarted growth—balanced against self-protective, conservative elements—must play a central, perhaps superordinate, role in the organization of the psyche (Kriegman and Slavin, 1989).

Repression, Regression, and Transference: A Coordinated Set of Adaptive, Developmental Processes

Repression and regression enable the temporary suspension of access to parts of one's inner experience, indeed, to vital aspects of the self, and to make use of this "reserve" in future negotiations/renegotiations with the environment. This capacity for reversible suspension of access to parts of the self serves as a major fulcrum for ongoing adaptation throughout the entire life cycle (Slavin and Kriegman, 1992). In addition to adolescence, as examples consider any of the times when one's own identity is called upon to complement another's, or to compensate for the loss of the other: marriage, divorce, death of a spouse. In all of these normal crises in relationships, one can well make use of that reserve of alternate identity elements and repressed wishes which natural selection has enabled the child to bequeath to the adult (Slavin, 1985, 1990).

Normal dynamic functioning entails a fluid, experimental shifting of the line between what is conscious and what is not (Stolorow and Atwood, 1989). In the evolutionary view, this fluidity derives from the fact that we are designed to synthesize aspects of self structure in a provisional way—a way that always remains highly contingent on the fit between our self-interest and the environment. Our selves are adaptively divided, nonunitary, and thus flexible (Slavin, 1996a).

SOME BASIC IMPLICATIONS FOR THERAPEUTIC CHANGE AND THE ANALYTIC PROCESS

The Psychoanalytic Situation

The psychoanalytic situation itself can be viewed as a human relationship that invites precisely the sort of regressive revival of repressed aspects of the self that were held in reserve for future renegotiation under altered relational conditions. The major reason we are able to mobilize powerful transferences and therapeutic regressions within the analytic situation becomes understandable as a heightened natural phenomenon: Our psyches are organized to experience new situations as opportunities for the revival of repressed aspects of the self and the reorganization of intrapsychic structure (cf. J. H. Slavin, 1994). Indeed, whatever modifications in personality psychoanalysis can achieve may be essentially patterned on this built-in human capacity for regressive renegotiation of identity under altered relational conditions.

Thus, transferences and therapeutic regressions within the analytic situation become understandable not simply in terms of the range of factors typically cited in the analytic literature: i.e., as drives pressing for gratification (Fenichel, 1945), as projections of internal objects (Racker, 1954), as the effective activation of a self-selfobject relationship (Kohut, 1984), as the creation of a transitional space (Winnicott, 1965), as the establishment of a sufficient "background of safety" (Weiss and Sampson, 1986), or as simply the ongoing "organizing activity of the psyche" (Stolorow and Lachmann, 1984). These represent essentially aspects of transference and of those conditions under which transference is likely to operate and be heightened.

Repression, regression, and transference appear to operate in a coordinated way throughout the life cycle to repeatedly heighten the experienced comparison of the fit between inner needs, old solutions—which we must remember were the best compromises individuals could effect earlier between their self interests and the competing interests of others—and current relational realities. This experiential juxtaposition of needs, solutions, and current realities enables, indeed, compels us (and the objects of our transferences) to engage in the renegotiation–revision process. The centrality of transference as the therapeutic vehicle is thus seen as a way in which psychoanalysis has capitalized upon a built-in set of coordinated biological functions designed to maintain and revise inclusive fitness. This conception of transference provides a needed conceptual rationale for Loewald's (1965) notion of "creative repetition" as a force for dynamic change, as well as for efforts such as Stolorow and Lachmann's (1984) to increase our basic appreciation of the critical subjective truths entailed in the phenomena of transference, and Hoffman's (1983) to recast the meaning of transference in terms of a social exchange. It broadens and lends considerable weight to constructs such as the "curative fantasy" (Ornstein, 1984) in which many of the so-called misperceptions and distortions of reality in the transference are

seen as expressions of the patient's overarching effort to generate the interactive conditions in which, for that individual, a
cure may be possible.

A CASE EXAMPLE: NANCY AND THE ANALYST'S CHILD

Nancy was a very troubled young woman who had been characterized by many previous therapists as "borderline." She described her family as a "horror show"—no one ever helping
her grow up or seeing anything that was real. She was, for
years, seen as the perfect child. Father was described as very
compulsive, trying to solve everything in life rationally; mother
as depressed, severely "out of it," yet anxiously very solicitous
about Nancy's welfare. Neither had really protected her from
an abusive older brother; and both felt fragile to her, afraid
of life.

   She quickly developed a powerful transference to her therapist in which he was clearly experienced as a good parent. He
seemed *present* to her, she said, as if he could take care of
himself. He found himself talking with her easily in colloquial
language, easily adopting an openness and flexibility with her.
The analyst had developed a countertransference experience
with her in which he actually felt an especially clear sense of
himself. This was like, he thought, the solid, reliable, soothingly
matter-of-fact, feet-on-the-ground parent she had never known
(cf. Slavin, 1996b). He would keep himself safe, and keep her
safe. He also felt he could, in a more interpretive vein, begin
to help her construct a picture of how the legacy of her childhood still haunted her creating expectations of danger and
rageful responses that undermined her constantly.

   After a few years of treatment, Nancy became increasingly
agitated and depressed after hearing that her analyst was about
to have a child. She felt his child would take him from her
and she would lose everything. The analyst felt and responded
warmly to her, recognizing her distress, and repeatedly trying
to capture empathically what he felt was her subjective perspective on the situation. "We've seen," he said "how much you

tend to feel that there is a limit to the amount of love and concern available in the world—the kind of 'zero-sum' feeling we've talked so much about. So what I might give to my child, will reduce what is available for you." And although he would invite her views of the current situation, he would tend to gravitate back to representing it to himself in terms of the repetitious experience created by her zero-sum organizing principle. He repeated versions of this in various ways, over time, linked more or less closely with the specifics of her early parenting experience.

The implication of his understanding was that the most significant dimension of Nancy's current experience was a set of subjective organizing principles carried over from a childhood during which she felt misunderstood by parents who were oblivious to her needs and her experience of intense isolation and jealousy with her two male siblings. The analyst's emphasis on her past was communicated in a compassionate way without any direct implication or sense of "distortion." In the analyst's "postmodern" perspective, the concept of distortion was felt by him to be a moot issue, one he had moved beyond. Yet, his understanding still inevitably implied that, in some way, her views did not fit the reality of the current situation (cf. Kriegman, 1996a, 1998). Nancy seemed to contemplate the analyst's words. But, after several sessions, she became more distraught and angry (in his view she became quite regressed) and suicidal.

Nancy's analyst was deeply invested both in his sense that there was a reparative dimension to their relationship, and—protecting his somewhat idealized, relatively nonconflictual view of the treatment process—in his assumption that Nancy's fear, rage, and regression now came predominantly from her idiosyncratic way of constructing the meaning of his having a child—her pathologically limited and rigidified way of organizing experience. He felt that her sense that there would be an inevitable disruption of her experience of him as a solid, reliable parental figure (because he was going to have a child of his own) must derive from her past experience of distracted, oblivious, unprotective parenting (Slavin, 1996b).

In his regular supervision on this case, various strategies had been suggested to the analyst for conceptualizing and dealing with Nancy's terror and rage over his "disappearing and abandoning her." He was reassured that, of course, he would have enough to give and that the crucial therapeutic question was why Nancy could not experience his caring. He was encouraged to look at how she had even managed to project her doubts and anxiety into him—managing to enlist him emotionally in a reenactment of her relationship with her rejecting parents—making him feel, at times, as though he was abandoning her. It was also pointed out that this was, simultaneously, a reversed side of the enactment: Nancy was now (by threatening to break off their relationship) in the role of her abandoning parents (with whom she was identified) engaged in a rejection of the vulnerable child (projected into the therapist).

The power of Nancy's "regression," her intense transference, set in motion an interactive process that led (with some help from a consultation) to a deeper reappraisal by the analyst of his own beliefs: specifically, of the way in which his views of Nancy shielded him from recognizing the elements of self-deception and self-protection in his own initial response to her. During this process, he also had the opportunity to experience the birth of his child—his own joyful preoccupation with it *and* the very real drain it created on his resources.

In his own thoughts and then in subsequent sessions, the analyst found himself ready to acknowledge the truth that Nancy's "transferential anxiety" had ultimately brought him to hear: namely, that, of course, his life energies were and would be significantly absorbed by a child of his own flesh. And that his relationship with his child did represent a different—in many ways, far more powerful—investment than his bond with her. He would physically hold his new child and, indeed, reorganize much of his time and life around him. In contrast, were the time-limited schedule of their meetings, her paying for them, their lack of physical touching when she longed for (and in many ways probably needed) it.

The analyst acknowledged and discussed the reality of these conflicts with Nancy, including his own struggle to recognize and articulate them. Nancy finally seemed to experience something in these discussions as genuine. She began, as she put it, to feel "real" again; she no longer felt her therapist had "disappeared." She became less afraid and, in her inimitable way, quipped that maybe her analyst would actually learn something about nurturing that might be of use to her.

As she recompensated, Nancy went on to talk more openly about (and to try to understand her participation in) the crisis: how and why she so deeply believed that the painful experience with her depressed and oblivious parents would automatically be repeated in the relationship with her analyst. Indeed, over the course of many years, Nancy's treatment revealed how Nancy had come to live in a walled off, dissociated inner world—an inner world built around powerful expectations of reenacted trauma precisely like what she had anticipated and then partially relived (and cocreated) with her analyst. Her repressed–dissociated self experience was built around an alternating sense of her own badness–dangerousness and the dangerousness–deceptiveness of others. Her constricted subjective world was maintained by a set of entrenched assumptions about herself and others that cut her off from whole aspects of her own inner emotional life and robbed her of a sense of solidity and legitimacy in interactions with others. The pathological structure of her inner world was sustained and reinforced by repeated experiences that, in one way or other, confirmed the "reality" of her worst fears—including, on countless occasions, the repetition of multiple versions of experiences with her therapist that in one way or other resembled this painful negotiation of the meaning surrounding his newborn child.

Slowly, through these repeated negotiations, she and her analyst developed what she called an increasingly "real" relationship—for years the only relationship in her life that felt real to her. The evolving negotiation about what was "real" in their relationship included both: (1) the identification of conflicts and related biases and self deceptions (on both parts), as well as (2) the development of an increasingly detailed, emotionally usable analytic understanding of how her adaptive effort at psychic survival (her use of dissociation/repression) had, nevertheless, ended up creating the entrapping, self-defeating structure of her inner world—the world in which she felt she had no right or capacity to live.

Conflict, Deception, Self-Deception, and
Negotiation in the Therapeutic Relationship

Thinking about the case of Nancy leads us to consider the complicated, conflictual, deception prone process through which the therapeutic endeavor unfolds. From an evolutionary psychoanalytic perspective, we emphasize the ways in which a meaningful engagement of patient and therapist requires that therapist and patient continuously negotiate together their separate interests and involvement in the therapeutic frame and the therapeutic process. Only through such a negotiation can they engage in the arduous process of disentangling the patient's entrapping inner world from the conflicting interests of others in a way that is emotionally usable and promotes change.

Our patients have lost versions of themselves, of their needs experiences—have put them somewhere that is minimally accessible—in the effort to maintain a familiar, if painful, story line about their lives. From an evolutionary perspective, both this pathological sequestering of a self–other schema as well as their revision is made possible by the evolved capacity for repression–dissociation operating in concert with what we have sketched as the adaptive capacity for regression and transference.

ASPECTS OF THE THERAPEUTIC ACTION

The Negotiation of Conflict

From an evolutionary vantage point, we begin with the sense that Nancy's therapist needed to be "pulled" by her away from many of his beliefs (as they fit within his particular relational psychoanalytic perspective) that his sustained empathy, flexibility, and affective responsiveness with her could, in a crunch, sufficiently provide the new object experience she needed to remain safe with him and grow. He was simultaneously pulled away from the more classically derived side of his thinking, from the interpretive framework and belief system of his training (and several trusted supervisors) in which the belief existed that the careful articulation of the historical roots of Nancy's transferential rage could provide the understanding she needed to contain her current anger and despair.

The painful process by which the analyst came to grasp some of the essential realities of Nancy's experience—his feelings of being terribly lost, responsible for a potentially tragic ending, and thoroughly confused—needed to be endured as he peeled away the various beliefs about their relationship and about psychoanalysis. These beliefs had provided structure, identity, safety, and self-esteem for him, yet he needed to risk reproach from his supervisors and to struggle with the disquieting sense of disloyalty. All of this inner process was in part precipitated and guided by her "regression," her "transference." We view this as a truly interactive, mutual process, perhaps a "mutually regulated" (thoroughly and profoundly negotiated) regression (cf. Pizer, 1992): She fell apart, became unreal and dissociated, in part, to provoke a parallel process in him—the deconstruction and renegotiated reconstruction of many of the familiar, less risky, and comforting views and beliefs that cohered nicely in his usual working identity.

Transference as an Adaptive Probe

The human capacity to develop and interactively use transferences may actually be geared, in significant part, to expressing and probing the potential for recognizing and negotiating the ambiguous mixture of real conflict and mutuality in human relatedness (cf. Aron, 1991; Hoffman, 1983). Nancy responded intensely to her sense of this potential deceptiveness in the transference. She was not part of the analyst's life in a way that permitted her to observe or directly influence his investment in her to anywhere near the extent that a child can affect the relative investment in a sibling. She thus needed to mobilize fantasy and emotion within her transference as a way of probing the analyst's capacity for candid reflection regarding their conflicting interests over the investment he made in his new baby.

In many respects, therapists must sustain an exquisite alertness to self-deception and avoidance of deception. For not only is the analytic relationship basically prone to the same complex web of conflict and deception as other human ties, but the analytic relationship must ultimately justify its potential influence without making the same kinds of real investment in the patient's life that is often found in other, more spontaneous and less contrived, reciprocal bonds. The negotiation between analyst and patient must serve to continuously transform the deceptive part of the relationship, its painful "unreality," into a more benign form, something that is experienced more as play and creative illusion (Winnicott, 1969; Modell, 1984; Pizer, 1992). Ultimately, it must be real enough on its own terms and in its own way (Greenberg, 1986) to justify the patient's using it effectively to question and revise fundamental conclusions about themselves and their ways of interacting with the relational world.

As Nancy compelled her analyst to recognize, one of the major ways in which therapists fail their patients revolves around the therapist's use of self-deceptive strategies for protecting or enhancing his or her interests in a fashion that is cast in terms of the interests of the patient. In our view, the danger that many patients sense in such a "confusion of interests" is not simply the "dread to repeat" a traumatic experience (Ornstein, 1974) or of major boundary violation in their past. Rather, within many ordinary enough, everyday deceptions, there lies the potential for further loss and erosion of the vital capacity to define, know, and promote one's own interests. We believe this tendency to engender a confusion of interests is, perhaps, the central feature of many less than good-enough, traumatizing, pathogenic family environments. And it is not uncommonly replicated in many therapies woven into what therapists codify as "technique."

This "confusion of interests" can be very destructive to a child and we would probably tend to call its effect "traumatic." However, it can operate in subtle ways over a long period of time and it is this confusion of interests in a conflictual relational world that can lead to a very familiar event: our dealing with very troubled and confused patients who continually exclaim, "What's my problem? I had a good family/childhood. Nothing *really* bad happened to me."

Negotiating the Frame and Becoming a "New Object"

In our focus on this transference–countertransference replay of Nancy's past experience, on the enactment, and the complex, mutually regulated dynamics of this process, let us not forget that this interaction seemed to be, at its core, a genuine negotiation around the painful reality of the existence of conflicting interests in this highly structured but otherwise intimate, collaborative, and mutually beneficial relationship (cf. Pizer, 1992). It was not, in this crucial sense, simply a replication of something that existed in Nancy's past that was badly negotiated back then and still lived, unresolved, within her—though it was, *in part,* that. Rather, it was primarily a negotiation of a new version of the same kind of conflict and deception that occurred not only with special regularity in Nancy's childhood, but that occurs in everyone's childhood to some extent. A conflict that was perhaps as debilitating as it was for her not simply because it replicated the past but because it was quite real in the present and could be expected to reoccur in the future. It is also very important to see that it is no accident that Nancy and her analyst entered what Havens (1993) calls the "realm of the real" precisely when they were struggling with the "unrealness" of their relationship—the ways the analyst's emotional investment and rules of engagement (the analytic frame) were not real in anything like the sense they were real with his own child.

Why does the genuine struggle with the "unreal" in the analytic relationship bring in, as it were, something more real? We believe it is because the analytic frame, the basic rules and rituals of the analytic engagement (set up by analyst) usually become a deep part of each analyst's professional identity in the basically honest belief that these rules (e.g., money, time, no touching) while serving the analyst's interests are also fundamentally aligned with what is ultimately in the interest of the patient.

In most cases, this alignment with the patient's interests is probably somewhat true. But, like any human arrangement, including the human family, the real balance of interests is highly ambiguous and shifting. Because analysts establish the "ground rules," they are exceedingly likely to be tilted and biased toward the analyst's interests more than those of the patient. The preexisting structure designed by analysts for their use with a wide variety of patients can only be relatively aligned with the particular needs and interests of a specific patient, needs that change over time. The bias toward the analyst's interests is often subtle, invisible, barely knowable by him or her. The patient's job, not unlike the job of the child in the family, is to, in whatever ways possible, use their own needs and transferences to ferret out the relative balance of interests: to separate the apparent or assumed alignment with their interests from what in other ways they actually feel to be the case. Our patients present their sense of this delicate, ever changing, tilting balance of interests through the multitude of continuing ways they react to and challenge the strange unrealness—i.e., the strange mixture of deep concern and intimate emotional involvement with the severe limits and fairly rigid structure of the therapeutic relationship—of our care and concern for them (Aron, 1991; Davies, 1994).

Why the Analyst Needs To Change

At the outset of an analysis, the analyst may start out as a "new object" in the sense of an individual whom the patient can experience as having different views, needs, and responsiveness from the patient's familial objects (Greenberg, 1986). Yet only through a prolonged interpersonal and internal negotiation with the challenge and influence of the patient does the analyst cumulatively become for the patient a more deeply usable "new experience" with a new object: "new" to the patient because the analyst is—through the negotiation process—new to him- or herself. That is, it is often the patient's experience of the analyst changing—of the analyst *struggling* to come to terms with something new—that provides the crucial knowledge that there is a genuine working negotiation occurring. Because the relationship between analyst and patient entails real conflicts between their identities, the negotiation process, ultimately involving real changes in the analyst, provides the crucial experience for the patient to risk reopening and re-working old conclusions about his or her self as well as the potential for more effective negotiations with others (Slavin and Kriegman, 1998).

Remember, in this view, pathology is due, in significant part, to failed or inadequate earlier negotiations that led to limited and limiting characterological compromise formations. These problematic characterological limits include: (1) re-pressed aspects of the self that are *unavailable* for flexible adap-tation to the relational world; (2) repressed aspects of the self that get *enacted* in disguised or distorted form; (3) debilitating *styles* of negotiating with others for one's needs; and (4) debili-tating *beliefs* (both positive and negative) about the possibilities for effective negotiation and the ultimate availability of needed responses from others. When analysts change, patients have the direct experience of having developed a working *style* of negotiation; in long, often difficult negotiations, they experi-ence the real impact they have had on an other as analysts struggle to discover something new about themselves. Patients also realize that their preconceptions regarding the extremely limited potential for responses from the world may be mis-leading; they see that, within the often painful limits of the analytic frame and despite the inevitable frustration of their wishes, it is possible to obtain a meaningful, real adaptation–accommodation to their interests and needs from an other. These experiences often carry the necessary emotional impact only when patients watch analysts struggle to become new and different people because the change is necessary for a meaning-ful relationship with their patients—and thus is valued by the analysts who, in a painfully limited but real way, care about their patients.

CONCLUSIONS: RESTORING THE CAPACITY TO KNOW AND LIVE INCLUSIVE SELF-INTEREST

We began this chapter with an offer to the reader of a different vantage point from which to view some of the central debates in contemporary psychoanalytic theory and practice. "Listening," as we put it, "with the evolutionist's ear" brings many themes to the fore. For us, the central evolutionary story of childhood is one in which parent and child are engaged, from the outset, in a far more complex version of "mutual regulation" than that which has, so far, been so usefully depicted in much recent literature (Beebe and Lachmann, 1988). In the evolutionary version of the developmental narrative, parent and child are, from the word go, involved in a negotiation process in which, despite overlapping interests, they each have differing, individual perspectives and somewhat different agendas. It is a natural negotiation in which both parties continuously attempt to tilt or bias the developmental process toward ends that are aligned with their own particular interests. Throughout the life cycle, the evolutionary realities of parent–offspring conflict translate into some of the most vexing, paradoxical questions posed by our children (and then, by our patients). These "questions" are actually ongoing, often unconscious, subjective inner dialogues—at times excruciating existential dialogues—around negotiating and living an inclusive sense of oneself (of one's own interests) amidst the ambiguous web of deceptions, self-deceptions, conflict, and genuine mutuality that has shaped us as well as shaped our very way of shaping ourselves.

How can this person, these people, this family who love me—whom I love and need, and whom I have used to build my very sense of self—simultaneously be multiple, divided, deceptive creatures in some ways out for themselves in ways that cause me great pain? Despite their self-presentations, I have sensed levels of deception and multiplicity (Bromberg, 1994, 1995; Slavin, 1996a)—painful contradictions. From the very beginning, we have had difficult struggles. Did they, do they now, how could they also care deeply about me and my real interests? I have come to represent myself, in good part, through them—my subjectivity, my very self-definition built on identifications and interactions with those ambiguously and imperfectly allied others. How can I (come to) know who I really am: to construct where, within my own multiplicity (among my own inner contractions), my real interests may lie and how to effectively define and live them? Can I be effectively out for myself? I must. Yet I must also experience myself as faithfully related to my own past—loyal to others, geared, somehow, to their real interests, part of a larger web of human purposes.

The Intertwining of Evolved, Adaptive Deep Structures and Pathological Structures

Our psyches have been shaped over millions of years to deal more or less effectively with the existential challenges posed by these universal, adaptive dilemmas. Every child is prepared—from the moment of conception onward (Haig, 1993)—to expect that the relational world will be filled with love and opportunity, as well as hard-to-recognize yet powerfully problematic conflict. And the conflict the child must be prepared for is almost always hidden, to varying degrees, behind rules and views that are represented as more tailored to the child's interests than in fact they are or could possibly be. The way we are prepared for this via our evolved, complex, psychological design, our intrapsychic "deep structure" of affects, fantasies, fundamental desires and strivings, adaptive and defensive strategies, make it possible to negotiate these life-long, paradoxical conflicts. We have evolved an extraordinary, but intrinsically precarious, working solution to the dilemmas of human development and relating (cf. Modell, 1989).

Analysts and therapists rarely see the ways in which, throughout human history and in a wide range of cultures, basic human dynamic capacities actually function well enough most of the time in a wide range of environmental circumstances. That is, well enough to often carry on despite severe, traumatic versions of these adaptive dilemmas. Yet, there are ironic (frequently costly) consequences of our very adaptive design. The adequate, dynamic strategies that have thus far been shaped by natural selection may function well enough in a range of developmental variations. Yet, these strategies introduce, by their very design, a certain precariousness in our overall adaptation as well as direct potentials for constructing very debilitating ways of trying to adapt to life's challenges.

Often enough—even in the absence of especially severe deprivation and frustration—we see patients who experience significant difficulty constructing effective ways to sense and live their inclusive self-interest. As an indispensable, built-in adaptive potential that operates through limiting access to awareness of aspects of experience, repression-dissociation can, nevertheless, become so entwined in an individual's way of experiencing him- or herself that it lends itself to the creation of walled off, self-perpetuating islands of experience as the only safe realms in which to experience life. So too, the crucial set of adaptive functions for counterbalancing the shaping power of relational influences—signified by what Freud called "drives" and Melanie Klein called "primal phantasies"—can be experienced (especially in the context of a walled-off self system) as posing dangers to others and ultimately oneself. Similarly, the vital "probing functions" of "regressive" transferences—so well suited to unearthing the hidden aspects of the subjectivity of others—can induce responses from others that are unlikely to be tolerable enough to be effectively negotiated and thus end up repeatedly reconfirming pathogenic beliefs (Weiss and Sampson, 1986). Within or outside of the clinical setting, few, if any of us, manage to utilize these adaptive functions without considerable difficulty at various points in life.

Thus, as in the emergence of autoimmune diseases ranging from allergies to cancers, our vital system of complex, dynamic psychological adaptations—the system that has evolved to protect and ultimately promote and enhance "inclusive self-interest"—can lend itself to the construction of self-structures that get turned against one's self-interest. A way of living, of experiencing self and others, can be created in which natural, adaptive capacities and strivings subvert and repeatedly impede the creation and living out of a vital sense of inclusive self-interest. As we view it, a wide range of psychological pain, symptoms, and dysfunctions signals precisely this sensed misalignment between one's current identity and one's genuinely inclusive self-interest as well as one's incapacity to create structures and meanings that allow one to actively "live" that inclusive self-interest day to day. Viewed as "disorders of inclusive self-interest" many forms of psychopathology challenge us to live with, identify, and understand the elusive intertwining of adaptive strivings and evolved capacities with repetitive, dysfunctional ways of living (see also Langs, 1978, 1996; Searles, 1975).

As our patients try to raise questions about their own entrenched, debilitating ways of experiencing themselves, we believe that they bring both powerful, residual adaptive strivings and repetitive, entrapping, pathological ways of organizing experience to the therapeutic relationship. They use the transference to ferret out and activate within the current therapeutic relationship precisely those areas of relational conflict and (failed) interpersonal negotiation in which old conclusions about themselves were formed. Nancy set out to more or less blindly recreate as well as to investigate (in part by recreating) whether her therapist (unlike her parents) would come to grasp and tolerate how, mixed with his devotion, his interests in certain ways clashed with hers.

Most of our theories, classical, self psychological, relational, etc., tend to deal with this entangled web of residual adaptive strivings and subverted (now pathological) adaptive capacities by emphasizing one or another aspect of this complex interweaving of dimensions in the therapeutic relationship. We believe that it is crucial for the therapist to recognize and identify the adaptive potentials embedded in the patient's ways of organizing experience as well as the patient's experience of the realities of conflicting agendas and interests in the therapeutic relationship (including those that are ambiguously built into the analytic frame). This emphasis on adaptive striving does not preclude the recognition and identification of what may be repetitive, problematic ways of organizing experience and relating within or outside the therapeutic relationship. As we see it, despite the comfort we must forgo in feeling that we are able to label and know what is and is not pathological, it is absolutely crucial that we do not separate the "adaptive" from the "pathological" aspects of the process too clearly; or try to use our inevitably biased perspective to decide too (self) confidently from whence (whom) the problems emanate. For as soon as we do so, we risk setting up the kind of

neat division, or dichotomy that quickly loses an essential quality, the paradoxical—indeed contradictory—quality of how
these dimensions work and how they feel (to the individual
and the other). As a result, with many patients we may cease
to invite the full potential for negotiated reliving and redefining of the pathological and adaptive dimensions of self organization and relating.

Mutual Adaptation and Genuine Negotiation in the Therapeutic Relationship

In a successful therapy, we may be able to tolerate and encourage (even enjoy) the adaptive potentials in the patient's transference to help us create an "as-if" reality, if you will, a
"potential space" for activating and exploring the past in the
present. But though this reliving or reenactment of the patient's transference is crucial, it often cannot be an end in
itself. Such analytic "play" must often lead, in turn, to a call for
the opening up of real—often unseen but inevitable—conflicts
within the analyst and between the conflicting needs of analyst
and patient. In this sense, transference often serves as a vehicle,
a means, to arrive at an arena in which the therapist's own
identity, own real strivings and interests, become deeply engaged in the negotiation process. Transference (and "projective identification") serve to bring the analyst into a realm in
which the past is not simply enacted (or "affectively resonated
with" by the analyst) in the present. The past is, in fact, redis-
covered by the patient in the present in a very profound
way—in the confluences and conflicts with the analyst's identity and the realities of being with the analyst-other. When analysts are able to deal with the personal and professional
conflicts evoked in them over the way in which the analytic
relationship becomes real, then, like Nancy's analyst, they often
truly change in the process because having a relationship with
the patient requires it. The patient is worth it. When the patient
senses this, something vital to both the developmental negotiation of parent–offspring conflict and to analyzing occurs.

The patient changes in significant ways through an adaptation to the therapist—an adaptation that, like all adaptive solutions to life's dilemmas, entails some accommodation and cost. This adaptation is in part possible because the therapist—in ways that may sometimes prove difficult and psychologically costly—also adapts to the patient. The experience of genuine negotiation entailed in this mutual adaptation entails the inner revival of and revisiting of old relational scenarios in order to create some of the "usable newness" in the therapist as an object. The patient gets a lived sense of both the process and the goal—the ongoing negotiating process entailed in constructing and maintaining "inclusive self-interest" within therapy and in life. Our patients come to experience and grasp the meaning of the central human organizing function of knowing their inclusive self-interest as well as the complex interplay between the inner sources of their identities and the interactive relational realities that shape, define, limit, and provide opportunities for its expression. It is in this manner that patients can "use" therapists as new objects who help them create and live their own inclusive self-interests in developmentally needed but hitherto unavailable ways.

REFERENCES

Aron, L. (1991), The patient's experience of the analyst's subjectivity. *Psychoanal. Dial.*, 1:29–51.

Beebe, B., & Lachmann, F. (1988), Mother–infant mutual influence and precursors of psychic structure. In: *Frontiers in Self Psychology*, ed. A. Goldberg. Hillsdale, NJ: Analytic Press, pp. 3–25.

Bibring, E. (1943), The conception of the repetition compulsion. *Psychoanal. Quart.*, 12:486–519.

Blos, P. (1979), *The Adolescent Passage*. New York: International Universities Press.

Bowlby, J. (1969), Attachment. In: *Attachment and Loss*. New York: Basic Books.

Brenner, C. (1976), *Psychoanalytic Technique and Psychic Conflict*. New York: International Universities Press.

Bromberg, P. (1994), "Speak!, that I may see you": Some reflections on dissociation, reality, and psychoanalytic listening. *Psychoanal. Dial.*, 4:517–547.

———(1995), Psychoanalysis, dissociation, and personality organization. *Psychoanal. Dial.*, 5:511–528.

Chomsky, N. (1972), *Language and Mind.* San Diego, CA: Harcourt Brace.

Davies, J. M. (1994), Love in the afternoon: A relational reconsideration of desire and dread in the countertransference. *Psychoanal. Dial.*, 4:153–170.

Eagle, M. (1984), *Recent Developments in Psychoanalysis.* New York: McGraw-Hill.

Erikson, E. (1956), The problem of ego identity. *J Amer. Psychoanal. Assn.*, 4:56–121.

———(1964a), *Identity, Youth and Crisis.* New York: W. W. Norton.

———(1964b), *Insight and Responsibility.* New York: W. W. Norton.

Fenichel, O. (1945), *The Psychoanalytic Theory of the Neurosis.* New York: W. W. Norton.

Freud, A. (1936), *The Ego and the Mechanisms of Defense.* New York: International Universities Press, 1966.

———(1958), Adolescence. *The Psychoanalytic Study of the Child*, 13:255–278. New York: International Universities Press.

Freud, S. (1920), Beyond the pleasure principle. *Standard Edition*, 18:3–64. London: Hogarth Press, 1955.

Fuss, D. (1989), *Essentially Speaking.* New York: Routledge.

Glover, E. (1955), *The Technique of Psychoanalysis.* New York: International Universities Press.

Gould, S. J. (1980), *The Panda's Thumb.* New York: W. W. Norton.

Greenberg, J. (1986), Theoretical models and the analyst's neutrality. *Contemp. Psychoanal.*, 22:87–106.

———Mitchell, S. (1983), *Object Relations and Psychoanalytic Theory.* Cambridge, MA: Harvard University Press.

Haig, D. (1993), Maternal–fetal conflict in human pregnancy. *Quart. Rev. Biol.*, 68:495–532.

Hamilton, W. D. (1964), The genetical evolution of social behavior. *J. Theoret. Biol.*, 7:1–52.

Havens, L. (1993), *Coming to Life.* Cambridge, MA: Harvard University Press.

Hoffman, I. (1983), The patient as interpreter of the analyst's experience. *Contemp. Psychoanal.*, 19:389–442.

Kitcher, P. (1985), *Vaulting Ambition.* Cambridge, MA: MIT Press.

———(1987), Confessions of a curmudgeon. *Behav. Brain Sci.*, 10:89–99.

Kohut, H. (1984), *How Does Analysis Cure?* Chicago: University of Chicago Press.

Konner, M. (1982), *The Tangled Wing: Biological Constraints on the Human Spirit.* New York: Harper & Row.

Kriegman, D. (1988), Self psychology from the perspective of evolutionary biology: Toward a biological foundation for self psychology. In: *Progress in Self Psychology,* Vol. 3, ed. A. Goldberg. Hillsdale, NJ: Analytic Press.

————(1990), Compassion and altruism in psychoanalytic theory: An evolutionary analysis of self psychology. *J. Amer. Acad. Psychoanal.,* 18:342–367.

————(1996a), On the existential/subjectivism-scientific/objectivism dialectic in self psychology: A view from evolutionary biology. In: *Progress in Self Psychology,* Vol. 12, ed. A. Goldberg. Hillsdale, NJ: Analytic Press, pp. 85–119.

————(1996b), Using an experience-near understanding of inherent conflict in the relational world in the treatment of a "psychotic" patient. Paper presented at the 19th Annual Conference on the Psychology of the Self, Washington, DC, October.

————(1998), Interpretation, the unconscious, and analytic authority: Toward an evolutionary, biological integration of the empirical/scientific method with the field-defining, empathic stance. In: *Empirical Perspectives on the Psychoanalytic Unconscious, Vol. 7, Empirical Studies in Psychoanalytic Theories,* ed. R. F. Bornstein & J. M. Masling. Washington, DC: American Psychological Association.

————Knight, C. (1988), Social evolution, psychoanalysis, and human nature. *Soc. Policy,* 19:49–55.

————Slavin, M. (1989), The myth of the repetition compulsion and the negative therapeutic reaction: An evolutionary biological analysis. In: *Progress in Self Psychology,* Vol. 5, ed. A. Goldberg. Hillsdale, NJ: Analytic Press, pp. 209–253.

———— ————(1990), On the resistance to self psychology: Clues from evolutionary biology. In: *Progress in Self Psychology,* Vol. 6, ed. A. Goldberg. Hillsdale, NJ: Analytic Press, pp. 217–250.

LaBarre, W. (1954), *The Human Animal.* Chicago: University of Chicago Press.

Langs, R. (1978), The adaptational-interactional dimension of countertransference. *Contemp. Psychoanal.,* 14:502–533.

————(1995), Psychoanalysis and the science of evolution. *Amer. J. Psychother.,* 49:47–58.

————(1996), *The Evolution of the Emotional Processing Mind.* New York: Brunner/Mazel.

Lichtenberg, J. (1989), *Psychoanalysis and Motivation.* Hillsdale, NJ: Analytic Press.

Lloyd, A. (1984), On the evolution of the instincts: Implications for psychoanalysis (typescript).

Loewald, H. (1965), Some considerations on repetition and the repetition compulsion. In: *Papers on Psychoanalysis.* New Haven: Yale University Press, 1980.

Mayr, E. (1974), Behavior programs and evolutionary strategies. *Amer. Scientist,* 62:650–659.

——(1982), *The Growth of Biological Thought.* Cambridge, MA: Belknap Press/Harvard University Press.

——(1983), How to carry out the adaptationist program. *Amer. Naturalist,* 121:324–334.

——(1988), *Toward a New Philosophy of Biology: Observations of an Evolutionist.* Cambridge, MA: Harvard University Press.

Mitchell, R. (1985), *Deception: Perspectives on Human and Non-Human Deceit.* New York: State University of New York Press.

Mitchell, S. (1988), *Relational Concepts in Psychoanalysis, An Integration.* Cambridge, MA: Harvard University Press.

Modell, A. (1984), *Psychoanalysis in a New Context.* New York: International Universities Press.

——(1989), Discussion of Slavin and Kriegman, "Beyond the classical-relational dialectic in psychoanalysis: A new paradigm from contemporary evolutionary biology." Paper presented at the Spring Meeting of the Division of Psychoanalysis (APA), Boston.

Ornstein, A. (1974), The dread to repeat and the new beginning: A contribution to the psychoanalysis of narcissistic personality disorders. *Annual of Psychoanalysis,* 2:231–248. New York: International Universities Press.

——(1984), Psychoanalytic psychotherapy: A contemporary perspective. In: *Kohut's Legacy: Contributions to Self Psychology,* ed. P. E. Stepansky & A. Goldberg. Hillsdale, NJ: Analytic Press.

Ornstein, P. (1989), Why self psychology is not an object relations theory: Clinical and theoretical considerations. Paper presented at the 12th Annual Conference on the Psychology of the Self, October 12, San Francisco.

Peterfreund, E. (1972), Information systems and psychoanalysis, an evolutionary biological approach to psychoanalytic theory. *Psychological Issues,* Monograph 25/26. New York: International Universities Press.

Pizer, S. (1992), The negotiation of conflict in the analytic process. *Psychoanal. Dial.,* 2:215–240.

Racker, H. (1954), Considerations on the theory of transference. In: *Transference and Countertransference*. London: Hogarth Press, 1968, pp. 71–78.

Rappaport, D. (1960), The structure of psychoanalytic theory. *Psychological Issues,* Monograph 6. New York: International Universities Press.

Searles, H. F. (1975), The patient as therapist to his analyst. In: *Tactics and Techniques in Psychoanalytic Theory, Volume II: Countertransference,* ed. P. Giovacchini. New York: Aronson, pp. 95–151.

Slavin, J. H. (1994), On making rules: Toward a reformulation of the dynamics of transference in psychoanalytic treatment. *Psychoanal. Dial.,* 4:253–274.

Slavin, M. (1974), An evolutionary biological view of the mechanism of repression. Presentation to the graduate seminar in social evolution, Department of Biology, Harvard University, Professor R. Trivers, Cambridge, MA. typescript.

———(1985), The origins of psychic conflict and the adaptive function of repression: An evolutionary biological view. *Psychoanal. & Contemp. Thought,* 8:407–440.

———(1986), A relational model of innate inner conflict: Drives, objects, and the self in evolutionary biological perspective. Paper presented to the Midwinter Meeting of the Division of Psychoanalysis (APA), Ixtapa, Mexico.

———(1990), The dual meaning of repression and the adaptive design of the human psyche. *J. Amer. Acad. Psychoanal.,* 18:307–341.

———(1996a), Is one self enough? Multiplicity in self organization and the capacity to negotiate relational conflict. *Contemp. Psychoanal.,* 32:615–625.

———(1996b), The reparenting dimension of psychotherapy: Negotiating conflict, deception, and self-deception in childhood and in the therapeutic relationship. Paper presented to the Annual Spring Meeting of Division 39 of the American Psychological Association, New York City, April.

———Kriegman, D. (1992), *The Adaptive Design of the Human Psyche: Psychoanalysis, Evolutionary Biology, and the Therapeutic Process.* New York: Guilford Press.

——— ———(1998), Why the analyst needs to change: Toward a theory of conflict, negotiation, and mutual influence in the therapeutic process. *Psychoanal. Dial.,* 8:247–284.

———Slavin, J. (1976), Two patterns of adaptation in late adolescent borderline personalities. *Psychiatry,* 39:41–50.

Stern, D. (1985), *The Interpersonal World of the Infant.* New York: Basic Books.

Stolorow, R., & Atwood, G. (1989), The unconscious and unconscious fantasy: An intersubjective developmental perspective. *Psychoanal. Inq.,* 9:364–374.

———Brandchaft, B., & Atwood, G. (1987), *Psychoanalytic Treatment: An Intersubjective Approach.* Hillsdale, NJ: Analytic Press.

———Lachmann, F. (1984), Transference: The future of an illusion. *Annual of Psychoanalysis,* 12/13. New York: International Universities Press.

Tooby, J., & Cosmides, L. (1990), On the universality of human nature and the uniqueness of the individual: The role of genetics and adaptation. *J. Personality,* 58:17–67.

Trivers, R. (1971), The evolution of reciprocal altruism. *Quart. Rev. Biol.,* 46:35–57.

———(1974), Parent–offspring conflict. *Amer. Zoologist,* 14:249–264.

———(1976), Foreword. *The Selfish Gene* by R. Dawkins. New York: Oxford University Press.

———(1985), *Social Evolution.* Menlo Park, NJ: Benjamin Cummings.

Weiss, J., & Sampson, H. (1986), *The Psychoanalytic Process: Theory, Clinical Observation, and Empirical Research.* New York: Guilford Press.

Winnicott, D. W. (1965), *The Maturational Processes and the Facilitating Environment.* New York: International Universities Press.

———(1969), The use of an object and relating through identification. In: *Playing and Reality.* Middlesex, U.K.: Penguin.

Wrong, D. (1963), The oversocialized conception of man in modern sociology. In: *Personality and Social Systems,* ed. N. Smeltser & W. Smeltser. New York: Wiley.

12.

The Communicative Approach

David Livingstone Smith, Ph.D.

INTRODUCTION

Historical Background

It is commonplace to note that Freud was a child of his time
as well as an explorer, who expanded intellectual horizons.
Many of the limits of Freud's work stemmed from constraints
imposed by the scientific and philosophical climate of his era
(Kitcher, 1991). One such limitation was Freud's belief in what
is now called *internalism.* Internalism is the thesis that meaning
is internal, imposed by the mind upon the world.

As the twentieth century progressed, the *zeitgeist* became
hostile to internalism. Philosophers eventually clarified a new
view of the mind that became known as *externalism.* According
to externalism, the world around us, our environmental context, enters directly into the mind and radically shapes its contents. Psychoanalysis reflected this shift by developing new
"relational" approaches. The British and American object relations approaches, as well as psychoanalytic self psychology have

I would like to thank Dr. Ulrich Berns, Mrs. Leonora Morphet, and Mr. David Morphet for their assistance in the preparation of this chapter.

been developments in this general direction that meet externalism half-way by emphasizing that the mind must be understood in terms of its relation to the world whilst retaining ideas such as transference and the inner world. Throughout the history of psychoanalysis there have been those prepared to entertain a more radical view of the relationship between mind and world. Among these were Ferenczi (1933), Balint (1955), Little (1951), Racker (1957, 1958), Laing (1959), and Searles (1948, 1972, 1973, 1975, 1979), all of whom, to a greater or lesser degree, viewed the mind as open to, constituted and constrained by the world.

DEVELOPMENT OF COMMUNICATIVE PSYCHOANALYSIS

Communicative psychoanalysis was developed by Robert Langs. Shortly after completing his classical Freudian psychoanalytic training Langs began research into the relationship between dreams and waking experiences (Langs, 1971). This line of investigation led, a few years later, to the development of the idea of the *adaptive context*. Adaptive contexts (or *triggers* as they are now called) are external events which evoke psychological responses. Treating this as a clinical concept, Langs argued that the clinical behavior of psychoanalysts (their interventions, omissions, and modes of structuring the setting) provides the adaptive context for the behavior of patients. His observations convinced him that patients are powerfully influenced, on both conscious and unconscious levels, by their analysts.

Langs had by this point developed the rudiments of a method for clinical psychoanalytic research. Each communication, resistance, and symptomatic act of the patient was to be understood in relation to the patient's life-context, including the analytic setting. Further research led to three critical discoveries. First, that the analytic setting or frame has an overwhelmingly powerful effect on patients' *unconscious* activity. Second, that unconscious responses express a penetrating and sophisticated understanding of the real implications of the events triggering them. Third, that these unconscious processes operate in a predictable, lawlike fashion. Langs argued that patients unconsciously supervise their analysts and in 1975 embraced Searles' (1975) thesis that patients attempt to cure their analysts. The new synthesis was presented in *The Bipersonal Field* (1976) and extended in a series of clinical works (e.g., Langs, 1978a,b, 1979, 1980, 1981, 1982a, 1988, 1992a). Langs argued that if we listen to patients' free associations as meaningful and valid commentaries on the implications of analysts' behavior, we must conclude that psychoanalysis as it is generally practiced possesses highly destructive qualities. Langs' *The Psychotherapeutic Conspiracy* (1982b) and *Madness and Cure* (1985) anticipated current controversies surrounding the destructive potential of psychotherapy.

Langs' concern with the scientific status of psychoanalysis led him to undertake quantitative research into the psychoanalytic process. This research measured variables previously identified in more impressionistic clinical studies. Hand in hand with this, he has attempted to develop a systems theory for psychoanalysis and elaborate new models of the mind incorporating the results of communicative theory and research. Most recently, Langs has developed an educational application of communicative psychoanalysis that he calls *self-processing* (Langs, 1993), has investigated the evolutionary history of the "emotion-processing mind" (Langs, 1995, 1996), and has made contributions to the clinical significance of death anxiety (1997).

Responses to Langs' work have been largely and often vehemently negative. Sadly, there have been few thoughtful and informed criticisms of the communicative approach. The contributions of Gill (1984, 1985) and Dorpat and Miller (1992) are notable exceptions.

The Society for Psychoanalytic Psychotherapy was formed in 1980 as a forum for communicative research and debate and was named the International Society for Communicative Psychoanalysis and Psychotherapy in 1991. The European Society for Communicative Psychotherapy was founded in 1990. In 1997 the Electronic Journal of Communicative Psychoanalysis was launched in 1997 to provide an independent international forum for debate and a clearing-house for information on communicative psychoanalysis.

BASIC THEORETICAL CONCEPTS

General Principles

Communicative psychoanalysis is committed to a *scientific attitude.* Communicative theory defines psychoanalysis as that branch of cognitive science that investigates the processing of emotionally charged information.

Commitment to a scientific approach means that we must be concerned about the evidential basis of our claims, welcoming objective tests and opening ourselves to criticism. We must also be prepared to look to the more highly developed sciences for support and inspiration. This does not mean that each practitioner of the approach must be a research scientist, but it does enjoin them to work in a broadly scientific spirit and to engage with the debates surrounding the issue of validation in psychoanalytic theory (e.g., Grünbaum, 1993).

A second principle is that communicative theory is designed to apply to all human beings. It has been all too common for psychoanalysts to exempt themselves from their own theories. For example, it has been quite rare to find psychoanalysts discussing the unconscious messages contained in their interventions or their propensity for transference on equal terms with that of their patients. Communicative theory is applied in equal measure to both analysts and patients. The acknowledgment of analysts' psychological vulnerability implies that all clinical efforts will include a large measure of error.

Finally, communicative psychoanalysis places special emphasis on the biological concept of *adaptation,* taking a strong adaptive or ecological stance. The human mind is an evolved product of natural selection. There must therefore be a special "fit" between the mind and its environment. According to the strong adaptive position, one cannot meaningfully abstract the mind of the patient from the total patient–therapist system

(Langs, 1992b). The view that mental events in the patient (or the analyst) can be reified and abstracted from the ongoing analytic interaction is still quite common within the psychoanalytic community. The folly of this general approach is graphically described by Millikan (1993).

> Imagine trying to study the inner mechanisms that produce migration of birds, or nest building, or mating displays and female reactions to them, or imprinting in birds, without making reference to the way these mechanisms have historically meshed with the bird's environments so as to perform the functions for which they are named. More vivid, imagine attempting to study the origins of the coordinated motions made by the eyes and the head and the hand that effect eye-hand coordination while leaving completely out of account that there is, normally, a seen and felt object in the environment that mediates this coordination. It is equally ludicrous to suggest studying the deeper systems that produce human behaviors . . . without considering how the environment has historically mediated the performance of their functions [p. 181].[1]

Communicative psychoanalysts attempt to understand the behavior of both patients and analysts as adaptations to the immediate analytic situation.

Theoretical Principles

The adaptive qualities of the conscious aspects of the mind have long been recognized by psychoanalysts (Hartmann, 1939). According to communicative theory there are also powerfully adaptive unconscious mental systems. In particular, there is an unconscious mental system specifically concerned with adaptation to the social or relational world. This system is called the *deep unconscious wisdom system.*

---

[1]Millikan's reference to "historical" mediation does not endorse theories such as transference. Millikan is referring to the way that historical selection-pressures produce mental systems evolved to deal with real environmental features, and which cannot be properly understood outside the context of those environmental features for which the psychological item was selected to deal.

This system monitors our relations with those around us, and is particularly sensitive to any indication that we are being exploited, deceived, or damaged. It evaluates interpersonal situations with great sophistication and rapidly draws conclusions about what is occurring. These conclusions are expressed as *encoded* narratives. Narratives that carry deep unconscious meaning are also called *derivatives*. Derivatives are always concrete, imagistic, and superficially unrelated to the immediate situation.

The deep unconscious wisdom system monitors the most fundamental aspects of social systems. These include the spaciotemporal boundaries of relationships, the number of people involved, issues of exchange and so on. These fundamental features are set all by the rules defining the system. In the psychoanalytic situation (a two-person social system) these are called the ground rules of analysis. The ground rules of a social system are constitutive: They define and demarcate the system. The constitutive role of ground rules makes them vastly important (Mooij, 1991). The modification or abandonment of a single ground rule can have a cataclysmic effect on the system that it defines. The ground rules, roles, and setting are referred to as the *frame*.

The deep unconscious wisdom system appears to contain prototypes against which it evaluates human interactions. These prototypes seem to be universal "deep psychological structures" (Slavin and Kriegman, 1992) evolved over countless generations to deal with the great complexity of human relations. According to communicative theory, the secured or ideal psychoanalytic frame consists of (1) set location; (2) set duration for all sessions; (3) set frequency for sessions; (4) set fee for all scheduled sessions; (5) total privacy; (6) total confidentiality; (7) neutrality on the part of the analyst; (8) relative anonymity on the part of the analyst; and (9) no physical contact between analyst and patient.

Departures from the ideal ground rules will normally[2] result in patients producing negatively toned narratives portraying

---

[2]Because biological systems can malfunction or genetically vary, it is not possible to give true exceptionless laws operating at this level. Communicative claims about the lawlike behavior of the emotion processing mind should nevertheless be regarded as reliable empirical generalizations.

the implications of the modification. For example, if an analyst extends a session for five minutes his or her patient may respond by describing at the start of the next session how her mother was destructively possessive to the extent of never allowing her husband out of her sight. The narrative about the patient's parents is a narrative model of the extension of the hour.

Communicative theory claims that such responses are lawful. Departures from the ideal frame normally evoke negatively toned narratives. This commits communicative theory to the closely related claim that the rectification or securing of the frame, the restoration of some aspect of the ideal frame, should evoke positively toned narratives. This is called derivative validation. These are testable hypotheses which cast new light on recent philosophical debates about the validation of psychoanalytic theories (Smith, 1991a, 1992a, 1994, 1995a; Berns, 1994).

Although frame-securing efforts are normally validated, they also generate or evoke specific anxieties referred to as death anxiety or secured-frame anxiety. These forms of anxiety are still poorly understood (see Langs, 1997).

The Role of the Past

I have discussed patients' true unconscious understanding of the here-and-now psychoanalytic situation. However, a great deal of mainstream psychoanalytic theory is concerned with the role of past (or, more precisely, infantile) configurations and their causal relevance for later symptoms, character traits, relational patterns, and so on. In rejecting the very idea of transference, the communicative approach appears to beg the question of the role of "genetic" factors.

Freud used the term *transference* to describe a hypothetical process of displacement of libido from unconscious representations of archaic objects onto preconscious representations of others, especially one's analyst. Freud formulated this theory to give an account of how unconscious ideas impact upon conscious thought and behavior as well as to explain just why it is that patients' relationships with their analysts may be so highly charged with emotions. In recent decades the meaning of the word *transference* has become blurred. It is now often used to denote the emotionally charged attitudes themselves rather than the unconscious mechanisms that are supposed to bring them about. If we use the word in this way it does not explain anything. Alternatively, "transference" is sometimes used to denote the totality of the ways that past events affect current experience. But the very breadth of this version deprives it of any explanatory significance. It therefore seems advantageous to retain Freud's more delimited, explanatory definition of transference.

It should be apparent by now that communicative psycho-analysis rejects the Freudian theory of transference by virtue of rejecting the concept of mind upon which that theory is based. The deep unconscious system just does not function in the manner required by the theory of transference: It analyzes the meaning of interpersonal events rather than unilaterally imposing archaic meanings upon them. This does not mean that communicative psychoanalysis cannot accommodate a the-ory of how it is that past events unconsciously influence present functioning. Past events may influence the mind inexplicitly through affecting the manner in which it processes informa-tion, an approach which has been given considerable attention in neural net theory (Clark, 1990). This can occur at three levels. Past experiences can influence perceptual sensitivities the way that associations are formed between ideas, or the way that mental processes lead to behavior (including verbal behav-ior). For example, a person who had been physically abused by his father during childhood might be especially sensitive to the violent properties of his analyst's interventions, might readily associate intimacy with abuse, and might express his unconscious perceptions of, say, a confrontative intervention with narratives of interpersonal violence. This patient's mind is particularly well adapted to deal with certain kinds of experi-ence. This is very different from saying that he imposes his unconscious wishes, phantasies, or memories upon the analytic relationship.

Like transference, the concept of *countertransference* has

undergone considerable modification since Freud's coinage in 1910. For Freud, countertransference was any unconscious response to patients' transferences that disturbed the analytic attitude; but the term is now also used to describe analysts' subjective responses to their patients, irrespective of their sources or nature. Indeed, since Heimann's (1950) seminal paper, many psychoanalysts regard their subjective emotional responses as unconsciously orchestrated by their patients.

Although the original idea of countertransference possessed a defensive quality it also possessed an important self-critical edge. Langs (1982b) substituted the term *therapist madness*, and later *therapist maladaptation or dysfunction* for *countertransference* in an attempt to redress the balance. The concept of therapist madness does not necessarily refer to psychopathology. Essentially, it denotes a set of tendencies that psychotherapists and psychoanalysts share with the rest of the human race: a tendency to exploit others, to deceive others, and avoid painful or humiliating realizations. If we abandon conventional idealizations of the analytic situation, the question of who, at any given moment, is predominantly "mad" must remain an open one. By the same token, Langs' clinical work seemed to corroborate Searles' hypothesis that patients have strong needs to resolve their analysts' madness, so it must also remain an open question whether it is analyst or patient who, at any given moment, is functioning most therapeutically.

The human propensity for self-destructive behavior has led Langs to postulate a second deep unconscious subsystem that he calls the *fear–guilt system*. The fear–guilt system is believed to affect behavior more directly than the deep unconscious wisdom system. The concept of the fear–guilt system has not been articulated in anything like the same detail as that of the deep unconscious wisdom system.

Theory of Technique

Before any psychoanalytic work can start it is necessary for the analyst to establish whether he or she stands a reasonable

chance of assisting the prospective patient with their presenting problem and whether there are any contraindications
for engaging this person in analysis. Consultations therefore
normally begin with an invitation for the potential patient to
describe what has brought them to seek help. The analyst's
decision will rest upon (1) his or her assessment of the presenting problem and (2) the identification of countervailing
frame factors (the analyst should, for instance, refuse to take
on an applicant with whom they share a friend). Should the
analyst conclude that he may be helpful, this is expressed to
the prospective patient, taking care not to promise a successful
outcome. Next, the analyst sets out the ground rules of analysis
and specifies the setting in which these will be realized. Analysis
cannot begin in the absence of an agreed set of ground rules.

Once the conditions and setting of analysis have been established, the analysis can begin. Communicative psychoanalysts allow their patients to unconsciously orchestrate the
structure and course of analysis. The analyst's role is largely to
function as a translator or assistant. Priority is given to the
listening process. The fundamental stance of the analyst is
therefore one of silent attentiveness.

Unconsciously meaningful *derivative communications* are
marked by their narrative structure: They appear as stories.
They are concrete, specific, and easily visualized by the listener.
Communications that are abstract, analytic, and reflective are
said to be *nonderivative communications.*

In traditional forms of psychoanalysis, derivatives are understood as expressing infantile drives, phantasies, and object
relations. In communicative psychoanalysis, derivatives are interpreted in light of the immediate context of the setting,
ground rules, and behavior of the analyst (Raney, 1984). We
cannot really understand the unconscious meaning of a derivative unless we have identified the event in the analytic setting
to which it is a response and of which it is an icon.[3] In other

---

[3]Considering the extended and ambiguous meaning of the more standard term *representation* in the fields of psychoanalysis, cognitive science, philosophy, and psychology, I
have adopted the term *icon* or *intentional icon* from Millikan (1993) to denote this particular kind of "representation." In addition to the fact that Millikan's theory neatly captures
a number of communicative principles, the term "icon" also conjures up the specifically
pictorial quality of derivatives. Readers should note, though, that this is not a standard
communicative term.

words, we match derivatives to their triggers. For example, when an analyst starts a session late, we expect the very first story that the patient tells after this event to be a portrayal of and commentary on the analyst's tardiness. It can be much more difficult to identify derivative icons of chronic, background triggers. If, for example, the analyst takes notes, works in a home office or has inadequate sound insulation these issues will suffuse the patient's unconscious communications.

Once we have identified a derivative and determined its trigger it becomes possible to *trigger decode* the derivative. This is accomplished by extracting the narrative themes.

Here is a real example of the derivative sequelae of an analyst beginning a session late. After the analyst, who had been on the telephone, began his hour five minutes late his patient began to describe how she had arranged for new carpet to be laid in her apartment. The workers had arrived late. She insisted that this was highly unprofessional and that businesspeople who make commitments should take care to honor them. It is very easy to interpret the patient's story as a commentary on the analyst's lateness. She seems to represent this by means of the icon of the workers' lateness. Furthermore, she comments on the *implications* of their lateness: It is *unprofessional.* To understand the unconscious meaning of this we simply make use of our Rosetta Stone, the trigger, to formulate that she unconsciously regards the analyst as having behaved unprofessionally. In this vignette there is a further statement expressed in the *imperative* mood: The patient claims that business people should honor their commitments. This is an example of a *model of rectification:* an indication of what the analyst ought to do to remedy some problem in the analytic situation.[4] Of course, not all unconscious communications are negatively toned. Some express positive images of people behaving insightfully and appropriately, of systems functioning well, etc. Positive icons are usually regarded as *derivative validations,* i.e., as indications that the patient unconsciously approves of some feature of the analyst's activity.

---

[4]Models of rectification are not invariably expressed by explicitly imperative or normative sentences. They are occasionally expressed by derivative contrasting desirable and undesirable states of affairs.

"Interventions" are any and all actions performed by analysts within the analytic setting.[5] There are three fundamental types of intervention used by communicative psychoanalysts: silence, frame management, and interpretation.

It sounds strange to describe silence as an intervention. However, silence is a mode of activity. Silence is indicated so long as interpretation is unwarranted. If silence is maintained beyond the point when an interpretation is required, it becomes inappropriate.

Frame management is the modification or maintenance of the ground rules and setting of analysis. Appropriate frame management involves maintaining the secured frame or modifying the frame at the patient's unconscious behest *(rectification)*. Inappropriate frame management involves initiating some deviation or participating in a frame modification that has not been derivatively validated by the patient.

Interpretation is the basic verbal intervention in communicative technique. As is the case in classical psychoanalysis, communicative interpretations are hypotheses offered to explain and resolve symptoms and resistances. Classical interpretations revolve around events within patients' minds, attempting to explain symptoms and resistances primarily in terms of internal motivational systems (drives, selfobject, or attachment needs, and so on), infantile anxieties, primitive object relations, and transferential engagements. Communicative interpretations attempt to explain disturbances within the patient in terms of his or her responses to real events within the psychoanalytic setting.

Communicative interpretations are made only when patients have supplied sufficient information. This recipe for interpretation consists of three elements. These are (1) representation of the *trigger(s)*; (2) well-developed network of *derivatives*; (3) *indications* of distress within the patient.

The target of interpretation is always the indication of distress. These indicators can take two broad forms, appearing either as psychological *symptoms* (in the broad psychoanalytic

---

[5]I use the term *action* here to encompass refraining from activity as well as engaging in it.

sense of the term) or as *resistance* (including efforts to modify the ground rules of analysis).[6] Indicators express a need for intervention. They are implicit requests for help.

Communicative interpretations try to explain symptoms and resistance in terms of their triggers. As I have already mentioned, triggers are specific stimuli within the analytic setting that provoke unconscious responses. Because of the communicative principle that it is the patient who directs the analytic process, the analyst is not free to invoke triggers unless the patient has already represented thcm. Triggers can be represented in two forms: (1) They can be *manifestly represented.* In such cases patients allude directly to some feature of the analytic situation, usually in passing; (2) They can be *derivatively represented.* In such cases patients offer a thinly disguised derivative icon of the trigger. Derivatively represented triggers can only be used in interpretations if a *bridge to therapy* (some nonspecific reference to the analysis) has also been provided.

It is the way that a trigger is unconsciously processed which determines whether or not it evokes a symptom or resistance. Before a trigger can produce any effects, the patient needs to make sense of it. This process of unconscious "meaning analysis" (Dorpat and Miller, 1992) is revealed by the derivatives. For practical purposes, it is important to allow patients to produce an elaborate derivative network: a sequence of narratives that unconsciously describe numerous features of the active triggers. All three elements, trigger, derivatives, and indicator, are required because they correspond to the input, processing, and output phases of a complete cognitive sequence. Communicative interpretations attempt to describe this full sequence by applying the following interpretative template: (1) *specification of the trigger:* I (the analyst) have done such-and-such; (2) *analysis of the derivatives:* You (the patient) have selectively taken this to imply so-and-so; (3) *interpretation of the indicator:*

---

[6]The communicative approach delimits the concept of analyzable resistance to gross behavioral resistance, unambiguous expressions of noncompliance with the analytic process, in order to avoid the arbitrary, subjective and theory-laden attributions of resistance that are unfortunately common in standard psychoanalytic practice. A second form of resistance, communicative resistance, refers to the anxiety-laden failure to symbolize unconscious perceptions as derivatives. Communicative resistances are never analyzed directly.

This, in turn, explains why you are experiencing this resistance or symptom.

As long as the patient has not yet supplied all three of these ingredients no interpretation is warranted. By the same token, patients unconsciously expect an interpretation to be given as soon as the "recipe" has been fulfilled. The failure to interpret at this point will call forth *missed intervention derivatives:* narratives expressing such themes as the failure to act, someone or something being delayed, the failure to communicate, and similar themes.

Once an interpretation has been voiced, communicative psychoanalysts use the subsequently emerging narratives to understand patients' unconscious evaluation of the intervention. Interventions are only regarded as correct if they are followed by positively toned narratives (i.e., if they are derivatively validated). It is not uncommon for patients to consciously concur with interpretations of which they unconsciously disapprove. In such cases a manifest endorsement of the interpretation (e.g., "Yes, that's just how I feel . . . ") is followed by a *derivative admonition* (e.g., "I dreamed that I was being mugged . . . ").

Communicative psychoanalysis does not yet have a clearly articulated theory of how it brings about the remission of psychological problems, of how it achieves "cure." At most, we can say that there appears to be some causal relationship between validated interventions within at least a relatively secured frame and therapeutic progress. This cannot be attributed to "making the unconscious conscious" because communicative interventions do not depend upon patients' conscious acceptance for their therapeutic effects. It seems unlikely that therapeutic effects can be explained as effects of suggestion (Smith, 1991a).

In the absence of well-designed outcome studies, we must maintain a cautious attitude toward the therapeutic efficacy of communicative psychoanalysis. Even if research were to demonstrate good therapeutic outcome, it would still be necessary to consider the possibility of placebo effects (Grünbaum, 1993). These constraints apply to all forms of psychoanalysis, but the communicative commitment to scientific reasoning demands that they be honored rather than ignored.

The communicative approach does have some interesting things to say about purported "cure" in psychoanalysis. First, communicative theory emphasizes patients' readiness to participate in and idealize "therapeutic" interventions that are prima facie destructive and bizarre (Langs, 1985). This feature of psychoanalysis casts doubt on the value of subjective reports and questionnaires to assess outcome. Second, it also seems to be the case that such interventions may at least sometimes paradoxically produce relief or remission. One of the mechanisms that may underpin such paradoxical effects is *cure through nefarious comparison:* Patients may sometimes experience relief when they realize that their analysts are at least as mad as they are. Third, communicative theory claims that such ostensible improvements must be offset against *iatrogenic side-effects.* Anecdotal evidence suggests that patients may act out the unaddressed destructive aspects of their analysis in their personal lives (Langs, 1985; Myers, 1994).

CLINICAL ILLUSTRATION

The following example is a realistic summary of two communicative psychoanalytic sessions. Of course, the clinical material has been extensively altered in order to secure the patient's anonymity.

The patient in this example is a female university lecturer who entered analysis because of a compulsion to seduce her students. The frame is secure except for the fact that analysis is paid by National Insurance (the analysis takes place in a European country in which this arrangement is mandatory). In the session preceding the present one, the patient's derivatives had led the analyst to realize that he had omitted to describe the fundamental rule of free association to her, had interpreted accordingly and had received derivative validation.

P: I don't know what to say. I don't know if I have anything useful to say. I'm thinking about Jacques (a student with whom she is having an affair). I always wonder if it will

bother you if I talk about this. I think of a paper that I
am writing. I was hesitant about it at first, but today I
finished it. That was great. I really think it's a good piece
of work. It was good to just get it done without worrying
over it too much.

The patient refers to her manner of talking in the session,
implicitly alluding to the analyst's intervention during the previous session (trigger). She also mentions that she has some
difficulty free associating and expresses concern that her analyst will find her associations disturbing, which are mild resistances (indicators). The reference to Jacques is ambiguous, as
it is not embedded in a narrative. The remaining icons are
positively toned and appear to pertain to the analyst's frame
rectification in the previous session (derivatives).

A: When you came in you had difficulty finding something
to say, and wondered if you would say anything useful.
This must connect with my remark in our last session,
when we talked about you letting go and saying anything
that came to mind. You went on to mention being hesitant at first but then writing the paper without worrying
over it. You felt this was great. It sounds like you are
happy with this way of working with me. You don't feel
that you have to worry over what you say so much, but
you are still rather concerned that it will bother me.

The analyst interprets this material in light of his prior
intervention. Although correct, this intervention was not necessary. It would have been better to wait for derivatives explaining
the source of the patient's resistances. The analyst's decision to
intervene probably reflects some form of countertransference
which will be unconsciously perceived and interpreted by the
patient.

P: Just then I thought of M. Sanglier and then I thought of
Jacques. I feel kind of excited, because I'm attracted to
four young men in today's class. This makes me feel

ashamed. The class had a nice, sexy atmosphere. I suddenly realized that Jacques actually cares for me, is really
interested in me. It's weird. Before, I used to plan out
my seductions to figure out if the reward was worth the
effort.

M. Sanglier was a teacher with whom the patient had a
sexual relationship during her adolescence. This, and her reference to her attraction to the four male students, portray intrusions of sexuality into professional relationships. The patient
has apparently detected something seductive in her analyst's
behavior. Taking the preceding intervention as the trigger, it
sounds as though the patient is unconsciously telling her analyst that his last intervention possessed seductive characteristics.
A moment's reflection will show how incisive the patient's interpretation is. The intervention unnecessarily emphasized his
own constructive impact upon the patient. This might be understood as an attempt to impress her: to solicit her love, gratitude, or admiration. The final sentence may portray the
impulsive quality of the intervention. The reference to Jacques
caring for her probably alludes to the accurate and caring aspects of the intervention. The absence of a fee may provide an
additional trigger for this material.

A: You seem occupied with what I've been saying to you
       recently. You thought of two men, M. Sanglier and
       Jacques, who were interested in you. Perhaps you thought
       of these men because you feel that my remarks show that
       I am interested in you. You no longer have to behave in
       a calculating way to gain my interest. On the other hand,
       this seems to have led to an erotic atmosphere of which
       you are ashamed. Maybe my interest has evoked a mood
       in you, like with Jacques and M. Sanglier, which in the
       past caused you to allow contacts that you were
       ashamed of.

Although this intervention does cover the possibility that
the analyst has behaved seductively, it does so in an ambiguous

and compromised fashion (the word *interested* may denote either appropriate therapeutic interest or inappropriate sexual interest). There is no reference to any specific trigger. It would have been preferable for the analyst to silently wait for the patient to provide more information.

P: I am thinking of my friend's little daughter running towards me and embracing me. What did I do to deserve this? Jacques came by yesterday. He came by and chatted for a while. We didn't have sex. I realized that he was interested in me not just for the sex. I have such problems finding a partner my own age. This week I didn't try. What a relief!

The vivid icon of the child embracing the patient may be a validating derivative, showing an image of care and affection, but might also be taken as a portrait of the analyst's neediness. The narrative about Jacques seems validating. The final sentences do not have much of a derivative quality: They do not concretely portray an event or sequence of events. The patient's difficulty finding an appropriate partner may, however, allude to some seductive aspect of the analyst's behavior, and can also be treated as an indicator.

The session ended at this point. The next session began as follows:

P: I feel queasy. I'm thinking about the cashier at the bookshop. He was friendly, but he had an unpleasant body odor. He touched me when he gave me my bag of books. His hand was unpleasantly soft. The thought of soft, fleshy people makes me feel sick. I don't like tough, boney people either. Great Aunt Malmedie was hard and boney but strong, not like my mushy mother who was always complaining and whining. I went to the dentist's this morning. She stood so close to me that her body touched me. It was a bit disgusting. I started to feel sick when I was sitting in the waiting room thinking that I would have to tell you these things.

Here the patient's derivatives deepen. In the first narrative someone offering a service is kind but repulsive and touches the patient. There is an image of a strong woman whom the patient also dislikes, and someone who is always complaining. Finally, she depicts a scene of repulsive physical contact with a professional. The feeling of sickness is an indicator. There is a general reference to therapy that can, in principle, be used as a trigger. The icon of a whining, accusatory mother is probably a portrayal of those aspects of the preceding interventions which ignore the analyst's contributions to the sexual aspects of the material that the patient has brought to analysis.

A: You felt a little sick thinking about telling me these things. On one hand this feels hard and strong, not mushy like your mother, dentist, and the bookseller. On the other hand it seems unpleasantly close, as though something came out of me that you had to inhale. Perhaps you were afraid that something evil smelling might come from you, which could also be the reason for your feeling sick.

Communicatively speaking, this intervention was rather off the mark. The analyst does not allude to any trigger, makes a general and vague reference to himself, and speculates on the patient's inner world.

P: I was thinking about today's session on the bus coming back from the dentist's. Analysis is more difficult now that we're getting into important issues. The things that I say surprise even me! I had a lover years ago who was really strange. The relationship didn't go anywhere. He was terribly uptight although this doesn't add up because he was tender in bed. But we couldn't be in bed all the time. Anyway, he was Dutch and lived in Holland. I tried to talk about all this to him, but he didn't understand a word of it. We were finished then. I had an appendectomy and it was only after that that I got over him.

The patient begins with an indicator: her reluctance to come to the session. Although consciously she attributes this to their touching on important issues, she appears to unconsciously attribute it to the analyst's counter-resistance. She is puzzled by his rigidity and inaccessibility, because she is aware that on some occasions he is open and caring. Taking the last intervention as the trigger, we can hypothesize that the patient experiences her analyst as remote, rigid, and unwilling to reflect upon his role in the relationship. The reference to the appendectomy may relate to unconscious thoughts of terminating the analysis.

A: Now that I've asked you to say everything that comes to mind you find yourself saying things that surprise you, and this makes it difficult for you to come to analysis. Also, you remember your relationship with the uptight man who was tender in bed. You seem to see my insistence on this as rigid, but at the same time this awakens tender sexual feelings in you, which seems to worry you. You have to talk about your feelings to me, but you feel that I may respond by ending the analysis, just like the man who ended the relationship.

This intervention, which brings the session to a close, seems strongly countertransference-driven in light of the preceding analysis. The root of this seems to be the analyst's difficulty coming to grips with the possible seductive implications of his interventions. This is particularly evident in the final sentence of the interpretation, which contradicts the patient's narrative (it was the *patient* who ended the relationship because of her partner's unwillingness to acknowledge his rigidity).

The movement between accurate intervention with consequent derivative validation and countertransference with derivative criticism, is typical of communicative work. The analyst must continually struggle against his readiness to lead himself and his patients astray. Every successful intervention entails an overcoming of the analyst's emotional resistance: an acknowledgment of some aspect of himself that he would prefer to leave unacknowledged. Communicative analysis therefore requires a high level of vigilance, discipline, and emotional resilience on the part of its practitioners.

RESEARCH AND CONTROVERSY

Research

I have already noted that the structure of communicative theory renders it particularly suitable for investigation. In order for a theory to be scientifically interesting it must have determinate consequences: It must be able to predict certain phenomena or patterns of phenomena while excluding the occurrence of others. Grünbaum (1984, 1993) has argued that although many aspects of classical psychoanalysis are scientifically testable, they are not testable "on the couch" using clinical evidence but must rely on experimental or epidemiological studies. This has grave consequences for psychoanalysis, as psychoanalysts generally justify their theoretical claims on the basis of the very "clinical evidence" the probity of which Grünbaum disputes. The core of Grünbaum's argument is that if "cure" is used to underwrite psychoanalytic theory, one must be able to exclude the possibility that it is brought about by factors other than the truth of the interpretations offered to patients. According to Grünbaum, it does not seem possible to exclude or even to distinguish such "false positives." The situation is made all the more insidious by the fact that virtually all forms of psychoanalysis explicitly or implicitly promise cure if and only if patients consciously concur with their analysts' interpretations (or at least, reach some interpretation that is compatible with their analysts' theoretical framework). The inevitable interpersonal pressure attendant upon this situation further contaminates psychoanalytic clinical data.

Unlike conventional forms of psychoanalysis, communicative theory is clinically testable (Smith, 1991a,b, 1992a, 1994, 1995a; Berns, 1994; Du Plock, 1992). As a theory of human interaction, the theory is sufficiently robust to explain and predict events outside the *communicative* psychoanalytic setting.

Communicative theory can, for example, be applied to data from classical Freudian psychoanalytic sessions to generate explanations, predictions, and retrodictions.

Communicative psychoanalysis has not yet attracted attention from philosophers of science or psychotherapy researchers. Langs and Badalamenti have engaged in extensive quantitative research into the psychoanalytic process (Langs, 1992b; Langs, Badalamenti, and Thompson, 1996). This research has concentrated mainly upon using communicative variables to investigate psychoanalytic and psychotherapeutic interactions. Communicative theory has been used heuristically rather than taken as the object of scrutiny. This strategy reflects Langs' commitment to creating a "bottom up" quantitative science of psychoanalysis. The results of these investigations have been striking and suggestive and await attempts at replication by other researchers. There have also been several attempts to investigate specific communicative hypotheses (Lindstrom, 1986; Quinn, 1994) which provide modest support for aspects of communicative theory.

On the more conceptual level, there has been growing interest in exploring the relationship between communicative psychoanalysis and cognitive science and neo-Darwinian formulations of communicative theory (Langs, 1992b, 1995; Smith, 1991a, 1992a,b,c, 1994, 1995a,b).

Controversy

Commitment to a scientific attitude entails commitment to criticism and self-criticism (Popper, 1963), in spite of narcissistic tendencies to protect and uncritically promote one's point of view. There are aspects of communicative theory about which there is considerable disagreement and a need for research to assess the objective validity of communicative propositions. I will therefore confine myself to those controversies that have been salient in the literature and discussion in recent years, but which are not overly technical or esoteric.

1. *Are the criteria for the secure frame universal?* Although "orthodox" communicative theory claims that the unconscious criteria for the secured frame are the same for all people

in all cultures, this claim has not been tested by means of extensive cross-cultural studies. Some (e.g., Troise, 1992) have argued that frame criteria are to some extent culturally relative. This criticism possesses considerable prima facie plausibility, as the items definitive of the psychoanalytic frame are almost without exception, social items. Smith (1991b) has argued that cultures may *instantiate* universal norms by means of diverse forms. Slavin and Kriegman's (1992) idea of "deep psychological structure" is helpful in this connection. It may be that just as according to Chomskian theory the universal and innate cognitive template for language is realized through numerous languages, so an innate unconscious social template finds many different cultural expressions.

2. *Can "external" triggers shape derivatives?* Langs initially claimed that analytic derivatives must be understood in light of triggering events and only subsequently argued that proximal stimuli occurring within or impinging upon the analytic frame are overwhelmingly potent instigators of unconscious mental activity. More recently, some analysts (e.g., Schaus, 1991) have suggested that this imposes an unnecessary constraint upon our ability to discover unconscious meaning. It is incumbent upon proponents of this view to present clinical evidence suggesting that distal triggers may take precedence over proximal ones.

3. *How can intrapsychic factors be understood in the context of communicative theory?* Early in his career, Langs adhered to the mainstream psychoanalytic view that the production of derivatives may be instigated by internal factors such as drive-cathected memories and phantasies. Recently, some communicative analysts (e.g., Quinn, 1992) have argued that derivatives can be to a significant degree self-referential. Quinn and others who have addressed this issue seem to be grappling with the fact that communicative theory does not yet have a theorized account of how it is that the "inner world" interacts with external events. Langs has suggested that we respond selectively to frame-events and that this selectivity is determined by intrapsychic concerns, but proposes no formal model of how such selectivity operates. I have already hinted at the idea that such items do not have to be imagined as explicit contents pressing for

discharge. It is probably more consistent with communicative theory to claim that the main impact of such "genetic" factors is on the *organization* of the mind. In this view our past constrains the ways in which we can make sense of the present. Thus, the way that we produce derivatives is a function of our early experiences, but this does not mean that memories of these experiences are themselves represented by means of derivatives.

Directions for Future Research

Given the impressionistic and objectively unvalidated nature of practically all of psychoanalytic theory, an exhaustive account of future pathways for research would occupy many pages. I can specify only a few of these issues in this place.

1. In common with other forms of psychotherapy, the communicative approach needs sensible methods of *outcome analysis* that are sensitive to negative as well as positive effects. In the absence of such studies, therapeutic claims must be expressed cautiously and tentatively.
2. Communicative psychoanalysis needs to devote more attention to developing theories of *psychopathology* and *affect,* the modification of the mind by *past experience.*
3. Communicative psychoanalysis needs to develop its interface with adjacent disciplines such as *developmental psychology, cognitive science,* and *evolutionary biology.*
4. Given the hypothesis that the deep unconscious wisdom system is an evolved unit of the mind, communication investigators need to study its operations *naturalistically,* in settings outside the psychoanalytic setting.

Most important is the need for independent investigators to objectively test communicative hypotheses. There is nothing easier than finding spurious corroboration for a position in which one has an investment. If the communicative approach is to fulfill its potential to be more than just another psychoanalytic belief system it is essential that it attract this sort of scientific scrutiny.

CONCLUSION

Throughout its brief history, communicative psychoanalysis has evoked dismissive and hostile responses from the proponents of other approaches and has attracted very little sober and thoughtful criticism. Extrapolating from its history, it would be easy to predict that the approach will gradually fade away. However, the human mind tends to respond adaptively to its contemporary context and the context of psychoanalysis in Western society is certainly changing. There is now widespread acceptance of the view that psychoanalysis can be a destructive as well as a healing process. Powerful philosophical criticisms of the knowledge-base of psychoanalysis have shown the scientific claims of psychoanalysis to be more pretense than reality (Grünbaum, 1993). Perhaps a common commitment to truth will now prevail over single-minded attempts to promote one's preferred doctrine, and the communicative approach will be given a fair scientific hearing. If not, psychoanalysis has a bleak future as a contribution to human knowledge.

REFERENCES

Balint, M. (1955), Notes on parapsychology and parapsychological healing. *Internat. J. Psycho-Anal.*, 36:31–35.

Berns, U. (1994), Die Übereinstimmungsdeutung: Ein Ergebnis der Evaluationsanalyse. *Forum der Psychoanalyse*, 10:226–244.

Clark, A. (1990), *Microcognition: Philosophy, Cognitive Science and Parallel Distributed Processing*. Cambridge, MA: Bradford/MIT.

Dorpat, T., & Miller, M. (1992), *Clinical Interaction and the Analysis of Meaning: A New Psychoanalytic Theory*. Hillsdale, NJ: Analytic Press.

---

*Recommended reading.

Du Plock, S. (1992), The communicative concept of validation and the definition of science. *Internat. J. Commun. Psychoanal. & Psychother.*, 7:113–118.

Ferenczi, S. (1933), Confusion of tongues between adults and the child. In: *Final Contributions to the Problems and Methods of Psycho-Analysis.* London: Hogarth Press.

Freud, S. (1910), The future prospects of psycho-analytic therapy. *Standard Edition*, 11:140–154. London: Hogarth Press, 1957.

Gill, M. (1984), Robert Langs on technique: A critique. In: *Listening and Interpreting: The Challenge of the Work of Robert Langs*, ed. J. Raney. New York: Jason Aronson, pp. 395–415.

————(1985), A critique of Robert Langs' conceptions of transference, evidence by indirection and the role of the frame. *Yearbook of Psychoanalysis and Psychotherapy*, 1:177–189.

Grünbaum, A. (1984), *The Foundations of Psychoanalysis: A Philosophical Critique.* Berkeley, CA: University of California Press.

————(1993), *Validation in the Clinical Theory of Psychoanalysis: A Contribution to the Philosophy of Psychoanalysis.* Madison, CT: International Universities Press.

Hartmann, H. (1939), *Ego Psychology and the Problem of Adaptation.* New York: International Universities Press.

Heimann, P. (1950), On countertransference. *Internat. J. Psycho-Anal.*, 31:81–84.

Kitcher, P. (1991), *Freud's Dream: A Complete Interdisciplinary Science of the Mind.* Cambridge, MA: Bradford/MIT.

Laing, R. D. (1959), *The Divided Self.* Harmondsworth, U.K.: Penguin.

Langs, R. (1971), Day residues, recall residues and dreams: Reality and the psyche. *J. Amer. Psychoanal. Assn.*, 19:499–523.

————(1976), *The Bipersonal Field.* New York: Jason Aronson.

————(1978a), *The Listening Process.* New York: Jason Aronson.

————(1978b), *Technique in Transition.* New York: Jason Aronson.

————(1979), *The Therapeutic Environment.* New York: Jason Aronson.

————(1980), *Interactions: The Realm of Transference and Countertransference.* New York: Jason Aronson.

————(1981), *Resistances and Interventions: The Nature of Therapeutic Work.* New York: Jason Aronson.

————(1982a), *Psychotherapy: A Basic Text.* New York: Jason Aronson.

————(1982b), *The Psychotherapeutic Conspiracy.* New York: Jason Aronson.

————(1985), *Madness and Cure.* Emerson, NJ: Newconcept Press.

————(1988), *A Primer of Psychotherapy.* New York: Gardner Press.

*———(1992a), *A Clinical Workbook for Psychotherapists*. London: Karnac.

*———(1992b), *Science, Systems and Psychoanalysis*. London: Karnac.

———(1993), *Empowered Psychotherapy*. London: Karnac.

———(1995), *Clinical Practice and the Architecture of the Mind*. London: Karnac.

———(1996), *The Evolution of the Emotion-Processing Mind: With an Introduction to Mental Darwinism*. Madison, CT: International Universities Press.

———(1997), *Death Anxiety and Clinical Practice*. London: Karnac.

———Badalamenti, A., & Thompson, L. (1996), *The Cosmic Circle*. New York: Alliance.

Lindstrom, M. (1986), *The Client's Direct and Indirect Communication in Response to a Planned Stimulus of the Worker*. Unpublished doctoral thesis, Adelphi University, New York.

Little, M. (1951), Countertransference and the patient's response to it. *Internat. J. Psycho-Anal.*, 32:32–34.

Macmillan, M. (1991), *Freud Evaluated: The Completed Arc*. Amsterdam: Elsevier/North Holland.

Millikan, R. G. (1993), Explanation in biopsychology. In: *White Queen Psychology and Other Essays for Alice*. Cambridge, MA: Bradford/MIT, pp. 171–193.

Milner, M. (1952), Aspects of symbolism and comprehension of the not-self. *Internat. J. Psycho-Anal.*, 33:181–185.

Mooij, A. (1991), *Psychoanalysis and the Concept of a Rule*. Berlin: Springer Verlag.

Myers, P. (1994), *Freud and Ferenczi: Layers of Meaning*. Unpublished M.A. dissertation, Regent's College, London.

Popper, K. (1963), *Conjectures and Refutations: The Growth of Scientific Knowledge*. New York: Harper & Row.

Quinn, B. (1992), *Tests of the Validity of Communicative Psychoanalytic Postulates*. Unpublished doctoral thesis, New York School of Social Work.

Racker, H. (1953), The counter-transference neurosis. In: *Transference and Countertransference*, ed. J. D. Sutherland. London: Hogarth Press, pp. 125–127.

———(1957), The meaning and uses of countertransference. *Psychoanal. Quart.*, 26:305–357.

———(1958), Countertransference and interpretation. *J. Amer. Psychoanal. Assn.*, 6:215–221.

*Raney, J., Ed. (1984), *Listening and Interpreting: The Challenge of the Work of Robert Langs*. New York: Jason Aronson.

Schaus, H. (1991), The adaptive context revisited. *Soc. Psychoanal. Psychother. Bull.*, 5:35–37.

Searles, H. (1948), Concerning transference and countertransference. *Internat. J. Psychoanal. Psychother.*, 7:165–188, 1977–1978.

———(1972), The function of the patient's realistic perceptions of the analyst in delusional transference. *Brit. J. Med. Psychol.*, 45:1–18.

———(1973), Concerning therapeutic symbiosis. *The Annual of Psychoanalysis*, 1:247–265. New York: International Universities Press.

———(1975), The patient as therapist to his analyst. In: *Tactics and Techniques in Psychoanalytic Therapy, Vol. 2: Countertransference*, ed. P. Giovacchini. New York: Jason Aronson, pp. 95–151.

———(1979), *Countertransference and Related Subjects*. New York: International Universities Press.

Slavin, M., & Kriegman, K. (1992), *The Adaptive Design of the Human Psyche*. New York: Guilford Press.

*Smith, D. L. (1991a), *Hidden Conversations: An Introduction to Communicative Psychoanalysis*. London: Routledge.

———(1991b), Psychoanalysis and dogmatism: A reply to Patrick Casement. *Brit. J. Psychother.*, 7:416–422.

———(1992a), Where do we go from here?' *Internat. J. Commun. Psychoanal. & Psychother.*, 7:17–27.

———(1992b), A revised communicative model of the mind. *Soc. Psychoanal. Psychother. Bull.*, 6:3–19.

———(1992c), Meaning, models and scientific reasoning: A reply to Vesna A. Bonac. *Internat. J. Commun. Psychoanal. & Psychother.*, 7:63–70.

———(1994), Riding shotgun for Freud: A reply to Ernesto Spinelli. *J. Soc. Existen. Anal.*, 5:142–157.

———(1995a), "It sounds like an excellent idea!": Part four of a psychological cliff-hanger. *J. Soc. Existen. Anal.*, 6:149–160.

———(1995b), Free associations and honeybee dancers: The unconscious and its place in nature. *Electron. J. Commun. Psychoanal.*

Troise, F. (1992), A re-examination of the universal framework concept in communicative psychoanalysis. *Internat. J. Commun. Psychoanal. & Psychother.*, 7:105–111.

Afterword

Robert Langs, M.D.

As reflected in the rich presentations of this book, the accomplishments of psychoanalysis in its first one hundred or so years have been monumental. However, as acknowledged by several of these writers, it is well to be reminded that psychoanalysis lacks a formal scientific foundation (Langs, Badalamenti, and Thomson, 1996) and is without a generally accepted definitive means of testing and validating its theories and techniques. In this light, its seems wise to conclude this volume by attempting to define areas and issues whose further exploration and clarification might well advance psychoanalytic thinking in ways not as yet fully realized.

What, then, lies ahead? Are there gaps to be filled? Revisions to be made? Indications of future directions for both psychoanalytic theory and practice? My answer, which will be made from the communicative vantage-point (see Chapter 12, and Langs, 1982, 1992a, 1993; Smith, 1991), will be broad and address the field of psychoanalysis as a whole.

THE ADAPTIVE DIMENSION

Human beings, including, of course, patients and therapists, are first and foremost adaptive organisms. Indeed, explorations of adaptations and the theory of evolution are among the most fundamental aspects of biology, the science of living organisms. It follows, then, that psychoanalysis, in its role as a science of human emotional adaptations, must embrace a strong and basic adaptive position. However, while adaptation is acknowledged or implied in current psychoanalytic thinking, with the exceptions of evolutionary and communicative approaches, adaptation is not a central dimension of existing theories and the practices they advocate. This relative neglect points to one aspect of psychoanalytic thinking that needs to be reconsidered and greatly expanded (Slavin and Kriegman, 1992; Langs, 1995b, 1996).

A strong adaptive position implies that both patients and therapists primarily are engaged in adapting to their environments—a term that alludes to both living-social and nonliving-physical impingements from the outside world. Adaptations first and foremost are triggered by and directed at stimuli and events that arise in one's immediate environment; they pertain to the interactions and transactions that an organism is dealing with at any given moment. Coping responses to internal events—thoughts, fantasies, memories, affects, and the like—are *secondary* adaptation-evoking triggers.

Adaptive responses are carried out by organ systems. In respect to processing emotionally charged impingements, the system responsible for this important endeavor is called *the emotion-processing mind,* a language-based, mental module that has evolved for emotional coping (Langs, 1995a). In humans, this module adapts on two, separate and distinct levels—one attached to consciousness and with contents capable of reaching awareness, and the other, not so connected (see below).

All in all, then, present theories of psychoanalysis tend to lack a strong adaptive position and as a result, they are without an essential understanding of the structure and functions of the emotion-processing mind—allusions to the all-too-broadly defined ego, superego, and id notwithstanding (Langs, 1992b, 1995a). Given that this mental module is the fundamental organ of adaptation in the emotional realm, the absence of an understanding of its capacities for relating, communicating, and coping is a serious deficiency that calls for future exploration and correction (see Chapters 11 and 12, and Slavin and Kriegman, 1992).

THE UNCONSCIOUS DOMAIN

The most fundamental identifying feature of psychoanalysis is its proposition that unconscious mentation, communication,

experiences, and adaptation (including relating and interacting) are among the most vital factors in human emotional
life and its vicissitudes. An essential theorem of this kind must
be carefully defined and honed, both theoretically and prag-
matically. In the absence of a specific delineation of this aspect
of human functioning, the term *unconscious* becomes nonde-
script. Its use is akin to the terms *atmosphere* and *protoplasm*
which had almost no utility because they were far too broad
and indefinite to meaningfully define the essential features of
their respective referents. Settling for the idea that "the unconscious" refers to anything—content, affect, motive, need, inclination, or behavior—that transpires or finds expression in the
absence of immediate awareness, fails to do justice to the concept and its role as the hallmark of psychoanalytic thinking and
clinical work.

The strong adaptive approach provides a definitive opportunity to study both conscious and unconscious coping, and to
thereby incisively define the nature of the unconscious realm.
To do so, it has provided another critical element that also is
missing from prevailing psychoanalytic approaches—a definitive means of attending to, formulating, and validating the
communications from both patients and therapists (Langs,
1992a, 1993; see below). This too is a challenge for future pursuits.

DEFINING THE NATURE OF INTERACTIONS

Implicit to adaptively oriented listening efforts is the thesis that
there is a single set of verifiable perceptions of the nature and
meanings of reality events. This implies, for example, that there
is an essential and limited group of validatable formulations of
a given sequence of communications from patients. It also
means that external reality exists in definable form and that it
is not open to an endless variety of interpretations jointly arrived at by patients and their therapists. The actual meanings
of an emotionally charged impingement are selectively perceived by patients in keeping with their life histories, sensitivities, defenses, and other aspects of their past and current

psychic state. While a valid definition of direct, conscious views of reality are, as a rule, difficult to establish because of the existence of massive conscious system defenses (see below), deep unconscious views tend to be very reliable and readily accessible to *encoded* validation. In most instances, deep unconscious experiences and perceptions, as communicated via encoded narrative communications from patients, allow for but a single cluster of decoded meanings—i.e., those interpreted meanings that obtain responsive indirect, encoded, unconscious validation (Langs, 1978, 1992a, 1993).

In essence, then, an organism's inner biases are constrained and channeled by the nature of imposing environmental incidents. Furthermore, while events are open to multiple levels of impact and understanding, it is also the case that there is a particular level of emotional experience that is far more powerful, meaningful, and relevant to emotional adaptations than all others. This level involves deep unconscious experiences and processes and operates entirely in the absence of direct awareness.

This discussion is grounded in the idea that natural selection insures that adaptations will be based on selective but incisive perceptions of the environment (Langs, 1996). For the emotionally charged events experienced by humans, these perceptions uniquely occur both consciously and unconsciously (subliminally)—and the latter, as noted, are especially critical to emotional life and the therapy experience. In this light, the concept of *transference*, defined as a patient's primary means of relating to his or her analyst in terms of misperceptions and distortions imposed by past life experiences (Freud, 1912), needs to be reexamined and modified (Langs, 1992b, 1995a). Present thinking, correct in its acknowledgment that a patient's past life experiences and current inner mental state affect contemporary reactions, appears to be erroneous in suggesting a dominance of fantasy over reality. The transference concept needs to be reassessed in order to provide a more valid picture of the complex nature of the relationships and interactions that transpire between patients and analysts—especially in respect to their unconscious aspects.

THE BASIC LISTENING PROCESS

As for the need for an effective listening process, here too we find that in general, psychoanalytic thinkers have failed to adequately define this fundamental aspect of their clinical work, one that also serves as the basis for the derivation of their theoretical ideas. In contrast, the strong adaptive position facilitates the careful formulation of both the conscious (surface and directly implied) and the unconscious (encoded) meanings in patients' free associations. This effort is carried out in light of the adaptation-evoking environmental stimuli or *triggers* to which patients are responding consciously and unconsciously (Langs, 1978, 1992a, 1993).

For psychotherapy and psychoanalytic patients, the immediate triggers for their adaptive responses are the *interventions* of their therapists—a term used in all-encompassing fashion to allude to anything therapists do or say, or meaningfully fail to do or say. Explorations of material from patients in response to these *specific triggering events* reveal a set of conscious responses that tend to be heavily restricted and distorted by intense defensiveness. As a result, patients show multiple failures to *consciously* appreciate and acknowledge many of the most significant emotionally charged meanings embodied in their therapists' interventions. In contrast, the encoded narrative responses of patients nondefensively reveal a deeply unconscious appreciation of the most critical meanings and implications of therapists' efforts, many of them outside of the awareness of therapists themselves.

Direct, consciously articulated communications, including their implied meanings, are, then, laden with communicative and psychological defenses such as noncommunication, denial, and repression (Langs, 1997). It follows, then, that the surface meanings of messages and their implications are an entirely *unreliable* basis for assessing the validity and utility of a therapist's interventions and are not especially useful as a basis for psychoanalytic theory building. This understanding casts another shadow across the ideas developed by current schools of psychoanalysis because their thinking is based on patients' manifest and directly implied reactions to interventions. This level of communication is constructed in important ways so as to use minor truths and falsehoods as a means of obliterating more painful, anxiety provoking, major truths.

Adaptively configured listening and formulating reveals that the *stories or narratives* told by patients—rather than the *intellectualizations* stressed in present thinking—are the vehicles for the encoded messages that reflect and reveal deep unconscious experience and coping efforts. Thus, after a therapist has intervened, the stories told by a patient about outside figures and events will contain displaced images and themes that encode the patient's selective unconscious perceptions of the most disturbing meanings of that intervention. Listening and formulating in this fashion reveal a deeply unconscious world of emotionally charged experiences that is far different from the world visualized through the methods of attending and formulating used by present-day therapists. We need, then, to develop ways to appreciate and define both levels of human experience—conscious and deeply unconscious—and to clarify their relevance to psychotherapeutic transactions and the process of cure.

ARCHITECTURE AND FRAMES

Examination of the results of *trigger decoding* patients' narrative themes—i.e., deciphering their disguised meanings in light of the interventions to which they are an encoded, unconscious, adaptive response—reveals a great deal about the evolved architecture and coping strategies of the emotion-processing mind (Langs, 1995a, 1996, 1997). This mental module is comprised of two basic systems. The first is termed the *conscious system* because its contents and workings, even when unconscious and transpiring in its *superficial unconscious subsystem,* ultimately are accessible to awareness either directly or through a minimal decoding effort—as when a therapist's lateness to a session is disguised through an allusion to a teacher who was late to class. The prevailing psychoanalytic theories reflect formulations made and clinical work carried out within the domain of this particular system of the emotion-processing mind.

The second basic system of the emotion-processing mind is termed the *deep unconscious system* because its adaptive intelligence and coping operations are, by evolved design and secondary psychodynamic factors, inaccessible to awareness in any direct or easily deciphered manner. This system relies on unconscious perception for its inputs and uses encoded narrative tales for its outputs. In principle, then, its workings and adaptive preference are revealed only through *trigger decoding* these disguised output stories—deciphering efforts that must account for deep unconscious responses to specific and currently active interventions by therapists.

The conscious system has evolved as our means of adapting to issues and conflicts related to immediate and long-term survival. In the emotional realm, the system is, as noted, defensively structured to an extreme degree. Beyond a certain level of intensity, emotionally charged impingements tend to disrupt rather than enhance conscious system adaptive functioning. To protect the system from overload and dysfunction, humans automatically and naturally make use of anxiety-sparing conscious system misperceptions, repressions, denials, omissions, obliterations, and other psychological and communicative defenses. However, these defensive structures greatly compromise our conscious emotional intelligence and direct adaptive capabilities, especially when powerful and emotionally disturbing meanings are inherent to the triggering events with which we are coping.

In contrast, the deep unconscious system is relatively free of psychological defensiveness because the meanings of the perceptions and experiences that it processes do not at any time have *direct access to awareness*. In consequence, the system is highly intelligent and its adaptive efforts and choices are far more enabling than those of the defense–laden conscious system.

There are many other critical differences between these two systems of the emotion-processing mind which operate quite independently of each other and on the basis of rather different perceptions, needs, motives, and values. For example, the conscious system scans many diverse aspects of the environment and self, but has a very limited repertoire of responses to this huge array of impingements and their meanings. In contrast, the deep unconscious system is concentrated almost entirely on a single dimension of human experience—*its settings, rules, and boundaries*—but reacts with multiple views and a wide variety of coping advisories (Langs, in press).

Surprisingly, the results of deep unconscious processing, although truly brilliant and constructive, do *not* influence conscious adaptations. The system's only link to awareness is *communicative* and is conveyed through *encoded narratives*—its perceptions and their meanings are too anxiety provoking and terrifying to reach consciousness in undisguised form. As a result, they are unavailable for the development of coping strategies.

There is, however, a deep unconscious influence on human behavior, but it stems from a second subsystem—*the fear–guilt subsystem*. This entity embodies the basic human fear of death and is as well a storehouse of deep unconscious guilt for misdeeds real and imagined, enacted by self and affiliated others. The most powerful motivating forces of human emotional adaptation are deeply unconscious, never directly experienced, and center around death anxiety and guilt-evoked needs for punishment (Langs, 1995a, 1997).

Because they do not embrace a strong adaptive position and fail to make use of trigger decoding, the entire world of deep unconscious experience is missing from existing psychoanalytic theories and practices. The two-dimensional world of human emotional experience receives a one-dimensional formulation. Practicing analysts and therapists do indeed have part of the puzzle, but they also are missing some of its most essential pieces. This oversight needs to be corrected.

THE BASIC ISSUE

In discussing the limitations of present psychoanalytic theory and practice, I have, to this point, taken a cognitive approach. I've identified some missing elements and have suggested that psychological and communicative defenses are at work in generating these omissions. This assessment is, however, insufficient; there's a root cause of these exclusions and it too needs to be identified and brought under the aegis of psychoanalytic theory and practice.

The critical missing piece can be discovered by detecting a significant void that exists in every present version of psychoanalytic theory, including until very recently, the communicative approach. Nevertheless, it is the single most fundamental source of human anxiety, conflict, and emotional dysfunction—and creativity as well.

I am referring here to *human mortality*, to *death*, and to *death anxiety* which exists in two forms—existential and predatory. And I am suggesting that every generally accepted version of psychoanalytic theory and therapy has been constructed in significant part as a means of avoiding the manifestations and processing of death related issues. Lesser conflicts and truths have been and are being used to deny and obliterate greater and more morbid conflicts and truths which have personal mortality at their center (Langs, 1997).

In terms of human evolution, the key factor in this state of affairs is the development, some 100,000 to 150,000 years ago, of the extraordinary capacity for language (Bickerton, 1990; Corballis, 1991; Langs, 1996, 1997). Because this occurrence is a very recent event on the time scale of evolutionary processes and because the adaptations of the emotion-processing mind are essentially language based, natural selection has had little time to fashion an effective and flexible adaptive instrument for emotional coping. It has consistently "opted" for two ways of increasing the chances for individual and species survival: first, through the creation of a two-system emotion-processing mind and second, by selecting for an enormous array of protective but obliterating and costly conscious system psychological and communicative defenses (Langs, 1995b, 1996, 1997).

These inherited design features protect the human mind from system overload, but do so at considerable cost because it entails an *enormous reduction in knowledge of the environment and self*—including the loss of possible psychoanalytic knowledge. Indeed, the conflicts and anxieties evoked by the awareness of personal mortality have been and are so powerful that they have served as major selection pressures for the design features of the emotion-processing mind of *homo sapiens sapiens*. As a result, the emotion-processing mind is basically organized and structured to function *consciously* first and foremost as a defensive instrument.

Language did, of course, facilitate the development of many remarkable capacities that have been the basis for extensive human achievements. Among these gifts, of considerable importance to this discussion is the human ability to define, articulate, and anticipate the future. A critical aspect of that future, as the young child begins to realize as he or she acquires language capabilities, is that all people die—including important others and oneself. The result is a universal experience of conscious and unconscious forms of *existential death anxiety* that unconsciously motivate a wide range of both adaptive and maladaptive behaviors. These include healthy forms of denial and creative acts, as well as extreme and pathological forms of denial, inappropriate sexual behaviors, and acts of violence that are directed against others and at times, even oneself.

Existential death anxiety is a motivating force in all aspects of personal growth and creativity, and is as well, a root cause of every form of maladaptation, psychopathology, and dysfunctional relatedness and interacting.

To date, humans have evolved only one basic means of adapting to existential death anxiety—the use of *denial* in its many, often disguised, forms (Becker, 1973; Langs, 1997). This mechanism can operate at the perceptual, communicative, psychological, and behavioral levels and it functions as a means of obliterating disturbing, death-related reality impingements and most of their more compelling meanings—often doing so through manic celebrations and activities, and frame modifications. Indeed, violations of rules and boundaries are among the most common denial-based defenses in the human repertoire. The defiance and breaking of a rule of any kind is in part motivated by the *deep unconscious illusion or delusion* that being an exception to a rule is tantamount to being an exception to the fundamental existential rule of life, namely that it is followed in all cases by death.

The manner in which humans manage, deal with, and respond to rules, frames, and boundaries is intimately connected with both forms of death anxiety—existential and predatory. *Secured frames,* which in psychotherapy means adhering to all of its essential, *unconsciously validated* ground rules (see Chapter 12, and Langs, 1992a, in press), generates extremely positive, growth promoting, and conflict-resolving unconscious experiences. Nevertheless, simultaneously, frame securing interventions evoke deep unconscious experiences of entrapment and a strong sense of dread related to the secured frame, existential death anxieties that are activated in this manner. These anxieties are so severe and overwhelming that they consistently motivate humans to engage in repetitive conscious system efforts to invoke frame modifications within and outside of psychotherapy—the existential death anxieties caused by secured frames are among the most dreaded affects experienced by humans.

In this regard, there is once more a striking contrast between the preferences of the two systems of the emotion-processing mind. On the one hand, based on a firm appreciation for the positive attributes of secured frames—they offer safety, trustworthiness, and sound, growth promoting, inherently supportive holding and the like—the deep unconscious system consistently and universally encodes for secured frames. On the other hand, the conscious system is both frame insensitive and inclined to favor frame modifications as a way of unconsciously dealing with and defending against the underlying existential death anxieties with which it is continually plagued.

In this light, we can appreciate the sources of the neglect of the management of the ground rules and settings of psychoanalysis and psychotherapy that characterizes present psychoanalytic positions. Developed on the basis of conscious system viewpoints, the attitudes and defensive biases of this system prevail. By focusing on etiological past experiences and the isolated psychodynamics of material from patients, a therapist will overlook the critical role of frame-related interventions in the dynamics of the therapeutic interaction and also fail to appreciate the importance of the exploration and understanding of present and future death-related incidents and prospects. A shift to trigger decoding and to the inclusion of the deep unconscious viewpoint would prompt a reconsideration of the critical role in therapy that is played by its ground rules and framework. The general neglect of frame issues would give way to a realization that a patient's deep unconscious experience is organized around unconscious perceptions of the multitude of meanings inherent to a therapist's management of the ground rules and setting. Technically, attention to ground rule issues would shift this aspect of human experience from the periphery to the center of psychotherapy and psychoanalysis. Frame related transactions are the main activators of the critical deep unconscious dynamics and genetics on which emotional maladaptations are based.

Frame modifications, which provide maladaptive, temporary relief from existential death anxieties, prove to be very costly to all concerned because they are persecutory and evoke predatory death anxieties. Without exception, a violation of a ground rule harms, assaults, and inappropriately seduces those toward whom it is directed. Nevertheless, humans in general, and patients and therapists in particular, prefer dealing with persecutory rather than existential death anxieties, and this unconscious preference has greatly shaped the forms taken by the theories and practices of psychoanalysis and psychotherapy.

Denial of death and of death anxiety was inherent to Freud's position—he denied its existence in "the unconscious" (Freud, 1923) and transformed death anxiety into a purported instinct or wish (Freud, 1920). This defensively oriented heritage has unwittingly been carried forward by latter-day psychoanalysts. In the spirit of the presentations of this book, with their efforts to transform Freud's one-person psychology into a two-person, interactional psychology, Freud's denial of death needs to be transformed into the realization that death is the single most powerful and fundamental problem of human existence and emotional life. The theories advocated by contributors to this volume are well positioned to make this transformation.

In concluding, it is well to realize that the viability of psychoanalysis as a theory and foundation for dynamic forms of psychotherapy depends on the recognition of unsolved puzzles and flaws and gaps in present-day thinking. Such realizations motivate research and stimulate the development of new and revised perspectives and theoretical and technical constructs of the kind that insure the constructive evolution and growth of psychoanalysis as a theory and heart-felt effort to heal psychic wounds.

REFERENCES

Becker, E. (1973), *The Denial of Death*. New York: Free Press.

Bickerton, D. (1990), *Language and Species*. Chicago: University of Chicago Press.

Corballis, C. (1991), *The Lopsided Ape*. New York: Oxford University Press.

Freud, S. (1912), The dynamics of transference. *Standard Edition*, 12:97–108. London: Hogarth Press, 1958.

———(1920), Beyond the Pleasure Principle. *Standard Edition*, 19:3–64. London: Hogarth Press, 1961.

———(1923), The Ego and the Id. *Standard Edition*, 19:1–66. London: Hogarth Press, 1961.

Langs, R. (1978), *The Listening Process*. New York: Aronson.

———(1982), *Psychotherapy: A Basic Text*. New York: Aronson.

———(1992a), *A Clinical Workbook for Psychotherapists*. London: Karnac.

———(1992b), 1923: The advance that retreated from the architecture of the mind. *Internat. J. Commun. Psychoanal. & Psychother.*, 7:3–15.

———(1993), *Empowered Psychotherapy*. London: Karnac.

———(1995a), *Clinical Practice and the Architecture of the Mind*. London: Karnac.

———(1995b), Psychoanalysis and the science of evolution. *Amer. J. Psychother.*, 49:47–58.

———(1996), *The Evolution of the Emotion-Processing Mind*. London: Karnac; Madison, CT: International Universities Press.

———(1997), *Death Anxiety and Clinical Practice*. London: Karnac.

———(in press), *The Ground Rules of Psychotherapy and Counselling*. London: Karnac.

———Badalamenti, A., & Thomson, L. (1996), *The Cosmic Circle: The Unification of Mind, Matter, and Energy*. Brooklyn, NY: Alliance Publishing.

Smith, D. (1991), *Hidden Conversations: An Introduction to Communicative Psychoanalysis.* London: Tavistock/Routledge.

Slavin, M., & Kriegman, D. (1992), *The Adaptive Design of the Human Psyche: Psychoanalysis and the New Evolutionary Biology.* New York: Guilford Press.

Name Index

Subject Index

Accommodation, 89–90
Adaptation
  in communicative psychoanalysis,
    300–301
  in control-mastery theory, 127–130
  definition of, 259
  evolutionary, 333–334
  facts concerning, 262–263
  of human child, 262–265
  mutual, 290–291
  selective, 328
  transference in, 281–282
Adaptation-evoking triggers, 326, 329
Adaptive context, 298
Adaptive deep structures, 287–290
Adaptive dimension, 325–326
Adaptive responses, 326
Addictive ties, 37
Adolescence, 92–93
  early, 83, 92–93
  late, 83
  regression in, 267–268
Adulthood, 83
  in interpersonal approach, 92–93
Affects
  confrontation of, 192
  pathogenic beliefs and, 133–134
  of selfobject experiences, 155–156
Affiliation, need for, 170–171
Aggression
  implications of, 199
  role in psychological development,
    207–208
Aggressive drive, 178
Alter ego transference, 155
Amplification, 242–243
Analyst. *See also* Therapist
  emotional need for validation of, 70
  "greediness" of, 98–99

holding function of, 46
internal conflicts of, 38
listening to patient, 17–19
need to change, 284–285
as neutral blank screen, 114–115,
  120
ongoing relationship with, 95–96
in patient's original trauma, 34–35
personality of, 17, 24–25
plan formulation by, 144–145
self-deception in, 280, 281–282
self-disclosure of, 52–53
self-reflection of, 45
silent, 40
subjective experiences of, 115–116
unformulated experience of
  patient, 119–120
Analytic dialogue. *See* Psychoanalytic
  dialogue
Analytic process, 274–276
Analytic relationship
  shared vision in, 46
  Sullivan's work on, 74
Analytic situation, conceptual pillars
  of, 39–44
Anger, 210
Anima/animus archetypes, 235–237
Anna Karenina, 236
Annihilation, fear of, 208
Anxiety. *See also* Death anxiety
  in children, 220–221
  in conflict, 179
  depressive, 205
  drive to avoid, 76, 94–95
  focus on, in psychotherapy, 182–183
  personifications and, 79–80
  role in psychological development,
    208–209
  with self-discovery, 85–87